NATIONAL GEOGRAPHIC

TRAVELER
Sicily

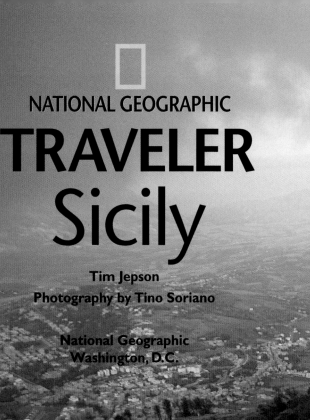

NATIONAL GEOGRAPHIC
TRAVELER
Sicily

Tim Jepson
Photography by Tino Soriano

National Geographic
Washington, D.C.

Contents

How to use this guide 6–7 About the author & photographer 8
The areas 41–158 Travelwise 159–85
Index 186–89 Credits 190–91

**Page 1: Festa Medievale,
Randazzo**
**Page 2-3: Castello Normanno di
Venere and Torre Pepoli viewed
from Erice**
Page 4: Aci Castello beach

How to use this guide

See back flap for keys to text and map symbols.

The *National Geographic Traveler* brings you the best of Sicily, in text, pictures, and maps. Divided into three main sections, the guide begins with an overview of Sicily today, its history and culture.

Following are six area chapters with featured sites selected by the author for their particular interest. Each chapter opens with its own contents list for easy reference. A map introduces the parameters covered in the chapter, highlighting the featured sites and locating other places of interest. (The Palermo chapter has a closeup map within the chapter as well as an area map located on

the inside back cover.) Walks, plotted on their own maps, suggest routes for discovering the most about an area. Features and sidebars offer intriguing detail on the area.

The final section, Travelwise, lists essential information for the traveler—pre-trip planning, special events, getting around, practical advice, and emergency contacts—plus provides a selection of hotels and restaurants arranged by area, shops, activities and entertainment.

To the best of our knowledge, information is accurate as of press time. However, it's always advisable to call ahead when possible.

158

Color coding
Each area of the city is color coded for easy reference. Find the area you want on the map on the front flap, and look for the color flash at the top of the pages of the relevant chapter. Information in **Travelwise** is also color coded to each region.

Cathedral
www.cattedrale.palermo.it
- ▲ Map p. 43
- ✉ Piazza della Cattedrale, off Corso Vittorio Emanuele II
- ☎ 091 334 376
- ⊕ Treasury & crypt: closed Sun.
- $ Treasury & crypt: $

Visitor information
Practical information for most sites is given in the side column (see key to symbols on back flap). The map reference gives the page number of the map and grid reference. Other details are address, telephone number, days closed, and entrance charge in a range from $ (under $5) to $$$$$ (over $25). Other sites have information in italics and parentheses in the text.

TRAVELWISE

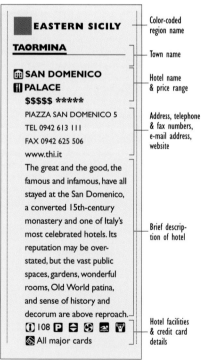

EASTERN SICILY — Color-coded region name

TAORMINA — Town name

🏨 SAN DOMENICO 🍴 PALACE — Hotel name & price range
$$$$$ ★★★★★

PIAZZA SAN DOMENICO 5 — Address, telephone & fax numbers, e-mail address, website
TEL 0942 613 111
FAX 0942 625 506
www.thi.it

The great and the good, the famous and infamous, have all stayed at the San Domenico, a converted 15th-century monastery and one of Italy's most celebrated hotels. Its reputation may be overstated, but the vast public spaces, gardens, wonderful rooms, Old World patina, and sense of history and decorum are above reproach. — Brief description of hotel

🛈 108 🅿 🔄 🅲 🖼 🈵 — Hotel facilities & credit card details
🅰 All major cards

Hotel & restaurant prices
An explanation of the price bands used in entries is given in the Hotels & Restaurants section (beginning on p. 168).

REGIONAL MAPS

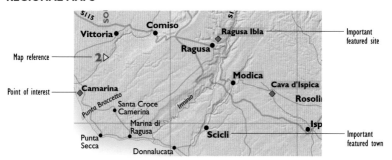

Important featured site

Map reference

Point of interest

Important featured town

- A locator map accompanies each regional map and shows the location of that region on the island.
- Adjacent regions are shown, each with a page reference.

WALKING TOURS

Direction of route

Building outline

Featured site (in bold) on walk route

Gray numbered bullets link site on map to descriptions in the text

Walk route

- An information box gives the starting and ending points, time and length of walk, and places not to be missed along the route.

DRIVING TOURS

Drive route

Point of interest on route

Gray numbered bullets link site on map to descriptions in the text.

Detour

Road numbers

- An information box provides details including starting and finishing points, time and length of drive, places not to be missed along the route, and tips on the terrain.

NATIONAL GEOGRAPHIC
TRAVELER
Sicily

About the author & photographer

Tim Jepson has been a passionate and lifelong devotee of Italy. Since graduating from Oxford, he has spent long periods of time living and traveling in the country and five years as a writer and journalist in Rome. Over the years he has written some 15 books on the country, as well as numerous articles for the *Daily Telegraph, Vogue, Condé Nast Traveler,* and other publications. He wrote the *National Geographic Traveler: Italy.*

Now based in London with the *Daily Telegraph,* Tim continues to visit Italy regularly, and, as a keen hiker and outdoor enthusiast, he takes a particular interest in the rural areas. He also revels in Italy's more sedentary pleasures—the food, wine, art, and culture.

Tim has also worked on Italian programs for the BBC and commercial television, and his career has included spells in a slaughterhouse, on building sites, and as a musician playing piano and guitar in streets and bars across Europe.

Born and raised in Barcelona, Spain, **Tino Soriano** divides his work between photojournalism and travel photography. He has received a First Prize from the World Press Photo Foundation as well as awards from UNESCO, Fujifilm, and Fotopres.

In addition to Sicily, since 1988 Tino has photographed in Spain (Catalonia, Andalucia, Galicia), France, Italy, Portugal, Scotland and South Africa on assignments for National Geographic. His work has also appeared in *Geo, Merian, Der Spiegel, Paris Match, La Vanguardia,* and *El Pais* as well as many other major magazines around the world.

Tino likes to write, and he has published *El Futuro Existe* (a story about children with cancer). He also regularly lectures and teaches workshops at the University of Barcelona.

History
& culture

The temple at Segesta dates
from the fifth century B.C.,
a golden age of Sicilian art
and architecture.

Sicily today

SICILY IS ONE OF THE GREAT ENIGMAS, AN ISLAND OF INCOMPARABLE BEAUTY and cultural wealth. Yet it is also a world apart, separated from mainstream European life by a tumultuous history that has left a troubled present and the monuments of a glorious past. The result is a society rich in ambiguity and an island almost unmatched for the myriad pleasures of its art and architecture, food, wine, landscapes, and outdoor activities.

Sicily's location has long been its blessing and its curse. At one time, when the known world barely extended beyond the Mediterranean, it was at the crossroads of Africa and Europe, a conduit for trade and peoples—and a prize for all the covetous states that have risen and fallen in this region. The island was once a paradise on earth, a wealthy and fertile

enclave of teeming seas, olive trees, citrus groves, vineyards, and rolling wheat fields. For three transcendent periods—under Greek, Arab, and Norman domination— the island was the cornerstone of the Mediterranean. Yet throughout its history, it was also ruled— usually badly—by foreigners.

Virtually all of Sicily's triumphs and present travails can be attributed to its invaders: Greeks, Romans, Vandals, Carthaginians, Arabs, Normans, the French, the British, the Spanish, and the Italian state, the last as much an ineffectual imposter to many Sicilians as its predecessors.

The degree to which Sicily has been misruled, and the poverty, alienation, enforced self-sufficiency, and mistrust of authority it has engendered, goes a long way to explaining the complex nature of Sicilians. Stereotyping is always a dangerous game, but there is no doubt that Sicilians are a curious hybrid, a melting pot of an ancient race—itself split between the "Greek" east and "Arab" west— and the other peoples who invaded the island.

The Sicilian character is a heady mix, at once brooding, suspicious, cynical, insular, fatalistic, and withdrawn, but also generous, sensuous, stoic, bright, calculating, curious, deeply cultured, and industrious. Sicilians have invariably been subjects not citizens, have felt oppressed rather than championed, and have cultivated a powerful sense of pride, vanity, and honor to confront the uncomfortable fact of their subjection.

Misrule has engendered a mistrust of authority, and with it a tendency to eschew many of the more conventional structures of society. Loyalty is first and foremost to one's family, as in much of Italy, though as Luigi Barzini, author of *The Italians* (1964), has observed: "Sicily is the schoolroom model of Italy for beginners, with every Italian quality and defect magnified, exasperated, and brightly colored."

The reluctance to take on social and civic roles, and the perceived absence of a reliable and trustworthy central authority, are partial reasons for the existence of the Mafia (see pp. 52-53), which is still a presence in Sicily, though not as profound or dramatic as portrayed in the media. Certainly no casual visitor will feel its effect, and in the last decade there have been signs both of a weakening of organized crime and a change in the attitude of ordinary Sicilians and the Italian state—once passive at best and complicit at worse—to an organization that once held both in thrall.

Signs of change in Sicily's economy are more elusive. The desperate poverty of the last century, when millions of Sicilians emigrated, has mostly gone, but Sicily still has Italy's highest levels of unemployment and illiteracy; a per capita income half that

A wedding at the church of San Giorgio, Modica, in southeast Sicily. Family ties are of great importance to Sicilians.

of northern Italy; an increasing problem with immigration from North Africa; and, with a quarter of all workers employed by the state, a suffocating bureaucracy and culture of *clientelismo* (patronage in return for political and other favors) that often stifle private initiative.

Tourism is now being championed as a panacea for Sicily's economic ills, and in this, perhaps, the island has a chance of change and partial prosperity. What could be more tempting than Europe's finest mosaics at Piazza Armerina; the Greek remains of Syracuse, Agrigento, Segesta, and Selinunte; the lure of resorts like Taormina; the many glories of Palermo; the cathedrals of Monreale and Cefalù; the medieval beauty of Erice; the brooding majesty of Etna; and the maritime charms of the Aeolian and other islands? Ironically, it could be Sicily's latest invaders—its visitors—who prove its ultimate salvation.

THE LAND

The Mediterranean's largest island, Sicily's breathtaking landscapes form a triangle (the ancients called Sicily Trinacria, or the Three Corners) measuring 9,926 square miles (25,709 sq km). It lies just 1.8 miles (3 km) from the Italian mainland and 87 miles (140 km) from Africa. To the east, its shores are washed by the Ionian Sea, to the north by the Tyrrhenian, and to the south by the Mediterranean. About 62 percent of the island is hilly, with 24 percent

Scopello, one of Sicily's small villages, sits on the rocky coastline above the Gulf of Castellammare.

classified as mountainous and the remaining 14 percent plain or lowland.

The principal mountains, the Appennino Siculo, touch 6,491 feet (1,979 m) and parallel the north coast for about 125 miles (200 km). They consist of three massifs—the Peloritani, Nebrodi, and Madonie—and are a geological

continuation of the Apennines that form a central spine down the Italian peninsula.

Western Sicily is more complex: a mixture of limestone outcrops, undulating clay escarpments, and swaths of olives and vineyards stretched across the plains of Trapani and Marsala. In the east, the prosperous agricultural plains of Catania give way to the Monti Iblei in the island's southeast corner, an enclave of tabletop uplands and steep-sided valleys.

The rolling interior is another landscape entirely: a region that the writer Giuseppe Tomasi di Lampedusa called "the real Sicily," a sort of petrified sea "aridly undulating to the horizon in hill after hill, comfortless and irrational…conceived apparently in a delirious moment of creation."

The interior is where Sicily's acute lack of water is most apparent (the island has erratic rainfall and poorly managed water distribution, made worse by centuries of deforestation). There are few rivers, those in the north

At a theater performance in Palermo, patrons enjoy Sicily's rich and diverse cultural heritage.

being short, tumultuous affairs that rush for a few days and then remain dry for much of the year. The most important rivers—the Dittaino, Simeto, and Gornalunga—drain and irrigate the plains around Catania in the east.

All of Sicily's natural features pale beside Mount Etna, a majestic geological anomaly that is both the island's highest point (at about 10,900 feet/3,323 m) and Europe's most active volcano. Its presence is due to Sicily's position astride major faults in the earth's crust,

making the island prone to occasionally catastrophic earthquakes. The same faults account for the Isole Eolie (the Lipari Islands) off the north coast, where the island of Stromboli is a dramatic volcanic presence, and the presently inactive islands of Pantelleria and Linosa off Sicily's southern coast.

Parts of the coast have been spoiled by industry and pollution, around Gela and Augusta especially, but other areas are still delightful: the Zingaro reserve and Capo San Vito west of Palermo, for example, or the beaches of Noto Marina and Cala Bernardo (south of Syracuse), Porto Palo (near Selinunte), Cefalù and Marina di Modica, Cava d'Aliga, and Donnalucata.

VEGETATION

Sicily's vegetation is as rich and varied as its landscapes. Mild winters, hot summers, fertile soils, varying altitude, and numerous habitats create a profusion of trees, plants, and flowers. Almond, peach, orange and other citrus fruits flourish, providing creamy, scented blossoms in spring, along with the silvery green of olives, the red and white of oleander, the perfumed white stars of jasmine, and the bold magenta and purple blooms of bougainvillea.

Wheat on the plains lends its own palette, from the green of winter shoots to the dark

ocher of the ripening crop. Introduced plants include cork (at Niscemi); manna ash (near Castelbuono); and papyrus, cultivated since Greek times on the Ciane River near Syracuse.

In the mountains, beech, pine, holm oak, chestnut, and other trees flourish in the woodlands, while the drier slopes below support prickly pears, cactuses, palms, agaves, capers, and the classic plants of Mediterranean scrub (*maquis*) such as myrtle, lentisk, euphorbia, and arbutus.

In Petralia Sottana and other rural hill towns, life has changed little over centuries.

Etna has its own fecund vegetation—1,500 species in all—from the rare Etna ragwort to plants such as the silver-gray lichen, which manage to survive on still warm lava. And everywhere in the countryside in spring are spectacular swaths of wildflowers: poppies, orchids, irises, narcissi, and many, many more. ■

Food & drink

FOOD IN SICILY STANDS OUT, EVEN IN A COUNTRY WITH AS CELEBRATED and varied a cuisine as Italy's. Numerous historical and geographical strands come together to create a culinary tradition that combines dishes from as far back as the ancient Greeks, Arabs, and Normans, and from as far afield as Spain, Greece, North Africa, and the Middle East. Added to the mix are Sicily's myriad natural ingredients, the bounty of a fertile land and teeming sea.

The ancient Greek city of Syracuse—then culinary capital of the classical world—produced the West's first school of chefs and first recorded cookbook: Mithaecus's fifth-century B.C. *Lost Art of Cooking*. Many of Sicily's distinctive sweet-and-sour dishes, notably *caponata* (slow-cooked vegetables, olives, raisins, and pine nuts), may well date from Greek times.

More distinct dishes, however, date from the late eighth century and the arrival of the Arabs, who introduced innovative culinary and agricultural practices, as well as rice, citrus fruits, couscous, cane sugar, cinnamon, saffron—and ice cream and

sorbets, made from the snow found year-round near the summit of Mount Etna. Later, Sicily's Spanish rulers would introduce tomatoes and chocolate from the New World.

The Arabs' sweet tooth accounted for many of Sicily's distinctive desserts and candies, notably *cassata* (sweetened ricotta cheese, sponge cake, candied fruit, and almond paste), which takes its name from the Arabic *quas-at*, the bowl in which it was made. They may also have had a hand in the *cannoli*, pastry shells filled with ricotta, chocolate, and candied fruit.

From the Arabs, too, came marzipan, used to make *pasta reale* or *frutta alla Martorana*, marzipan shaped and painted to resemble other foods, and "virgins' breasts" *(minni di vergini)* or "chancellor's buttocks" *(fedde del cancellerie)*. The frutta was made traditionally by nuns, in particular the nuns of Palermo's La Martorana convent, hence its name.

The Arabs were probably also responsible for one of Sicily's key pasta dishes, *pasta con le sarde* (with sardines, wild fennel, olive oil, raisins, saffron, and pine nuts). It is said the chefs with the Arabs' first invading army

Above: Frutta alla Martorana, made from marzipan, was introduced by the Arabs. Left: Pescheria market cheeses

devised the dish simply by throwing together the ingredients that were at hand as the army marched through the countryside.

Available ingredients also accounted for the island's other pasta classic, *pasta alla Norma* (with sun-ripened tomatoes, salted ricotta, and eggplant), which may take its name from the fact that it was simply the basic, or "normal," pasta dish in eastern Sicily.

Whatever the derivation, Sicilian food remains wedded to simple ingredients and a peasant culinary tradition. Fish and seafood are more common than, and generally superior to, meat, notably sardines, clams *(vongole)*, anchovies *(acciughe)*, tuna *(tonno)*, or swordfish *(pesce spada)*. The exceptions are the lamb *(agnello)* and pork *(maiale)* from the Madonie,

Nebrodi, and other mountain regions. From these same regions come superb cheeses, especially ricotta, *caciocavallo* (like a mature mozzarella), and pecorinos, or sheep's cheeses.

Vegetables, particularly eggplant *(melanzane)*, often take the place of meat in pasta and other dishes, which rely for zest on

Innovative producers and new techniques have revolutionized the wine industry.

raisins, capers *(capperi)*, wild fennel *(finocchio)*, herbs, seeds, garlic, and other inexpensive gifts of field and forest. Beans, nuts and pulses such as fava *(fave)*, pistachio *(pistacchio)*, almonds *(mandorle)*, chickpeas *(ceci)*, and lentils *(lenticchie)* are also common. Rice, less prevalent than it was, still appears in many excellent street and snack foods, notably as *arancini* (breaded and deep-fried rice balls with peas, ham, or meat ragout).

WINE

Archaeologists suggest that wine has been made in Sicily since at least 1400 B.C., though it was the Normans who established viticulture as an enduring part of the island's economy.

Sicily's climate and terrain are good, almost too good, for making wine, and the intense sun, long summers, and high and dependable yields, meant that until recently the island produced quantity rather than quality where wine was concerned. Many wines were strong *vini da taglio*, literally "wines of cut," as they were produced in bulk and sent to "cut" with weaker wines of France and northern Italy to boost their color and alcoholic content.

Recently, however, there has been a dramatic change in Sicilian winemaking. Modern techniques of viticulture and viniculture have been introduced and the island is now one of the world's most exciting wine destinations. It has been dubbed the "new California," and a measure of its success is the current clamor by European and other wine companies to buy land and plant vineyards on Sicilian soil.

Italy has a complicated and outmoded system of classifying wines, but one that is of little practical use when trying to assess quality. Best to ignore the ratings, therefore, and follow a particular producer (see below for recommendations) or stick to restaurants' house wines *(vino della casa)*, which are generally far better in Sicily than in much of rural Italy.

The reasons for Sicily's dramatic improvement are the same as elsewhere in Italy, namely that the land's natural advantages for winegrowing finally have been matched by innovative winemakers prepared to use modern techniques and native and foreign varietals.

Special account has also been taken of Sicily's often extreme conditions. Low, bush-trained vines that develop vast amounts of sugar under the Sicilian sun were replaced with wire-trained grapes farther from the heat-reflecting soil. Vines are pruned to improve quality; grapes are harvested early and at night (to prevent acidity levels dropping and help them retain flavor); and pressed grapes are stored in cool vats to prevent fermentation beginning too quickly.

Producers have not totally abandoned the old, however, and make a point of combining local traditional grape varieties with the international staples. With white wines, where the

Sicilian wine revolution began, this has meant combining the age-old Grecanico, Catarratto, Inzolia, and Grillo grapes with Chardonnay, Sauvignon Blanc and the occasional Viognier.

Good whites include Vigna di Gabbri and more basic Donnafugata from the big Tenuta di Donnafugata winery; the premium Colomba Platino, Bianco di Valguarnera, and lowlier Corvo Bianco from the Corvo label; and Inzolia, Tasca, and Nozze d'Oro from Regaleali. Among smaller estates, Cometa and Chardonnay from the Planeta winery near Noto are excellent, as are the wines of Rudini, Calabretta, Fondo Antico, and Racalmare di Morgante.

Sicilian reds are now overtaking the whites, but the basis of improvement has been the same: the blending of Cabernet Sauvignon, Cabernet Franc, Syrah, Pinot Nero, and merlot grapes with traditional Sicilian varieties. The most notable of these is the Nero d'Avola, which makes deep-colored, fruity, and robust wines that are similar to syrah. Good Nero d'Avola wines include Planeta's Santa Cecilia, the Duca Enrico of Duca di Salaparuta, and Fazio's Torre dei Venti.

Other reds of note with mixed blends include Donnafugata's Tancredi DOC Contessa Entellina and Mille e Una Notte Contessa Entellina; Spadafora's Don Pietro; the Terre d'Agula of Duca di Salapurata; Planeta's Burdese and La Segreta Rosso; Morgante's Don Antonio; the Tripudium of Duca di Castelmonte; and Cusumano's Sagana, Noà, and Benuara.

The new wines should not obscure the virtues of some of Sicily's more established names such as the basic Bianco d'Alcamo and Cerasuolo di Vittoria. Marsala has acquired a bad name, but at its best from producers like Florio, Pellegrino, and Marco de Bartoli (and the older Vergine, Riserva, or Soleras versions), it is a fine, dry, smooth sherry-like wine.

Even better are the dessert wines conjured from the volcanic soils of Pantelleria and the Eolie Islands. These are some of the best wines of their kind in Europe, in particular the delicate Moscato di Pantelleria, the richer Moscato Passito di Pantelleria, and the Eolie Islands' sublime Malvasia di Lipari, especially the version from Salina. ∎

The Mercato della Pescheria in Catania is one of numerous markets in towns across Sicily that sell fresh produce and seafood from the island's fertile land and waters.

History of Sicily

SICILY'S EARLY HISTORY BEGAN GLORIOUSLY, WITH SEVERAL CENTURIES OF Greek domination, and flowered again under Arab and Norman dominion. For almost a thousand years, however, the island suffered grievously at the hands of less cultured and more rapacious foreign rulers. Only today, almost 150 years after Italian unification, are the effects of this long period of misrule being unraveled.

The first peoples to reach Sicily from mainland Italy are thought to have settled around 20,000 B.C., though the earliest known memorials to these Stone Age inhabitants are cave paintings from around 8700 B.C. Neolithic cultures are also known to have flourished around 4000–3000 B.C., especially on the Eolie Islands.

More coherent artifacts survive from around 1250 B.C., when the island was probably inhabited by three distinct groups: the Sikans (or Sicani), who dominated western Sicily, and were probably of Iberian (modern-day Spanish and Portuguese) origin; the Elymians (or Elimi), possibly of eastern Mediterranean origin, who settled in present-day Erice and Segesta; and the Sikels (or Siculi), a people from the Italian mainland who occupied eastern and central Sicily, and from whom the island took its name.

Sicily's proximity to Greece meant that all three peoples, and probably cultures before them, had strong trading and cultural links with the Greeks. It also meant that the more westerly peoples had ties with the Phoenicians from the eastern Mediterranean, who probably established trading outposts on Sicily's southern coast.

In time, the growing population of Greece, together with the Greeks' need to secure westerly trading routes—notably the Straits of Messina between Sicily and the Italian mainland—meant that the Greeks began to establish colonies on the island's eastern coast.

The first of these was Naxos around 735 B.C., followed a year later by Syracuse. Many more were quickly founded, the new colonists generally living side by side or assimilating with the Sikans, who, while resolute and civilized, lacked the Greeks' abilities as sailors and traders. The Greeks' relationship was less happy with the Phoenicians who, in 814 B.C., had established a trading base in North Africa called Carthage. In time this city forged its own empire and its people, the Carthaginians, traded and formed alliances with and against many of the Sicilian Greek colonies.

The first great encounter with the Carthaginians ended with victory for the combined forces of Syracuse, Agrigento, and others at the Battle of Himera (480 B.C.). The ensuing peace allowed most Sicilian colonies to prosper, Syracuse in particular becoming one of the most powerful forces in the known world. So powerful, in fact, that it aroused the envy of Athens, the most dominant of Greece's home cities.

Angered by Syracuse's support for Sparta, another Greek colony, Athens dispatched a vast fleet against Syracuse in 415 B.C. The result was one of the great battles of the ancient world, and a victory for Syracuse that marked the end of the Athenian empire and, effectively, of Greece's golden age.

While Sicily prospered and Greece declined, a new power was emerging in central Italy. By the beginning of the third century B.C., Rome had already defeated most of the Greek colonies on the southern Italian mainland. It had also come into conflict with Carthage in the so-called First and Second Punic Wars (264–241 B.C. and 218–201 B.C.), during which Sicily was one of the main

Above: Fresco "Triumph of Rome over Sicily" by Jacopo Ripanda (circa 1508-1513) depicts the conquering heros of the Punic Wars. Left: Decadrachm of Syracuse (413 B.C.)

battlegrounds. When Syracuse sided with Carthage in the second war, it was besieged and captured by the Romans in 212 B.C., cementing a Roman hold on the island that would endure for some 600 years.

Sicily was one of Rome's first colonies, and one of its most important: Sicilian taxes and tributes are estimated to have covered a fifth of all Rome's expenses in its early years. The island became the empire's breadbasket, supplying grain and other resources. It also provided the conquering Romans with vast feudal estates, or latifundia, whose aristocracy of absentee landlords would be the curse of Sicily until the land reforms of the 1950s.

Such was the rapacity with which Rome exploited the island that when the Roman Empire crumbled in the fifth century A.D., the invading Goths and Vandals found so little of

value that they left Sicily almost unscathed.

Much the same went for the Byzantines, the rulers of Constantinople (modern-day Istanbul), the capital of an eastern empire formed when Rome was divided in A.D. 286. The Byzantines' power outlived that of Rome, and saw them recapture parts of the old western empire, including Sicily, for some 300 years.

During the seventh century, Sicily came under the eye of a new invader, the Arabs of Egypt and North Africa, who made their first incursions on the island in 652. Little else happened until 827, when an inept Byzantine governor asked the Arabs for help to quell a revolt. A force of 10,000 Arabs, Berbers, and Spanish Muslims duly landed near Mazara in southwest Sicily. Within three years it had swept through the west of the island and taken Palermo.

From 878, when Syracuse fell, the Arabs

effectively ruled Sicily. Their reign would be a golden age, the incomers promulgating new ideas in science, philosophy, learning, the arts, and agriculture. Irrigation was introduced, along with crops such as dates, citrus fruits, cotton, silk, sugar, flax, rice, nuts, and henna. Trade blossomed, and with it Palermo, whose wealth and dazzling court made it the Mediterranean's leading cultural and trading center.

In the tenth century, however, unrest in North Africa saw Palermo's role as the center and other mercenaries across Europe, but especially in the strife-torn lands of southern Italy. Here, the outstanding Norman fighters were a group of 12 brothers by the name of de Hautville. One of them, Roger (1031–1101), captured Palermo in 1072. By 1091, when Syracuse, the last Arab stronghold, was taken, he ruled the island and took the title of Count Roger, or Roger I.

The new ruler displayed great toleration of Sicily's mixed population as did his son and

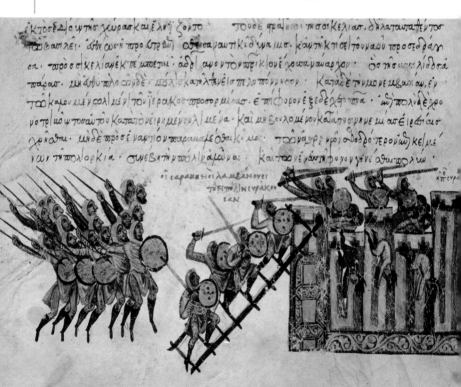

Part of an illuminated medieval manuscript portraying the siege and capture of Syracuse by the Romans in 212 B.C.

of the Arab empire pass to Egypt. This, combined with the fact that the Arabs never established a powerful central authority in Sicily, left the island vulnerable to attack.

The Normans, who originated in Scandinavia, settled in northern France in 911. Renowned fighters, they found work as papal successor Roger II (1095–1154), who ruled from 1101. Sicily prospered again, bolstered by Roger's fusing of the best of Arab, Norman, and Byzantine traditions in art, architecture, administration, and agriculture. His court at Palermo became probably the wealthiest, and certainly the most cultured, of any in Europe.

Count Roger, or Roger I (left), was a popular ruler in Sicily during the 11th century, unlike his 13th-century French counterpart, Charles of Anjou (right).

The Norman system of rule, however, was a feudal one, and relied on the king's supporters being rewarded with grants of lands and titles. This compounded the effects of the Roman latifundia and also created numerous semi-independent barons. Roger's less able son William I (1120–1166) would face several baronial rebellions, though it was the inability of William's son William II (1153–1189) to produce an heir that would have more far-reaching consequences.

In the absence of a natural successor, William II nominated his father's sister Constance (Constanza) as his heir. She was married to Henry of Hohenstaufen (1165–1197), the son of the great Holy Roman (German) Emperor Frederick I, better known as Barbarossa. Thus Sicily's destiny became linked to that of the northern imperial powers.

Henry duly became Emperor Henry VI (and king of Sicily), but died soon after his coronation, leaving Constance as the regent for their three-year-old son, the future Emperor Frederick II (1194–1250).

A man of prodigious talents, Frederick was a consummate statesman, commander, scholar, and legislator, known to contemporaries as Stupor Mundi, or the Wonder of the World. He reestablished Palermo as a court of European stature and rejuvenated Sicily as a whole, but when death removed his firm hand, his empire began to unravel.

His son Conrad IV (1228–1254) died within four years of assuming the throne, leaving Conrad's own son Conradin too young to assume power. Manfred (1232–1266), Frederick II's illegitimate son, then stepped into the breach. In a short time, much to papal horror, he soon controlled much of Italy.

The popes, nominal suzerains of Sicily and Italy, were forever in conflict with the empire, and ever anxious to deprive the Hohenstaufens of territory and influence. With the powerful Frederick II gone and helped by Manfred's illegitimacy (which weakened his claim), they saw their chance. Pope Urban IV, a Frenchman, awarded the title of King of Sicily and Naples to Charles of Anjou, the ruthless younger brother of the French king Louis IX.

On its own the title might have meant little in practical terms, but the Anjou, or Angevins, had an army to back up their new claims. They defeated Manfred and the imperial Hohenstaufen forces in southern Italy in 1266. Manfred was killed during the battle, and his nephew and heir, the 14-year-old Conradin, captured and beheaded by Charles in Naples in 1268.

The unpopularity caused by this act was soon compounded in Sicily by heavy taxes and a vicious campaign of revenge against former

Hohenstaufen supporters. In desperation, Sicilian nobles began to plot against Charles with an antipapal faction in Aragon, part of present-day Spain, whose ruler, Peter III of Aragon (1239–1285), was married to Manfred's daughter, Constanza. This, in his eyes and those of most Sicilians, gave him a claim to Sicily and the rest of the

Giuseppe Garibaldi began his successful military campaign to unite Italy on the west coast of Sicily in 1860.

Hohenstaufens' original domain.

As Charles's oppression continued, 1282 saw a popular revolt against the Angevins that precipitated the arrival of the Aragonese in Sicily. The Sicilian Vespers, as the revolt became known, allegedly was sparked on Easter Monday when a French (Angevin) soldier insulted a woman as the bell of Palermo's Santo Spirito church was calling her to vespers. The congregation reacted with fury, provoking a riot that quickly spread, eventually consuming the whole of Sicily in a frenzy of chaos and killing.

Five months later, Philip of Aragon landed at Trapani in western Sicily. Within days he had been acclaimed king of Sicily in Palermo, though the Vespers war, waged mostly in Spain and at sea between Aragonese and Angevin forces based in Naples, would last another 21 years.

If the Spaniards were initially welcomed, their continued presence in Sicily for the next 578 years would ultimately bring death, chaos, stagnation, corruption, revolution, and a complex legacy that survives to this day. As Sicily turned to Spain, and the Ottoman Turks began to dominate the eastern Mediterranean, an island that had once been at the center of European affairs found itself consigned to the fringes. When Spain itself looked west to the riches of the New World after 1492, Sicily became even more marginalized.

Things started reasonably well. Peter of Aragon's son Frederick II (1296–1337) continued his father's strong, centralist government, but thereafter weaker Spanish rule saw the rise of the barons and civil war between Aragonese and lingering Angevin supporters. To take things in hand, Spain ruled Sicily directly after 1410, nominating a series of viceroys to control the island. None of these, after 1460, would be of Sicilian origin. In all the 300 years of vice-regal rule, only one Spanish monarch ever visited Sicily—Charles V, who made a fleeting call while returning to Spain from Tunisia in 1525.

Spanish rule, and Sicily's isolation, meant it was cut off from most of the great reforms and cultural movements of the Middle Ages. Not only did feudalism survive; it was reinforced as large estates were granted to Spanish nobles in return for military service. The Renaissance had virtually no impact on the island, and after the crowns of Aragon and Castile in Spain were united under Ferdinand and Isabella, the introduction in 1487 of the Inquisition (an oppressive Church court) saw intellectual and cultural life circumscribed.

A conservative Church, long a pillar of Sicilian society, fell in step with a wealthy and conservative aristocracy. This, combined with the widespread corruption in the government, maintained a status quo of prosperity for a few, and poverty and ignorance for the many. The expulsion of the Jews from

Sicily in 1492 was just one example of the repressive tenor of the times.

Almost utter stagnation marked the 16th and 17th centuries in Sicily. This was compounded by natural disaster, notably the cataclysmic earthquake of 1693 and, in time, by the gradual decline of Spain itself.

This decline, and the extent to which Sicily had become a pawn to be bartered by the great powers, was underlined by the Treaty of Utrecht (1713) after the Wars of the Spanish Succession left Spain isolated. This saw the victorious European powers award Sicily to the House of Savoy, rulers of Piedmont in northern Italy.

They then traded it for Sardinia with the Austrians, who in turn, hardly caring for their distant possession, allowed the Spanish, this time under Charles of Bourbon (1716–1788), to capture the island in 1734. If the Aragonese had been bad, the Bourbons were even worse. Any and every means was devised to squeeze money from Sicily.

During the Napoleonic Wars that followed the French Revolution in 1792, Sicily remained the only part of Italy not conquered by Napoléon. Indeed, under its then ruler Ferdinand IV of Bourbon, Sicily supported Britain and her allies in their war against Napoléon, earning Britain's gratitude and support.

Noting Sicily's strategic importance, Britain assumed effective control of the island in 1811. Shocked at what it found, its envoys attempted far-reaching reforms, only to lose interest when Napoléon was defeated. Ferdinand IV returned, and with him—and his successors—a cycle of repression, exploitation, and occasional rebellion that continued until 1860, when the Risorgimento, or campaign to unify Italy, reached its climax.

Italy at the time was divided between the House of Savoy, who ruled much of the northwest; Austria, who controlled the north and east; the French-backed papacy, whose domain extended across much of central Italy; and the Bourbons, who controlled Sicily and southern Italy.

Skillful diplomacy on the part of the Savoys, who spearheaded the unification campaign, won them the backing of Britain and France, and the help of a French army, which

In 1943 Allied forces under Lt. Gen. George Patton invaded Sicily, the first area of mainland Europe to be recaptured from the Nazis in World War II.

duly dislodged the Austrians in 1859.

A year later Giuseppe Garibaldi (1807–1882), a charismatic soldier, who was frustrated by what he saw as the Savoys' slowness in advancing unification, raised a band of troops —the Mille, or Thousand—and decided to force the issue.

Auto workers protest against the closure of their factory near Palermo, a sign of the economic difficulties Sicily faces.

On May 11, 1860, Garibaldi landed at Marsala on Sicily's west coast. Four days later his small band defeated a Bourbon force of 15,000. By the end of July, Messina had been taken and Sicily was at last un-equivocally free of Spanish rule for the first time since 1282. As Garibaldi moved up from the south, revolts and events elsewhere saw the new Kingdom of Italy proclaimed on March 14, 1861.

The distant, northern-based government soon proved as unable, and as reluctant, to address Sicily's ills as any previous Spanish administration. Unrest was quelled not only by repressive government action, but by gangs employed by landowners or their shadowy middlemen—a contributory factor in the growth of the Mafia, a term which began to be current in the 1860s. So desperate was the lot of most Sicilians that the only option was emigration. An estimated 1.5 million left for the Americas, Australia, and elsewhere between 1880 and 1914.

For 50 or 60 years after unification, Sicily simmered or slumbered, beaten, resentful, and impoverished, not only in the grip of political, social, and economic inertia, but also the increasingly strong hold of the Mafia.

After 1922, when Mussolini came to power in Italy, it would be the Fascists, ironically, who would come closest to defeating this criminal elite, thanks to the violent, illegal, and remarkably successful methods of Mussolini's infamous chief of police, Cesare Mori. Even more ironically, it would be the liberating British and Americans during World War II that would reestablish and consolidate Mafia power.

In July 1943, Sicily's strategic position saw it chosen by the Allies as the obvious bridge-head for an attack on Europe's "soft under-belly". During Operation Husky, U.S. and British forces landed on the island's southeast coast, liberating Sicily after 38 days of tough fighting that saw many towns and cities heavily bombed. Their progress on the ground was helped by "prominent citizens" provided by the only men in the United States with the

appropriate contacts: Lucky Luciano and other U.S. Mafia dons. As the Allies marched on, they replaced Fascist mayors and officials in countless towns with these influential men or others who had been "recommended."

After the war Sicily despaired of the new Italian Republic and toyed briefly with separatism, not least under the infamous bandit Salvatore Giuliano (1922–1950), who was eventually conscripted by shadowy anti-Communist forces and died under myster-ious circumstances.

To placate the island, the Italian government awarded it semiautonomous status, with its own regional parliament. This was to little avail, however, because the old

reactionary forces, often in collusion with a Mafia growing rich on the postwar building boom, again stifled reform. Once more the Sicilians' only recourse was emigration; a million people left the island between 1951 and 1971 for the factories of Germany, Switzerland, and northern Italy.

Certain land reforms were gradually pushed through, but centuries too late, because by the 1970s and 1980s the number of people working or dependent on the land was rapidly diminishing.

A gradual change in attitude toward the Mafia, both on the part of Sicilians and of central government, followed the shocking assassination in 1982 of General Della Chiesa, a tough chief of police, and the murders in 1992 of Giovanni Falcone and Paolo Borsellino, two respected Mafia investigators. Crackdowns appeared to have more bite and Sicilians lost some of their old fear.

At the same time the Mafia question remains unresolved as do the evils of poverty and the curse of unemployment, crumbling infrastructure, and a political and bureaucratic system of often dubious reliability. It is depressing to think that a place must remain a prisoner of its past, but in the case of Sicily, sadly, the deep-rooted historical problems engendered by centuries of exploitation and foreign misrule still run deep. Only belatedly, and very slowly, are they being resolved. ■

The arts

THE THREE HIGHEST POINTS OF SICILIAN ART AND ARCHITECTURE—
the temples of the Greeks, the sublime decorative skills of the Arabs and Normans,
and the majesty of the baroque—were forged by Sicily's extraordinary history and its
long periods of isolation from the mainstream of Italian and other artistic traditions.

Sicily's earliest known works of art are ninth-century B.C. incised and painted figures in the Grotta Genovese, a cave on Levanzo. Some 5,000 years passed before its next body of coherent works was created, namely the incised pottery of the Stentinello, a Neolithic culture that was probably found in pockets across much of the island. The pottery's decorative motifs suggest the influence of traders and settlers from as far afield as Cyprus, Syria, Anatolia, the Aegean, Egypt, and North Africa.

Such cross-cultural influences found their most obvious monuments in the art and architecture of the Greeks, whose earliest legacies were the sixth-century B.C. fortresses and fortifications of colonies such as Syracuse. A far greater legacy, however, was the temples of the Sicilian Greeks. Today, more Greek temples survive in Sicily than in Greece itself, with sublime examples at Segesta, Selinunte, and Agrigento—among them the largest and best preserved temples in the Hellenic world.

Most temples in Sicily are Doric, the style of the Parthenon in Athens. A sober but majestic form that originated in the Peloponnese in southern Greece, it is distinguished by its monolithic and slightly fluted, tapered, and baseless columns, and by a relatively unadorned upper section, or entablature. This lack of decoration, and of sculptural reliefs in particular, contrasts with the more ornate temples of mainland Greece and has yet to be properly explained.

By the fifth century B.C., Sicily's temples showed a remarkable uniformity. They were usually peripteral (meaning they were surrounded by a line of columns) and hexastyle (meaning their front elevation contained six columns).

Similar uniformity was found in theaters from the same period. These were the Greeks' other major architectural legacy. Like temples, Greek theaters had a sacred as well as a cultural function. And, like temples, they often were situated in isolated or elevated locales where their impact would be most striking.

Stone theaters, which were often carved from the available surrounding rock, replaced wooden structures after the fourth century B.C. Sicily's most notable examples were the theaters at Taormina, Syracuse, Tindari, and Segesta. Like temples, their design was almost uniform and consisted of the cavea, a semicircular series of tiered ledges; the orchestra, a circular area occupied by the chorus and actors; and the proscenium, an area for scenery and backstage storage.

Piecemeal changes to these theaters were one of the very few legacies left by the Romans in Sicily. Their lack of interest in the island is reflected in an absence of major temples, baths, or other monuments. Although they laid the foundations of Sicily's road network, the Romans' only other significant memorial is the Villa Imperiale del Casale (see pp. 104–107). While this is an isolated example of Roman art, it is also an exceptional one and features the finest collection of Roman mosaics in Europe.

Other art from the period of the late Roman empire is scant: a few traces of wall frescoes in the catacombs at Syracuse, the earliest example of Christian art on the island.

Also lacking are any major monuments to Sicily's next invaders, the Arabs, though their very considerable artistic and architectural acumen survives in the influence they would have on the Normans and their successors.

Prolific builders, they introduced all manner of mosques, gardens, and palaces, as well the skills and imagination required for the decorative conceits that provide their most lasting memorial: the use of colored ceramics, for example; and the introduction of the

The mosaics in the Cappella Palatina in Palermo fuse the best of Arab, Norman, and Byzantine artistic traditions.

Festivals

That Sicily is Italy magnified is clear in its countless festivals, where the many strands of the island's pagan and Christian traditions, its multifaceted history, its food, and the dramatic and visceral aspects of the Sicilian temperament find their most colorful expression.

Take Noto, a small town in Sicily's southeast corner, where there are events that embrace all aspects of the island's festival tradition—religious, pagan, and cultural: There are celebrations of the town's patron saint and protector. Then there is a festival, the Infiorita, with pagan roots that celebrates spring when the streets are carpeted in vignettes of fresh flowers. Finally there is La Notte di Giufa, a night devoted to music and storytelling.

This is Noto, but it could be almost anyplace in Sicily. Every community has its saint—and the larger the town, the more lavish the festival. In Palermo, the U fistinu festival dedicated to Santa Rosalia lasts for six days, but even the tiniest hamlets enjoy at least a day's worth of festivities in honor of their patron.

Religious festivals peak on Good Friday when many towns stage processions and celebrations that have not changed for centuries. Some of the most enthralling are in Trapani, Marsala, and Enna, where hooded penitents carry statues of the dead Christ and Addolorata (Our Lady of Sorrows).

Elsewhere, historical tradition is marked in Piazza Armerina, where the Palio dei Normanni celebrate the town's liberation by the Normans, while Gangi continues the pagan tradition of Sagra della Spiga, dedicated to the goddess Demeter (Ceres). Local products, always a source of pride and an excuse for feasting, feature in many small festivals. ■

Left: Villagers in traditional dress during Randazzo's Festa Mediovale. Below: Randazzo's Processione della Vara. Above: Mosaics of flowers fill the streets during the Festa della Infiorita.

horseshoe arch, intricate geometric and arabesque designs, gloriously carved and painted wooden ceilings, and delicate honeycombs of stalactite plasterwork *(muqarnas)*.

While the Normans were supremely tolerant of their Muslim subjects, most of the Arabs' buildings were appropriated and altered, the result being the distinctive Arab-Norman hybrid that represents Sicily's second great artistic flowering. To the Arabs' decorative skills the Normans added their own Roman-

Normans' demise proved anathema to art and architecture. As a result, Sicily largely failed to register the impact of the Gothic art then being forged in the developing city states of central and northern Italy.

The exceptions were in Syracuse, Catania, and Enna, where Gothic forms were introduced when the towns' castles were refortified in the middle of the 13th century. The Gothic new wave also made mild ripples in Palermo, where the so-called Chiaramonte style fused

Left: Doric columns support one of Selinunte's eight temples. Right: Mosaics decorate the columns of the cloister at Monreale, a masterpiece of Norman art.

esque forms, notably the rounded arches and carved capitals and cloisters copied from France's great Burgundian and Provençal churches. In embracing Greek- and Byzantine-influenced mosaics, the Normans also added a third element to what would be a remarkably coherent composite style.

The results of this hybrid were not only some of Sicily's finest medieval buildings, but some of the finest buildings of any era anywhere. Most of them are religious rather than secular, the most notable being Palermo's Cappella Palatina and the cathedrals of Cefalù and Monreale, places where decorative elaboration, and mosaics above all, reached its apotheosis.

The political instability that followed the

classic Gothic mullioned windows with Arab-Norman decorative features to create a widespread local Gothic idiom.

By the middle of the 15th century, the consolidation of Aragonese (Spanish) rule in Sicily further stifled the development of the flamboyant Gothic style then reaching its zenith in northern Italy. Instead, the island's ruling Spanish viceroys and their architects naturally looked to Spain, where a more sober Gothic style was prevalent—a form that can be seen in the main doorway of Palermo's cathedral and the Palazzo Corvaja in Taormina.

The key Sicilian exponent of the style was Matteo Carnelivari (active in the late 15th century), a native of Noto in southeast Sicily who was responsible for Palermo's Abatellis and Ajutamicristo palaces.

The same Spanish bias, together with Sicily's increased isolation from the Italian mainstream, also accounts for the almost total absence of any great artists of the caliber emerging in Florence and elsewhere in the mid-15th century. This bias and underlying stagnation continued for the next hundred years, a period that embraces the height of the Italian Renaissance, an artistic reawakening

galleries in Messina, Cefalù, and Syracuse, and his masterpiece, the "Annunciation" (1476), in Palermo's Galleria Regionale.

In Renaissance sculpture, the story was similarly limited, with only two artists making an impact on the greater Italian stage. The first was Francesco Laurana (1430–1502), a Dalmatian artist who spent five years in Sicily (1466–1471) during which time he worked on the Cappella Mastrantonio in Palermo's church of San Francesco and com-

Left: Torre dell'Orologio and Orion Fountain in Messina. Right: One of the palaces of the Quattro Canti, the baroque heart of Palermo

that passed Sicily by almost completely.

That it did not leave the island entirely untouched was due to Antonello da Messina (1430–1479), the only Sicilian painter in the first rank of Renaissance artists. Even then, da Messina had to leave Sicily to forge his career, probably learning his craft in the workshops of Naples and Venice, where he would have come into contact with Flemish painters and leading Italian artists such as Giovanni Bellini and Piero della Francesca.

From the Flemish he acquired a consummate skill in the handling of oil paint, then a relatively new and exacting medium. Just four of his typically understated and subtly colored paintings survive in Sicily: one each in

pleted his celebrated bust of Elenora of Aragon (now in Palermo's Galleria Regionale).

The second was Domenico Gagini (circa 1430–1492), a sculptor from Lombardy in northern Italy who founded a dynasty of sculptors that included his son, Antonello, born in Palermo in 1478. Gagini's descendants continued to thrive in Sicily until the mid-17th century.

If the Renaissance eluded Sicily, the period of the baroque during the 17th and 18th centuries marked the island's third period of artistic transcendence. One reason was the ornate and theatrical nature of baroque style, which suited the Sicilians' love for the decorative, a passion that dated back to the Arab period. With this came

Above: Ornate decoration, a main characteristic of baroque architecture, on Palermo's church of San Ippolito. Below: "The Annunciation" was the last painting of Antonello da Messina.

the Sicilians' natural flair for color, marble, gilding, and other effects and embellishments.

Another reason was that the baroque found favor in Spain, and thus Sicily, which was still under Spanish rule. Yet another was the catastrophic 1669 earthquake, which destroyed swaths of southeast Sicily, opening the way for the creation of new or nearly new towns such as Noto, Ragusa, and Scicli, where architects could give full rein to their baroque ambitions.

The greatest of such architects, Messina-born Filippo Juvarra (1676/8–1736), abandoned his native Sicily in 1700, achieving fame in Rome, Madrid, and Turin. Of those that remained, nearly all were priests, and nearly all trained in Rome, then the epicenter of Italian baroque. Their training notwithstanding, most added a peculiarly Sicilian twist to their work, giving lie (as with the Normans' reworking of Arab and Byzantine idioms) to the notion that Sicilian art only copied or recycled the imported styles of its many foreign rulers.

Scholars still debate the precise influences and intricacies of Sicilian baroque. But briefly put, whereas baroque elsewhere in Italy reveled in geometry and the complex interplay of light and shadow, Sicilian baroque was more exuberant and concerned with detail and fantastical decoration. Some of its earliest proponents were Paolo Amato (1633–1714), responsible for Palermo's San Salvatore, the first Sicilian church built on a curvilinear plan, and Giacomo Amato (1643–1732), who built numerous palaces and churches in his native Palermo. Better known were Giovanni Battista Vaccarini (1702–1770), who redesigned 18th-century Catania virtually singlehandedly, and Rosario Gagliardi (circa 1700–1770), the most important of the architects who created the "new" towns of the southeast corner after the 1669 earthquake.

Sicilian painting and sculpture in their purest forms may have been negligible during the baroque period, but the work of the craftspeople responsible for the decoration of palaces and churches was second to none. The island's greatest decorative artist was Giacomo Serpotta (1656–1732), whose extraordinary work in stucco (plaster) graces the oratories of Santa Cita, San Domenico, and San Lorenzo in Palermo.

Thereafter, the art and architecture rarely touched the heights, with the exception of brief visits from mainland artists such as Caravaggio (1573–1610) in 1609, and the flowerings of the neoclassical and Liberty, or art nouveau, styles in the 19th and early 20th centuries.

More recently, the energetic expressionistic paintings of Renato Guttuso (1912–1987), born in Bagheria just east of Palermo, have achieved fame in Italy and beyond, as have the bronzes and other works of Catania-born sculptor Emilio Greco (1913–1995).

LITERATURE

Sicily's early literary glory was borrowed or reflected. Many of the episodes in Homer's Greek epic *The Odyssey,* for example, take place in Sicily, and the island was the setting envisaged by the Greek writer and philosopher Plato (circa 427–347 B.C.) for the utopian state propounded in his *Republic.*

Later, the wealth of patrons in the island's Greek colonies lured other Greek writers, notably poets such as Pindar (522–443 B.C.) and the great playwright Aeschylus (525–456 B.C.), both of whom worked in Syracuse. Home-grown talent included Syracuse-born Theocritus (circa 300–260 B.C.), who is credited

with inventing pastoral poetry.

In medieval times, a pure form of Sicilian, stripped of its colloquial idioms, became one of Europe's foremost literary languages. The genre reached its zenith under Emperor Frederick II in the 13th century, when his court played host to exponents of the Sicilian School of Poetry. The schools's poets included Giacomo da Lentini (circa 1210–1260), who is often credit-

Bust of Aeschylus, the fifth-century B.C. Greek playwright who worked in Syracuse

ed with inventing the sonnet form, and who, with his contemporaries, looked to the Provençal troubadour tradition for the style and content of his tales of courtly love. While this tradition would fade, Sicilian literature, even today, has never lost its taste for dialect and the vernacular.

Nor in its greatest writers has it flinched from confronting the travails and complexity of life in Sicily. This has naturally required a strong sense of realism, an approach pioneered in the 19th century by the poems of Mario Rapisardi (1844–1912) and the theoretical writings of Luigi Capuana (1839–1915).

It also formed the cornerstone of the writings of Giovanni Verga (1830–1922), the first

**Luigi Pirandello, 1934 Noble Prize winner in literature, aboard the S.S. *Conte Di Savoia*
October 5, 1935**

major Sicilian writer to make a lasting impact on the greater international stage. In novels such as *I Malavoglia* (1881), he explored what he saw as the real Sicily, portraying the lives of ordinary Sicilians in a characteristically somber prose style.

Realism also influenced the early work of Sicily's best known writer, Luigi Pirandello (1867–1936), whose plays and experiments with form and content won him the Nobel Prize for Literature in 1934. His play *Six Characters in Search of an Author* (1921) explored the theme of isolation and the role of individuals in societies or situations alien to them.

Pirandello's body of work was in contrast to the single, lyrical masterpiece of Giuseppe Tomasi di Lampedusa (1896–1957), an aristocrat whose posthumously published novel *Il Gattopardo (The Leopard)* is a magnificent study of the profound social changes in Sicily in the mid-19th century. Today, Lampedusa is one of only a few Sicilian writers whose works are available in translation, an honor shared by Elio Vittorini (1908–1966), a staunch anti-Fascist best known for *Conversation in Sicily* (1937), a deceptively simple novel that follows an emigrant returning to Sicily and his encounters with fellow travelers and everyday Sicilians.

Vittorini continued Sicilian literature's affinity for realism and the use of Sicilian as part of literary language. So, too, did the widely translated Leonardo Sciascia (1921–1989), who, in novels such as *The Day of the Owl* (1961), used the conventions of crime fiction to explore the complexities of the Mafia and Sicilian life. Similar political and social issues were also the concern of the poet Salvatore Quasimodo (1901–1968), awarded the Nobel

Prize for Literature in 1959.

The principal traits of Sicilian literature continue to flourish in the work of Andrea Camilleri (born 1925), whose crime novels—popular in Italy and abroad—are not only highly realistic, but they use Sicilian expressions and dialect to powerful and original purpose.

CINEMA

Sicily is a filmmaker's dream: The island's complex and often contradictory nature make it ripe for interpretation and cinematic exploration. The people, similarly, are both generous and hospitable, but also proud, passionate, and inscrutable. The ravishing countryside and historic towns and villages provide locations galore. And in the Mafia lies a subject that, for good or bad, is tailor-made for the big screen. No wonder that the island has attracted some of the world's finest directors.

Many of the best early films set in or inspired by Sicily were based on the island's great literary works. The Italian director Luchino Visconti, for example, used Giovanni Verga's masterpiece *I Malavoglia* as the inspiration for his 1948 movie *La Terra Trema (The Ground Trembles)*, the tale of an impoverished fishing community near Catania. The same director looked to another literary masterpiece, *Il Gattopardo*, by Giuseppe Tomasi di Lampedusa for his eponymous 1963 epic starring Burt Lancaster, Alain Delon, and Claudia Cardinale.

Landscape was part of the inspiration for Roberto Rossellini in *Stromboli: Terra di Dio (Stromboli: Land of God)*. The 1950 movie stars Rossellini's real-life lover, Ingrid Bergman, as a Lithuanian refugee involved in a torrid affair with a native fisherman amid the harsh volcanic landscapes of Stromboli, one of Sicily's Eolie

Actors Burt Lancaster and Claudia Cardinale in the film version of di Lampedusa's great novel *The Leopard*.

Roberto Rossellini (left) and Ingrid Bergman during the filming of *Stromboli: Terra di Dio* on Sicily's Stromboli Island

Islands. The same islands feature as settings in the Taviani brothers' visually stunning *Kaos* (1984), based on several often mournful and bittersweet stories by Luigi Pirandello.

A more poetic view of the Aeolians appears in Michael Radford's touching 1994 movie *Il Postino (The Postman)*, set on Salina in the 1950s. Massimo Troisi plays a postman hired to deliver mail to the exiled Chilean poet, Pablo Neruda, who guides him to a love of poetry (which gets him the girl) and a greater political awareness (which results in his death). The film garnered several Oscar nominations and was hugely popular abroad, echoing the success of Giuseppe Tornatore's autobiographical *Cinema Paradiso* (1988), a wonderfully nostalgic, comic, and exuberant look at the arrival of the talkies in Sicily.

Films about crime and the Mafia in Sicily had an early pedigree, notably *Salvatore Giuliano* (1961) by the great Italian director Francesco Rosi, one of several Italian filmmakers to adapt the subtle, crime-based novels of Leonardo Sciascia for the big screen. The 1976 movie *Cadaveri Eccellenti (Excellent Corpses)* is one of the most accomplished of these adaptations.

Over time, though, Mafia films became a debased cinematic staple in Italy, portraying a dramatic but biased view of Sicily. It took an Italian American to redefine the genre—Francis Ford Coppola, whose *The Godfather* trilogy (1972–1990) was set partly in Sicily.

Recently, Italian films have followed his more intelligent lead, notably Tullio Giordana's *I Cento Passi (The Hundred Steps)*, the story of a journalist who was murdered by the Mafia, which won the best screenplay award at the 2000 Venice Film Festival. ■

Sicily's many artistic, cultural, and historic strands come together in its colorful capital, Palermo, a teeming, decaying, fascinating city that provides a magnificent introduction to the island's rich past and occasionally troubled present.

Palermo

Detailed stonework decorates the exterior of the cathedral in Palermo.

Nuns approach La Martorana, or Santa Maria dell'Ammiraglio, on Piazza Bellini.

Palermo

BIG, BATTERED, AND BUSTLING, PALERMO IS NOT A CITY FOR ALL TASTES; ITS traffic, poverty, and decaying sense of baroque grandeur are not for the fainthearted. At the same time, it is one of Italy's most vibrant and atmospheric cities, a sultry, sensuous place of ancient origin that still bears the stamp of its Arab, Norman, and Spanish rulers. Monuments to past glories rise amid the modern tenements and cramped backstreets, fighting for space in a city whose Arab bazaars, flourishing port, seedy dives, and teeming thoroughfares offer a dramatic contrast between past and present.

Palermo's stupendous site has long been its lure: a natural harbor, a ring of encircling mountains, and, between, the sweeping amphitheater of the Conca d'Oro, or Golden Shell. Once a fertile hinterland of palms, citrus groves, and vineyards, the Conca d'Oro now is virtually lost under the apartment blocks of the 720,000 people who call the modern city home.

The area's earliest inhabitants were probably the prehistoric dwellers whose engravings adorn caves on Monte Pellegrino, the 1,988-foot-high (606 m) mountain to the north. From about the eighth century B.C., the city was a port and trading post for the Phoenicians and Carthaginians, peoples of North African origin, The latter prevailed until the city fell to the Romans in 254 B.C. A golden age began under the Arabs—from 831 to 1072—and continued in the 12th centu-

ry with the Normans, under whom Palermo became the most cultured, cosmopolitan, and prosperous city in Europe.

The Normans bequeathed Palermo its greatest monuments—the cathedral at Monreale and the Cappella Palatina in the Palazzo dei Normanni—but the flavor of Arab rule is apparent in the labyrinthine streets, busy markets (notably Vucciria), the love of flamboyant decoration, and the city's exotic and colorful air. But so, too, is the mark of later epochs, the accretion of the centuries being one of Palermo's defining and most alluring qualities.

Extravagant baroque and Renaissance churches, for example, are found at every turn—notably La Martorana, San Giuseppe dei Teatini, and the oratories of San Domenico and Santa Cita. Then there are the museums,

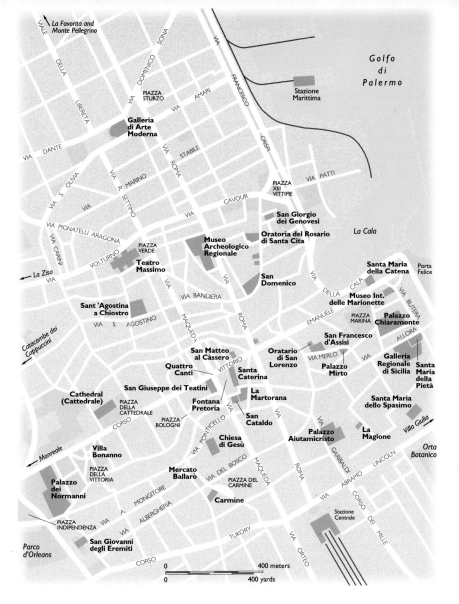

La Favorita and
Monte Pellegrino

VIALE

DELLA

LIBERETA

VIA DANTE

VIA

VIA S. OLIVA

VIA CARINI

VIA PIGNATELLI ARAGONA

La Zisa →

VIA

Catacombe dei
Cappuccini

Monreale

Parco
d'Orleans

SCINA

DOMENICO

PIAZZA
STURZO

AMARI

Galleria
di Arte
Moderna

VIA ROMA

STABILE

VIA R. MARINO

VIA SETTIMO

VIA

PIAZZA
VERDE

VOLTURNO

Teatro
Massimo

PIAZZA
VERDE

Sant 'Agostina
a Chiostro

VIA S. AGOSTINO

MAQUEDA

San Matteo
al Cassero

VITTORIO

Quattro
Canti

San Giuseppe dei Teatini

Cathedral
(Cattedrale)

PIAZZA
DELLA
CATTEDRALE

CORSO

PIAZZA
BOLOGNI

VIA PONTICELLO

Fontana
Pretoria

Santa
Caterina

La
Martorana

San
Cataldo

Villa
Bonanno

PIAZZA
DELLA
VITTORIA

Chiesa
di Gesù

Mercato
Ballarò

VIA DEL BOSCO

MAQUEDA

Palazzo
dei
Normanni

PIAZZA
INDIPENDENZA

VIA A. MONGITORE

ALBERGHERIA

PIAZZA DEL
CARMINE

Carmine

VIA

San Giovanni
degli Eremiti

CORSO

TUKORY

VIA ORTEO

SCINA

VIA FRANCESCO

CRISPI

CAVOUR

PIAZZA
XIII
VITTIME

VIA PATTI

VIA BANDIERA

ROMA

San
Domenico

Museo
Archeologico
Regionale

San Giorgio
dei Genovesi

Oratoria del Rosario
di Santa Cita

DELLA CALA

EMANUELE

Oratorio
di San
Lorenzo

Oratario di San
Francesco
d'Assisi

VIA MERLO

Palazzo
Mirto

San
Domenico

Stazione
Marittima

Golfo
di
Palermo

La Cala

Santa Maria
della Catena

Porta
Felice

Museo Int.
delle Marionette

PIAZZA
MARINA

Palazzo
Chiaramonte

VIA BUTERA

ALLORA

Galleria
Regionale
di Sicilia

Santa
Maria
della
Pietà

Santa Maria
dello Spasimo

Palazzo
Aiutamicristo

La
Magione

Villa Giulia

Orta
Botanico

GARIBALDI

LINCOLN

ABRAMO

ROMA

CORSO DEI MILLE

Stazione
Centrale

0 ————— 400 meters

0 ————— 400 yards

---

the equal of anything in Italy, such as the
Galleria Regionale and Museo Archeologico
that showcase the centuries' art and artifacts.

Yet for all the splendor, there is no doubt
that Palermo is damaged: traffic is a curse,
noise cacophonous, poverty endemic, and grim
modern building—a legacy of corrupt local
government and Mafia malfeasance—a terrible
blight. And yet not irreparably damaged, for in
the last few years honest administrators have
begun to turn the city around, directing considerable sums from the central government
and the European Union to the restoration of
the historic center. Decadent decay will always
be one of Palermo's defining charms, but at least
now there is the certainty that this decay will
remain picturesque rather than terminal. ∎

Palermo visitor information

📍 Map p. 43 & inside back cover

✉ Piazza Castelnuovo 34–35

☎ 091 583 847 or 091 605 811

Corso Vittorio Emanuele II and the streets around the **Quattro Canti** make up the bustling hub of historic Palermo.

Quattro Canti
 Map p. 43

✉ Via Maqueda & I Corso

Around Quattro Canti

THE QUATTRO CANTI HAS NOT ALWAYS BEEN AT PALERMO'S heart. The center of the ancient and Arab-Norman city was bounded by two small rivers, the Kemonya and Papireto (now a street), and focused on an area to the west of the crossing around the site of the present cathedral. Its main thoroughfare was known as the Càssaro, which derived from the Roman *castrum* or the Arabic *kasr,* both meaning "castle." As the city grew and the rivers became silted, the Càssaro—now the western half of Corso Vittorio Emanuele II— was extended eastward in 1565, eventually reaching the sea in 1581. Via Maqueda, the street that crosses the Corso at the Quattro Canti, was laid out in 1600, thus cementing the easterly shift of the city center.

The **Quattro Canti** itself was created between 1608 and 1620. Initially it took the name Piazza Vigliena, after the duke of Vigliena, the Spanish viceroy who commis-

sioned the crossing and its four **baroque palaces.**

Each palace's facade is divided into three sections, and each section boasts a central statue and one of

Fontana Pretoria (1554–55), a magnificent central fountain that lends the square its colloquial name, the Piazza della Vergogna, or Piazza of Shame, after the uninhibited nudity of its many male and female figures. Local nuns, it is claimed, were so outraged by the work that they broke off the noses of the male statues, only modesty preventing them from removing the more obvious male protuberances. The fountain is the work of a Florentine, Camillo Camilliani (active 1550–1586), and was commissioned by the city's then Spanish viceroy, Don Pedro of Toledo, for his Tuscan villa. The viceroy's son eventually sold the statue to Palermo, where it was reassembled to mostly lascivious approval in 1573.

The fine buildings around the square add to the fountain's considerable theatrical effect, notably the flank and dome of the sumptuously decorated but rarely open Dominican church of **Santa Caterina** (1566–1596) and the **Palazzo Pretorio** *(tel 091 740 1111, open occasionally Sat. a.m.),* also known as the Palazzo delle Aquile, after the eagles *(aquile)* that adorn its exterior.

Begun in 1463, but much remodeled since, the palace has long served as the seat of the city's council and is still the Municipio, or City Hall. The facade contains a statue (1661) of St. Rosalia (1132–1166), a niece of the Norman king, William I, who became Palermo's patron saint after a procession of her bones, found in 1624, was believed to have saved the city from a plague epidemic. The facade's many plaques commemorate a variety of events witnessed by the square, including visits from Pope John II and Giuseppe Garibaldi, one of the leading lights of the campaign to unify Italy in the mid-19th century.

three orders of classical columns: Doric, Ionic, or Corinthian. The fountains and statues on each of the lowest registers symbolize the four seasons; the central statues represent the four Spanish kings of Sicily (see p. 26); and the upper statues portray the four patron saints (Christina, Ninfa, Oliva, and Agatha) of the old city quadrants defined by the Quattro Canti—the Kalsa (southeast), Amalfitania (northeast), Sincaldi (northwest), and Albergheria (southwest).

Once this was a natural meeting place, but the intense traffic now means that pedestrian respite is best enjoyed on **Piazza Pretoria** immediately to the south. Here, the most eye-catching feature is the

The 12th-century decorations in the church of La Martorana are some of the oldest and most magnificent in Palermo.

Across Via Maqueda from the piazza is **San Giuseppe dei Teatini** *(closed noon–5 p.m.),* a plain-faced church built between 1612 and 1645 with a lavish baroque interior. Just north of the square, on the Corso, is the more modest and only intermittently open **San Matteo** *(tel 091 334 833),* another richly decorated mid-17th-century church with links to the Miseremini, an order devoted to the hearing of Masses for souls suffering in Purgatory.

Of more note are the churches on Piazza Bellini adjoining Piazza

Pretoria to the south: San Cataldo and **La Martorana** *(tel 091 616 1692, closed Sun. p.m. & daily 1:00–3:30 p.m.)*, the city's most compelling church after the cathedral.

Begun in 1143, this glorious building is also known as Santa Maria dell'Ammiraglio, or St. Mary of the Admiral, after its Syrian founder, Georgios Antiochenos, who became Norman king Roger II's "commander of the ocean," or *amir al-bahr* in Arabic, from which English derives the word "admiral." The church's more common name comes from a now vanished convent nearby founded in 1146 by Eloisa de Marturanu, whose nuns were presented with the church in 1433. These were the same nuns who invented Sicily's celebrated *frutta martorana*, or *pasta reale*, marzipan cakes and candies shaped and colored to resemble fruit.

Sadly, the nuns were less inspired when it came to their inherited church, where their many alterations destroyed much of the original Norman building and its decoration. They left untouched, however, the magnificent mid-12th-century mosaics of the dome, the side vaults, and the left and right apses. By the door on the west end, on both sides of the steps, look for two mosaic panels in baroque frames: One shows a kneeling Antiochenos presenting the church to the Virgin; the other depicts Roger II (labeled *Rogerios Rex*) being crowned by Christ. The latter is the only known portrait of the king in Sicily.

Next door to the south, **San Cataldo** *(tel 091 872 8047, closed p.m.)*, with its distinctive bulbous domes, lacks its neighbor's mosaics, but is still a captivating Norman building. It was founded by Maio di Bari, William I's chancellor, but left largely undecorated on his death in 1160. The interior's columns are from an older structure and the

marble pavement survives from the original church.

Walk south from San Cataldo on Via Marqueda and after a few steps Via Ponticello leads to a square containing the **Chiesa del Gesù** *(Closed Sun. p.m. & daily 11:30 a.m.–5:00 p.m.)*. Built between 1564 and 1636, it was the first church founded by the Jesuits after their arrival in Sicily. Their masterpiece on the island, it shows the Jesuits' typical love of decorative excess, a trait designed to awe potential doubters after the advent of Protestantism with a show of sheer grandeur.

Just beyond the church, Via Ponticello continues to Piazza Ballarò, the northern limit of the **Mercato Ballarò**, a superb general market *(closed Sun.)* which infiltrates the streets and alleys to the south as far as Piazza del Carmine. This is the fringe of the **Alber-gheria district**, one of Palermo's poorest quarters, an area that has never really recovered from bomb damage suffered in 1943. This said, its tiny streets, moribund palaces, and ancient tenements are wonderfully atmospheric to explore.

The soaring, tile-covered dome of **Chiesa del Carmine** *(Piazza del Carmine, tel 091 651 2018, closed Sat.–Sun., & p.m.)*, strikes an incongruously grand note amid the market's picturesque squalor. Inside, the highlights are two extravagantly decorated altars in the transepts.

From the church, retrace your steps, heading toward **Piazza Bologni**, a large baroque square off the corso that leaves you well placed to visit the cathedral and Palazzo dei Normanni. ■

A carved stone angel exemplifies the exuberant baroque sculpture adorning the church of San Giuseppe dei Teatini.

Cathedral

www.cattedrale.palermo.it

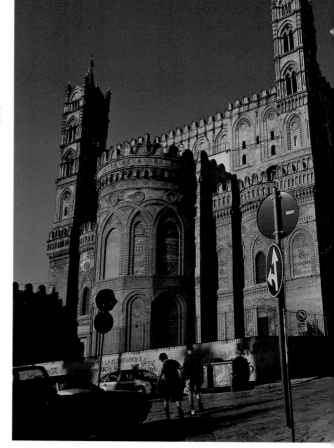

Map p. 43

Piazza della Cattedrale, off Corso Vittorio Emanuele II

091 334 376

Treasury & crypt: closed Sun.

Treasury & crypt: $

The Western City

PALERMO'S WESTERN QUARTER WAS THE HEART OF THE ancient city, its high ground the site of the fortresses and palaces of Sicily's rulers over almost three millennia. Its principal sights are the cathedral, built over a former mosque, and the majestic Palazzo dei Normanni, whose tiny Cappella Palatina is the city's most compelling Norman monument.

Palermo's **cathedral,** had it not been tampered with over the centuries, would rank as one of Italy's foremost churches. Built on the site of a Byzantine church and later ninth-century mosque, it was founded in 1185 by William of the Mill, Palermo's English archbishop. William had been sent to Sicily by King Henry II to tutor William II, in anticipation of the future Norman king's marriage to Joan

Plantagenet, the English sister of King Richard I, better known as Richard the Lionheart. Once in Sicily, the tutor insinuated himself into Sicilian politics, gaining the office of archbishop, in the words of one contemporary historian, "less by election than by violent intrusion." His foundation of the cathedral was in response to his former pupil's foundation of Monreale (see pp. 64-67), the great

Old and new:
Moorish motifs
of Palermo's
12th-century
cathedral con-
trast with the
whimsical art
of a later era.

cathedral just outside Palermo, designed in part to undermine the archbishop's power.

It is unlikely that the church would have matched Monreale, but enough survives of the original to suggest that its mosaics (these were removed in the 15th century) and decorative stonework would have been of the first rank. That they are not is mostly the fault of Ferdinando Fuga, an 18th-century architect commissioned to "improve" the cathedral with a baroque and neoclassic makeover. Fuga ripped out the wooden ceiling, tore down several walls, and whitewashed much of the interior. Perhaps his worst crime was the addition of the anomalous dome (1781–1801).

On the exterior, only the wonderful Islamic-inspired stonework at the church's eastern end hints as to what might have been, along with the Catalan Gothic **main porch** on the south side (*Piazza della Cattedrale*), begun around 1426. This is noted for the fine portal and doors (1426–1432), the early painted decoration (1296) above the three main arches, and a column on the left beneath the porch inscribed with a passage from the Koran, evidently a surviving fragment of the earlier mosque.

The **chapel** in the cathedral's southwest corner contains six Norman and Aragonese **royal tombs,** including that of the Norman king Roger II (died 1154; rear left), removed, against his wishes, from the cathedral at Cefalù; that of his daughter, Constance (died 1198; rear right);

The Palazzo dei Normanni was built on the site of an early Arab and Roman fortress.

and the grave of Frederick II (died 1250; left front), the great emperor and king of Sicily. Also buried here is Constance of Aragon (died 1222; far right),

PALAZZO DEI NORMANNI

West of the cathedral, the Palazzo dei Normanni, or Palace of the Normans, occupies the highest point in the old city, a position that probably has contained either the castle or royal palace of Sicily's rulers since Phoenician times. Even today, the present building on the site is the seat of the Assemblea Regionale Siciliana, the Sicilian regional parliament, housed here since 1947. The area's first documented fortress was an Arab castle, abandoned by the ruling emir for reasons of security in 938, when the royal residence was moved to the Kalsa district to the southeast. The castle was later reoccupied and enlarged by the Normans, when it became the seat of the most splendid European court of its day.

Much has been added since, notably the long facade (1616), a legacy of Spanish rule, and little of the Arab-Norman building now exists. The principal exceptions are the **Torre Pisana** at the northern end, the only survivor of four original towers, and the **Cappella Palatina,** an exquisite fusion of Arab, Norman, Byzantine, and Sicilian art and architecture. Be prepared to stand in line at this popular site during busy periods.

The Cappella was begun as a private chapel by Roger II in 1130 and largely completed by about 1140. Once it would have stood alone, but over the years it has been enveloped by the burgeoning palace. Inside, the chapel is split into two, with a lower nave divided into three aisles by ten granite columns, and the raised chancel and apses at the eastern end. The latter area contains the older mosaics, the chief glory of the chapel's extraordinary decorative scheme. Probably the work of Byzantine artists, these panels (circa 1140–1150) cover the apse and cupola, with the dominant image

Cappella Palatina

🅰 Map p. 43

✉ Palazzo dei Normanni, Piazza Indipendenza

☎ 091 705 6001

🕐 Closed Sat. p.m. & Sun.

Frederick's wife, whose crown was removed from her tomb and is one of the exhibits in the cathedral's fascinating little **treasury,** entered at the top of the south (right) aisle. Equally interesting is the **crypt,** entered from the north transept, where among 23 numbered tombs is the sarcophagus (No. 16) containing the remains of William of the Mill, the church's founder.

the apse figure of Christ Panto-crater *(see photo p. 31)*. The later nave mosaics (circa 1150–1170) portray scenes from the Book of Genesis on the south wall. The aisles show episodes from the lives of Sts. Peter and Paul.

This Islamic influence is more marked in the glorious wooden ceil-ing, carved from Lebanese cedar and decorated by Arab craftspeople with scenes from an idealized daily life. Roman and Norman artists left their mark in the 12th-century Cosmati stone floor, marble walls, and majes-tic pulpit. (The Cosmati were Roman masons who gave their name to a style of decorative stone inlay.) The same artists made a greater impact in the large candlestick, a spiraling sculpture with over a hundred fig-ures topped by Christ holding the Gospels. A figure in the garb of a bishop kneels below, and two ranks of birds (vultures and storks) sup-port three figures symbolizing the three ages of humankind.

Elsewhere in the palace only a limited area is open to the public, notably the Sala di Re Ruggero *(Palazzo dei Normanni, Piazza Indipendenza, tel 091 705 1111 or 091 705 7003, closed Sun., Tues.– Thurs., & p.m. daily)*, or Salon of King Roger, which can be seen on a 30-minute guided tour. Part of the former Royal Apartments, it echoes much of the Cappella Palatina, par-ticularly in its mosaics (1140), which portray hunting scenes in typical Sicilian countryside, and symbolic animals: the lion, suggesting royalty and strength, and the peacock, whose supposedly incorruptible flesh made it a symbol of immortality.

SAN GIOVANNI DEGLI EREMITI

The picturesque red domes of this deconsecrated church (1132–1148) make it one of the city's most dis-tinctive landmarks. Situated south of the Palazzo dei Normanni, it is Palermo's most romantic Norman monument, not so much because of its austere interior, but because of its Moorish domes, its beautiful clois-ters, and the little garden, a scented pocket of green calm, full of palms, bougainvillea, jasmine, and orange trees. The church was built on the orders of Roger II, and almost

The distinctive domes of San Giovanni degli Eremiti reveal the work of Arab-influenced architects.

certainly stands on the site of an ear-lier mosque, part of which probably survives in the shape of the simple hall to its right.

If the gardens here whet your appetite for escape, then the **Villa Bonanno** is a larger oasis just to the northeast of the church. Entered from Piazza della Vittoria, the large public park is a perfect place to relax and watch the Paler-mitans at play. ■

San Giovanni degli Eremiti
🅐 Map p. 43
✉ Via dei Benedettini
☎ 091 651 5019
🕐 Closed Sun. p.m.
💲 $$

The Mafia

Everyone has heard of the Mafia. The word first appeared in Italian around 1860. By 1866, it was quoted by Sicily's British consul, who reported to his superiors that "*maffie*-elected *juntas* share the earnings of the workmen, keep up intercourse with outcasts and take malefactors under their wing and protection." Both the word and the organizations of which the consul spoke have ancient origins: The linguistic roots probably lie in an Arab word, *mu'afàh*, which means many things—protection, skill, beauty, ability, and safety.

The organizational roots are more elusive. Many scholars believe the seeds were sown as early as the 12th century, when secret societies were created to resist the imposition of rule by the Holy Roman Empire. Others point to the Bourbons, who used ex-brigands to police the remote Sicilian interior, a system that quickly led to the brigands taking bribes in exchange for turning a blind eye to the activities of their former criminal colleagues. Many also cite the rise of the so-called *gabellotti*, middlemen who acted as rent collectors or mediators between peasants or landowners and quickly grew rich by intimidating the former and acting as agents for the latter. United by similar aims, the gabellotti quickly became a separate class, bound by distinct codes of honor, behavior, and semiformal organization.

All theories are linked by a common thread: The centuries-old gulf between Sicilians and agents of authority, a gulf fostered by Sicily's long succession of exploitative foreign rulers. Nowhere was the breach more keenly felt than by landless peasants forced to work on the island's latifundia, vast feudal estates owned by absentee landlords in Naples or Palermo. The system went back to Roman times and survived until well after World War II. Where conventional justice and authority were either lacking or despised, it was only a matter of

time before the gap was filled by all manner of local arbitrators—the so-called *amici* (friends) or *uomini d'onore* (men of honor).

The traveler Patrick Brydone, writing in *A Tour through Sicily and Malta*, summarized the situation in 1773: "These banditti," he wrote, "are the most respectable of the island, and have the highest and most romantic notions of what they call their point of honour…with respect to one another, and to every person to whom they have once professed it, they have ever maintained the most unshaken fidelity. The magistrates have often been obliged to protect them, and even pay them court, as they are known to be extremely

A policeman regards the impromptu shrine to Paolo Borsellino, the popular anti-Mafia investigator murdered by a car bomb in 1992.

determined and desperate; and so extremely vindictive, that they will certainly put any person to death who has ever given them just cause of provocation." He might easily have been describing events two centuries later.

What many people do not know is that Italy once came within a whisker of overturning this state of affairs. Under Mussolini, the legendary police chief Cesare Mori used brutal and entirely illegal measures to combat the Mafia, and, but for World War II, might have crushed it entirely. Ironically, it was the intervention of the Americans that foiled the venture. In preparing for the invasion of Sicily in 1943, the Allies had only one source of intelligence and logistical support—the Mafia—with whom it forged links by exploiting the contacts of Italian-

American gangsters such as Lucky Luciano.

Once the Allies had taken the island, they further reinforced Mafia power by drafting its often highly placed members onto the new Allied Military Government—of 66 Sicilian towns, 62 were entrusted to men with criminal connections. Mafia power was further consolidated in Italy's postwar boom, when huge fortunes were made in construction. Money was then laundered into legitimate businesses or funneled into narcotics, a trade that altered forever the nature of Mafia business. Despite occasional judicial successes, the Mafia's dismemberment remains highly unlikely largely because its tentacles are now so tightly entwined in Italy's legitimate economy: Not for nothing do the Italians refer to the Mafia as *la piovra*—the octopus. ■

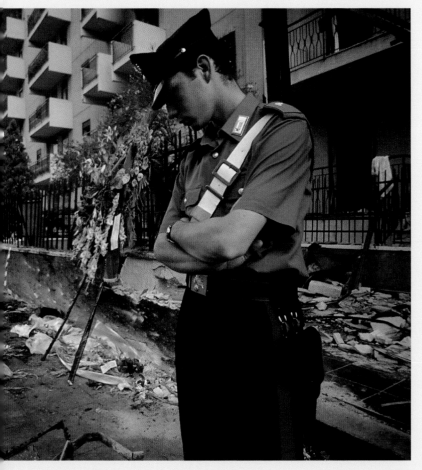

The Eastern City

THE EASTERN QUARTER OF PALERMO FROM THE QUATTRO
Canti to the harbor embraces the Kalsa, the old Arab and medieval
heart of the city. Badly damaged by Allied bombing in 1943, it is a traditionally poor area, but one that is undergoing belated restoration,
and includes many palaces, churches, and the excellent Galleria
Regionale, the city's foremost art gallery.

Start a tour of eastern Palermo at
the Quattro Canti and walk east
along Corso Vittorio Emanuele II
to Via Roma, a relatively modern
street that was pushed through the
district in 1922.

Just beyond it, Via Paternostro
leads right to **San Francesco
d'Assisi** (*Piazza di San Francesco,
tel 091 582 370*), a 13th-century
church much altered over the centuries. Outside, the main Gothic
portal and pretty rose window are
the key features, while inside the
highlight of the stripped-back interior is the Cappella Mastrantonio,
the fourth chapel on the south
(left) side. Its lovely carved arch
(1468), the work of Francesco
Laurana (1430–1502), was the first
major Renaissance work in Sicily.

Also noteworthy are the eight
statues in the nave by Giacomo
Serpotta (1656–1732), who was
responsible for the outstanding
stucco work of the **Oratorio di
San Lorenzo** (*entrance at Via
dell' Immacolatella 5*) next to the
church on the left. The artist's masterpiece, the decoration depicts
events from the lives of St. Laurence
(Lorenzo) and St. Francis of Assisi.

Via Merlo leads from Piazza San
Francesco to the 17th-century
Palazzo Mirto on the right (*Via
Merlo 2, tel 091 616 7541, closed
Sun. p.m.*), the seat of the Lanzi-
Filangeri family before it was
donated to the city in 1982. The
interior offers a good idea of how
a princely family residence of the
period might have looked, with

lovely furniture, antiques, and a
series of well-preserved rooms.

Via Merlo opens out beyond the
palace onto the large **Piazza
Marina,** part of the old port
before it silted up. Most activity
centers on the central Giardino
Garibaldi and its magnificent
banyan trees. The area was once
close to two prisons, including one
run by the Spanish Inquisition, and
was the scene of burnings and
other public executions.

Palazzo Chiaramonte
dominates the piazza's eastern
flank, built in 1307 for the Chiaramonte, Palermo's most flamboyant
14th-century family. The building
was later appropriated by Palermo's
Spanish viceroys and handed to the
Inquisition. Between 1782, when
the Inquisition was abolished in
Sicily, until 1972, it served as the
city's law courts. Today, it is used
for occasional exhibitions. Note the
wonderful lower windows, whose
decoration is so distinctive that the
name Chiaramonte is given to the
style, which is used in many buildings around the city.

Not far from the palace is one
Palermo's most charming museums, the **Museo Internazionale
delle Marionette** (*Piazzetta
Niscemi 5, tel 091 328 060, closed
Sun.*). Devoted entirely to puppets,
its fabulous 3,000-strong collection
embraces marionettes from across
Sicily, where puppet theaters were
an important cultural phenomenon
for centuries before their decline in
the 1960s. Today there has been

**The Museo Inter-
nazionale delle
Marionette holds
one of the world's
largest collections
of puppets, includ-
ing this knight.**

Guests dine alfresco at the Antica Foccaceria on Piazza San Francesco in the heart of old Palermo.

something of a revival of the old plays and courtly characters. Along with performances, the museum also devotes considerable space to puppets from around the world.

North of the museum and Piazza Marina is La Cala, all that remains of the old Arab and Norman port, which once extended much farther into the heart of the city. On its south side, on the corso, stands **Santa Maria della Catena** *(tel 091 326 597, closed Aug., & Sat.–Sun. & daily p.m.),* an elegantly restored 16th-century church whose name—St. Mary of the Chains—probably derives from the chain *(catena)* that was once stretched nightly across the harbor from this point.

To the east, at the end of the corso, is the modern **waterfront,** entered via the Porta Felice (1582) gateway. In its day, this was one of Italy's great promenades, but the current area, cut through by the busy Foro Italico-Umberto I,

though still a popular meeting place, is an unattractive affair.

Backtrack through the Porta Felice, passing the **Passeggiata delle Cattive,** or Walkway of the Mean-Spirited, on the south (left) side of the corso. One of the last fragments of the old Arab wall that once enclosed the Kalsa, it takes its name from the old women who used to look disapprovingly on the antics of couples promenading below.

Just beyond, turn left off the corso on Via Butera, passing the impressive 17th-century Palazzo Branciforti on the left and, alongside it, the site of the Trinacria, Palermo's smartest hotel between 1844 and 1911. Soon after comes Via Butera's intersection with Via Alloro, traditionally the Kalsa's main street, though its once fine palaces have suffered greatly from years of neglect.

One that hasn't is the Palazzo Abatellis (1484–1495), home to the **Galleria Regionale di Sicilia**

(Via Alloro 4, tel 091 623 0011, closed Sat.–Mon. p.m.), Palermo's foremost gallery of paintings and sculpture. The pictorial highlight is the "Triumph of Death" (circa 1449), the work of an unknown (but possibly Flemish or central Italian) painter. Many later artists, including Pablo Picasso, were inspired by the work. Other highlights include Francesco Laurana's 15th-century bust of Eleonora of Aragon and the paintings in rooms that trace the history of Sicilian art from Byzantine times. Here are several works by Antonello da Messina, Sicily's foremost Renaissance painter, and in particular his "Annunciation" (1476), considered his masterpiece.

Before leaving the vicinity of the gallery, look quickly at the churches immediately to its east and west on Via Alloro, both with fine facades and richly decorated interiors: the 17th-century **Santa Maria della Pietà** *(tel 091 616 5266, closed Sat. & Sun. p.m.)* is on the left as you face the gallery and 15th-century **La Gancia** *(tel 091 616 5221, closed Sun. p.m.)* is on the right.

Turn left off Via Alloro beyond La Gancia and Via Vetriera leads to Piazza dello Spasimo, named after the nearby **Santa Maria dello Spasimo** (1509), a rare piece of Sicilian Gothic architecture. The church's name probably derives from the first spasm of pain endured by Mary when she saw Christ on the Cross. Now deconsecrated, the building serves as an important cultural center, and has become a symbol of the restoration underway in the Kalsa.

Further evidence of this restoration can be seen in the blossoming **Villa Giulia** *(Via Lincoln)* to the south, once a park (created in 1778) in which no self-respecting Palermitan would venture by day, never mind night. Next door is Palermo's delightful botanical garden, the

Orto Botanico *(Via Lincoln 2b, tel 091 623 8241, closed Sat. & Sun. p.m.),* first opened in 1795.

If the green spaces do not appeal, turn west (right) on Via dello Spasimo to see the isolated **La Magione** *(Piazza Magione),* a sensitively restored Arab-Norman Romanesque church founded in 1151. From the church, Via Magione leads west to Palazzo Aiutamicristo (1490) and Via Garibaldi, named after the eponymous Italian revolutionary who led his troops up this very street in 1860 during the campaign to unify Italy. ■

The deconsecrated church of Santa Maria dello Spasimo has been transformed into one of Palermo's cultural centers.

The colorful Vucciria market trades in fish, meat, cheese, vegetables, and other foodstuffs.

A walk around the Northern City

Northern Palermo hinges around two districts: The Capo, one of the most impoverished and battered parts of the old center, and the Vucciria, an area centered around a superb market. The latter lies close to the city's main historical museum and two oratories that contain some of Palermo's finest baroque decoration.

Start a tour of the northern city by walking east from the Quattro Canti on Corso Vittorio Emanuele II. After two blocks on the left stands the little church of **San Matteo al Càssero** ❶ *(tel 091 334 833, closed Sun. p.m.),* whose interior features 17th-century statues by Giacomo Serpotta, a foretaste of the superb works you will see later in the walk by this master of stucco (plaster) decoration.

A left turn up Via Roma leads past the church of **San Antonio** ❷, rebuilt after an earthquake of 1823, which commands the highest point in the eastern quarter of the old city. Steps alongside the church, and streets to the north and the south, lead to

The 1640 Chiesa de San Domenico contains the tombs of many of the city's illustrious citizens.

the **Mercato Vuccirìa** ❸, Palermo's wonderful main market *(closed Sun. & daily p.m.)*. Less a feast for the senses than an assault on them, the narrow streets here are crammed with stalls selling everything from cascades of brains, tripe, swordfish, and live octopus (among many other foodstuffs) to fake designer bags, contraband cigarettes, and bargain-priced household goods such as porcelain pasta bowls and espresso cups.

At the market's northern limit, and just off Via Roma, stands the large church of **San Domenico** ❹ *(Piazza San Domenico, tel 091 329 588, closed Mon.–Fri. p.m.)*. It was rebuilt in its present form in 1640, only the lovely cloisters surviving from the 14th-century original. Inside are the tombs of numerous illustrious Palermitans, but here the interest is found not in the main church but in the tiny oratory to its rear—the 16th-century **Oratorio del Rosario di San Domenico** ❺ *(Via Bambinai 2, closed Sat. p.m. & Sun.).*

The interior of the oratory is filled with some of Palermo's finest baroque decoration, namely the extraordinary stucco work of Giacomo Serpotta, who was born in the city in 1656 and devoted most of his life to working in a medium with little of the versatility, tradition, or potential for artistic glory of paint or marble. This oratory was his last work (1720)

- See area map below
- Quattro Canti
- 1 miles (1.6 km)
- 4 hours
- Teatro Massimo or the Capo

NOT TO BE MISSED
- Vucciria
- Oratorios del Rosario di San Domenico and di Santa Cita
- Museo Archeologico Regionale

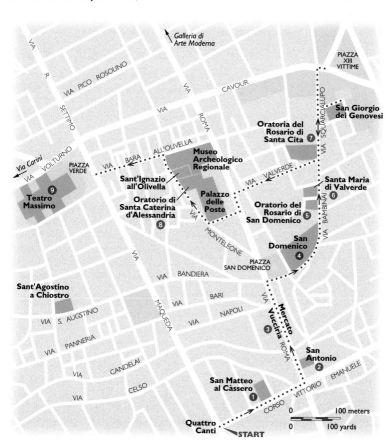

The restored 19th-century Teatro Massimo has become a symbol of Palermo's recent cultural rebirth.

and one of his most joyful and vivacious. The cream of Palermo's high-society ladies provided the models for the many allegorical figures. Gracing the main altar is a painting by Anthony Van Dyck, the "Madonna with St. Dominic and the Patron Saints of Palermo" (1628), completed in Genoa after a plague epidemic forced the artist to flee Palermo.

Continue north on Via Bambinai, passing on the left **Santa Maria di Valverde** ⑥ *(tel 091 332 779, closed Sat. p.m. & Sun.)*, another 17th-century church with a majestic baroque interior. A few steps beyond stands **Santa Cita,** or Zita, rebuilt between 1586 and 1603, but badly damaged by bombs in 1943. Here, as in San Domenico, the main attraction is not the main church, but its oratory, the **Oratorio del Rosario di Santa Cita** ⑦ *(Via Squarcialupo, tel 091 332 779, closed daily p.m. & Sun.)*, usually entered through the church.

Here, too, the lure is the work of Serpotta, who between 1686 and 1718 created another

mesmerizing swirl of stucco angels, miscellaneous figures, and numerous cherubs (for which Palermo's street children provided the models). The centerpiece at the rear of the nave is a depiction of the Battle of Lepanto (1571), in which a Christian fleet defeated the Ottomans (Turks). During the battle the victorious fleet looked for protection to the Madonna of the Rosary, hence the stucco reliefs elsewhere in the oratory portraying 15 Mysteries of the Rosary. The south (right) wall depicts the so-called Sorrowful Mysteries—including Calvary, the Thorn of Crowns, and Christ's Flagellation—and the left wall the Joyful Mysteries, notably the Resurrection, Ascension, and Assumption of the Virgin.

To the north and east of Santa Cita is an area badly damaged in 1943, a forlorn part of the city best avoided except for a brief few steps down Via Squarcialupo to glance at **San Giorgio dei Genovesi** (1581), a now deconsecrated church built for Palermo's Genoese merchants, and **Piazza XIII Vittime** beyond, a square with monuments

The Museo Archeologico Regionale displays Greek, Roman, and other artifacts from archaeological sites across Sicily.

to the 13 nationalists shot by the Bourbons in 1860 on the eve of Italian unification. Also here is a shrine (1989) to victims of the Mafia.

Walk back to Santa Cita and turn right (west) down Via Valverde to emerge on Via Roma in front of the city's colossal post office, a brutal Fascist-era monolith (1933). Walk behind it on little Via Monteleone past the **Oratorio di Santa Caterina d'Ales–sandria** ❽ on the right at No. 50 *(tel 091 872 8047, open Thurs. mid-day),* which has stuccos (1719–1726) by Giacomo Serpotta's son and apprentice, Procopio. Also visit the church next door, **Sant'Ignazio all'Olivella** *(tel 091 586 867, closed Sun. p.m.),* a gloriously opulent baroque affair built in 1598 on the reputed birthplace of Santa Rosalia, Palermo's principal patron saint.

Alongside it is the northern quarter's main highlight, the **Museo Archeologico Regionale** *(Piazza Olivella-Via Bara all'Olivella 24, tel 091 611 6805, closed. Sun. p.m. & Mon.).* Devoted to the history and archaeology of western Sicily, this museum's only Sicilian rival is the museum in Syracuse, which performs a similar role for the eastern part of the island. Most eras of Sicily's long past are covered, with wonderful displays of Neolithic, Phoenician, Greek, Roman, Arab, Norman, and other artifacts. The highlights are the metopes, or sculpted reliefs, removed from the temples at Selinunte (see pp. 92-94); 12,000 votive offerings to Demeter Malophoros from the same site; a fine collection of Greek ceramics; and seven Roman bronzes, including a celebrated third-century B.C. bronze ram.

Round off a tour of the northern city by following Via Bara west from the museum to see the **Teatro Massimo** ❾ (1875–1897), Europe's third-largest opera house. Then, if time and spirits allow, venture southwest into the heart of the **Capo,** Palermo's least developed and least savory popular neighborhood, and in particular the **market** in and around Via Carini—but be prepared for a very poor and often shabby area. ∎

Convento dei Cappuccini

🅰 Map p. 43
✉ Via Pindemonte-Piazza Cappuccini
☎ 091 212 117
💲 $

Catacombe dei Cappuccini

LONG AFTER OTHER MEMORIES OF YOUR VISIT TO SICILY have faded, the chances are that you will recall the Convento dei Cappuccini with a sort of grisly fascination. In one of Italy's most bizarre and macabre sights, the corpses of some 8,000 people are preserved in period dress and in various states of bodily decay.

Dressed as in life, preserved corpses of monks, priests, and others interred in the Capuchin catacombs offer a macabre window on the past.

Little in the entrance to the Capuchin convent on Palermo's outskirts suggests what is to come. A long, whitewashed corridor curves underground, a faint, unearthly smell of damp and decay assaulting the nostrils. Then comes a scene from somewhere between a horror film and a canvas by Hieronymous Bosch. Row after row of lolling heads, faces twisted in grimaces, frozen screams, and

skeletal smiles gaze down from cobwebbed corridors. Men, women, and children, dressed as they were on the day of death, or in clothes they chose for the afterlife, stand shackled to the walls. Skulls and splintered bones break through stretched and shrunken yellow skin. Time has been kind to a few. Some are simply theatrical, others, in slippers and top hats, almost comical. Many, hooded and funereal, are the Grim Reaper incarnate.

This bizarre catalog of death is unique. Other catacombs have their ossuaries, vast repositories of bones and skulls, but only here has the effort been made to immortalize corruptible flesh. At first, the dubious honor of cheating death was reserved for the convent's Capuchin monks. The first was placed here in about 1599. In time, however, rich patrons of the monastery came to share the perverse privilege. Eventually, anyone with sufficient funds could buy a place. Business was brisk until outlawed in 1881.

Various methods were used to preserve bodies. During plague epidemics, corpses were preserved in baths of arsenic or covered in a protective coating. Upon others, doctors performed crude surgery to leave only skin, hair, and nails. The most common method was simple desiccation, bodies being left in special terra-cotta urns or placed in closed cells in the area's dry tufaceous subsoil. After eight months of burial or drying, corpses were pickled in vinegar, baked in the sun, and then sent to join the bodies already in the catacombs. Once, all the corpses were fitted with glass eyes, but U. S. troops carried them off as souvenirs in 1944.

The collection is divided into sections: men, women, priests, and so-called professionals, the last rewarded with a coffin, albeit one that is open or has windows cut into its sides. Whether as a reward or perverse prudery, virgins are also segregated, as are cardinals and archbishops, distinguished by the faded glory of threadbare vestments. In fact, it's the clothes and other memento mori that are most poignant: bones pushing through kid gloves, fine silks and satins crumbled almost to powder, and the fading Sunday best of some inmates, the peasant burlap of others.

The family groups are particularly moving. In one corner, a small group stands under an Old Testament quote from Job: "I said to putrefaction and the vermin: You are

my mother and father." Nothing, however, is as affecting as the corpse of two-year-old Rosalia Lombardo, who died in 1920, but whose auburn hair and honeyed skin are almost perfectly preserved. Her embalmer, a local doctor, took the secret of his successful (and illegal) techniques to the grave. ■

Living and the dead: Visitors view rows of corpses (above), which are segregated by gender, social rank, and profession.

Monreale

Visitor information

✉ Piazza Vittorio
   Emanuele II

☎ 091 656 4501

Monreale

🗺 Map p. 43

✉ Piazza Vittorio
   Emanuele II

☎ Cathedral: 091 640
   4413. Cloister: 091
   640 4403

💲 $ (Tower, treasury,
   & cloister only)

🕐 Cathedral: open
   daily. Cloister: closed
   Sun. p.m.

MONREALE IS ONE OF EUROPE'S SUPREME CATHEDRALS, a monument to the greatest traditions of Arab, Norman, and Byzantine art and architecture. Sadly, it has the misfortune to be stranded in a town almost subsumed by the seething suburbs of present-day Palermo. Brave the surroundings, however, because the church, and its mosaics in particular, constitute Sicily's single greatest treasure.

Monreale was built on the whim of one man—the Norman monarch, William II (1153–1189). The king's royal predecessors had all endowed or created magnificent religious foundations in Sicily. William—who liked to be called al Musta'izz bi'llah, or "He who exalts in God"—was determined to do the same. The impulse to build the

church, he claimed, was the result of a dream-vision he experienced in 1174 in which the Madonna revealed the location of a great treasure concealed by his father, William I (1120–1166). The treasure was hidden on Monte Reale, or the Royal Mountain, a royal hunting estate in the hills above Palermo. It was to be used, the vision instructed,

Walter. Second, in turning over the completed church to the Benedictines, William was able to create a new archbishopric to challenge that of Palermo, for the abbot of a religious order thus endowed automatically became archbishop.

Walter's response was to begin work on his own pet project—the enlargement of Palermo's cathedral—though he could scarcely match the colossal financial outlay of William. As for his response to the new archbishopric, there was little to be done, especially when Pope Alexander III gave Monreale his special blessing, further undermining Walter's authority.

Exactly where William found the resources necessary to build so sumptuous a church is one of Monreale's many mysteries. Unlike projects of a similar scale—the cathedral in Orvieto, for example, which took 350 years to complete—the Sicilian cathedral took a little over 10 years from vision to consecration. Such speed must have required prodigious numbers of laborers and craftspeople, not to mention considerable sums for precious marble and other materials—the mosaics alone consumed 4,885 pounds (2,200 kg) of the highest quality gold.

The effects of so rapid a creation were significant. That the project was so personal to William

The sublime mosaics (left) and carvings (above) in the Monreale cathedral represent the pinnacle of Arab-Norman art and architecture.

to build a magnificent church.

In truth, the motives for creating so magnificent a building were as much political as religious. In Walter of the Mill, Palermo's powerful English archbishop, William had a significant political foe. The autocratic archbishop had vast lay as well as religious powers, and the support of much of the nobility. The king, by contrast, was more kindly deposed toward the papacy, an institution for which the independently minded nobles had little sympathy.

The creation of Monreale would have two advantages: First, an awe-inspiring building would underline William's worldly power—and undermine the prestige of Archbishop

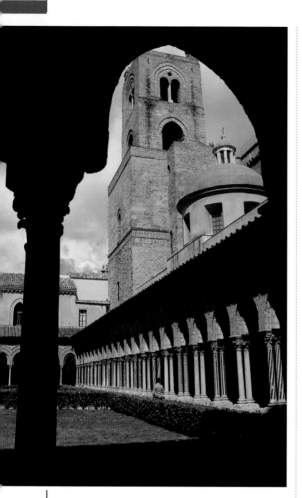

The 228 pairs of decorated columns in the cloisters at Monreale display an extraordinary blend of classical, pagan, religious, and other influences.

meant that Monreale's political influence survived only as long as the king, who died just four years after the cathedral's completion. More significantly, it meant that the building achieved an architectural and decorative unity that would have been compromised by a longer gestation. Thus in Orvieto, and most other major medieval building projects, the changing architectural taste over several decades or centuries was often reflected in a medley of Romanesque, Gothic, and other styles.

In Monreale the result was not only Europe's finest Norman building and its finest synthesis of Arab and European styles, but also the world's most extensive array of medieval Christian mosaic work.

Little on the cathedral's **exterior**, however, suggests the splendor within. The two towers on the west end facing Piazza Guglielmo II (William II Square) frame a banal porch added in the 18th century, an approach that is lifted by the fine portal and superb **bronze door** (1186). The latter is the work of Bonanno da Pisa, the architect largely responsible for the Leaning Tower of Pisa. The door's 46 panels depict scenes from the Old and New Testaments, their earthy, Romanesque simplicity in marked contrast to the more intricate Byzantine-influenced panels of the door (1179) by Barisano da Trani on the left (north) side of the cathedral on Piazza Vittorio Emanuele II.

Inside, the building is a marvel, shimmering with gold leaf, paintings, richly colored marble, and a staggering array of mosaics. If you have seen Palermo's Cappella Palatina (see pp. 50–51), founded by Roger II, William's grandfather, both its interior and decoration are similar, though on an massively grander scale. The arches of the nave, the main central body of the church, are carried on 18 slender columns, all made from granite except for one, which is of *cipollino* (onion) marble, probably designed to symbolize the office of archbishop. The columns clearly come from some earlier pagan temple or temples, though from where scholars are unsure, for the stone is of northern European origin.

The **mosaics,** one of Europe's great artistic glories, surpass even those of Ravenna (on Italy's east coast) and the Basilica of St. Mark in Venice. Covering an area of

64,000 square feet (5,950 sq m), the cycle was probably completed around 1182 by a combination of Greek, Byzantine, and Sicilian craftsmen. Some of the mosaics, notably those that line the nave and walls, are probably later works, dating from after William's death. These panels have a greater naturalism and sense of movement, suggesting that they are the work of Venetian artists sent south on the orders of the papacy.

The nave mosaics depict episodes from the Old and New Testaments, starting with the Creation in the upper tier at the nave's far end on the right (south) side and moving clockwise around the church. Mosaics in the crossing and transepts portray scenes from the Nativity and Christ's Passion, while the central apse's vast centerpiece is the majestic half figure of Christ Pantocrater, hovering above the traditional hierarchy of Madonna, angels, and named saints.

The right (south) transept contains the tombs of William I and William II, while across the church in the opposite transept are the tombs of Margaret, Roger, and Henry, the wife and sons of William I. To their right is an inscription recording the presence in 1270 of the French St. Louis, whose body was laid in the cathedral en route to France after his death in Tunis during the Crusades. His heart is buried here.

Close to the tombs is the entrance to the cathedral **treasury,** home to numerous precious reliquaries, though your time is better spent climbing the 180 steps to the roof for superlative views of the cathedral, the cloisters, Palermo, and the town of Monreale. The entrance is in the lower right (southwest) corner of the church. The climb should whet your appetite for a closer look at the **cloisters,** a sight which alone is worth a visit to Monreale. They are entered outside the cathedral from Piazza Guglielmo II.

The cloisters, part of the old Benedictine abbey attached to the cathedral, represent another pinnacle of Arab-Norman art, their

Children play around a statue of William II, Monreale's Norman founder, who is portrayed presenting his cathedral to God.

myriad arches borne by 228 paired columns and capitals, very few of which are alike. Most of the fabulous 12th-century Romanesque capitals are the work of Burgundian and Provençal masons, and display a bewildering range of decorative themes, mixing religious, pagan, classical, mythical, and other iconography.

Be sure to visit the monastery **gardens,** usually entered from the southeast corner of Piazza Guglielmo II. They are a lovely spot with some fine old plants, including several magnificent banyan trees. ■

Getting there

Monreale is easily reached from central Palermo by organized tour (inquire at visitor center); by cab (can be hard to secure for return trip); by 389 bus, which departs from Piazza Indipendenza every 20 to 30 minutes. By car, park in one of the lower lots, take stairs to center.

More places to visit in Palermo

LA FAVORITA
This large park, created in 1799 at the foot of Monte Pellegrino (see below), is best visited in daytime to see the **Museo Etnografico Siciliano Pitrè** *(Via Duca degli Abruzzi 1, tel 091 740 4893, closed Fri.)*. This is Sicily's largest ethnographical museum and an essential visit for anyone interested in folk traditions. Among the many aspects and objects of traditional Sicilian life shown here are the beautifully painted carts for which rural Sicily was once famous.
 Inside back cover

LA ZISA
The best of the few surviving Arab-Norman secular buildings, **La Zisa** *(Piazza Zisa 1, tel 091 652 0269, closed Sun. p.m., $)* is one of the Norman palaces built on the city's outskirts. The 12th-century palace has been beautifully restored and the gardens screen the encroaching modern world. To the north is the **Villa Whitaker Malfitano** *(Via Dante 167, tel 091 681 6133, closed Sun. & daily p.m.)*, built in 1887 by an English wine merchant. It is full of exquisite furniture and fittings, and the large park and garden contain rare trees and shrubs.
Inside back cover

MONDELLO
Palermo's seaside resort, with its 1.25-mile (2 km) sandy beach, lies 7 miles (11 km) northwest of city center between Monte Pellegrino and the headland at Capo Gallo. In summer many people come for the waterfront trattorias, where the morning's catch of fish and seafood is laid out for inspection. For quieter resorts, continue west around the headland to the Golfo di Carini and the towns of Sferracavallo, Isola delle Femmine, and Terrasini .
Inside back cover Bus: 806 and 833 from Piazza Sturzo or Via delle Libertà.

MONTE PELLEGRINO
Rising 1,988 feet (606 m) northwest of Palermo, this rocky redoubt is a popular destination for hikers and picnickers. Take the panoramic Via Pietro Bonanno to the Santuario di Santa Rosalia *(tel 091 540 326)*, an unexceptional 17th-century sanctuary built over the cave in which were discovered the bones presumed to belong to St. Rosalia. A road and steep trails continue beyond here to the mountain's summit, a fine viewpoint just 9 miles (14 km) from Palermo's Viale delle Libertà.
Inside back cover ■

The beach at Mondello sheltered by the craggy slopes of Monte Pellegrino

The area south and west of Palermo is one of the most culturally and scenically varied in Sicily, a patchwork of ruggedly beautiful islands, magnificent coastlines, and historic towns of ancient origin.

Western Sicily

Tins of tuna from the island of Favignana, where fishing has been an economic mainstay for hundreds of years

Western Sicily

WHERE EASTERN SICILY LOOKS HISTORICALLY TO ANCIENT GREECE, THE island's seafaring western region leans to Africa, and to the age-old cultures of the Arabs and Carthaginians. Although marginalized and wracked by poverty, it retains several glorious medieval villages, some resplendent ruins, and a handful of Sicily's most beautiful islands and maritime landscapes.

The farther south you travel in Italy, the poorer and harsher life becomes. Western Sicily, the country's most peripheral region, graphically underscores that point. Only recently, with the opening of the A 29 autostrada, has this insular and rather indefinable area become more integrated with Sicily, never mind Italy.

Parts of the region have a reputation as a Mafia heartland, and though times are changing, the names of villages in Palermo's hinterland such as Prizzi and Corleone have the most sinister resonance of any on the island.

Casual visitors, though, will find little or

no evidence of Mafia activity. On the contrary, they will find a region of complex history and wonderfully varied attractions.

On the west coast, the provincial capital, Trapani, is closer to Tunisia than it is to the Italian mainland, which lends the area's landscape and manners a distinctly African hue. Elsewhere, there are straggling whitewashed villages (the names of which can be traced to Arabic roots), a summer light of shimmering intensity, and festivals and traditions—notably the *mattanza*, the ancient, ritual springtime slaughter of bluefin tuna —in which distant cultures still resonate.

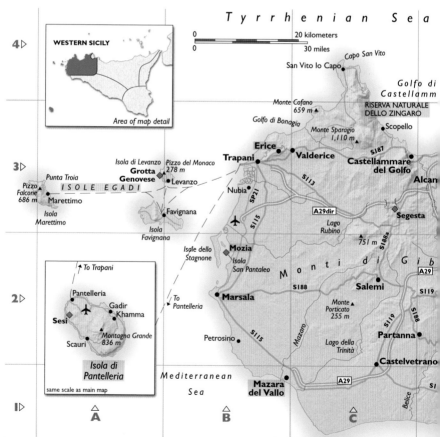

The majestic silhouette of Monte Cofano dominates the coastline near San Vito lo Capo.

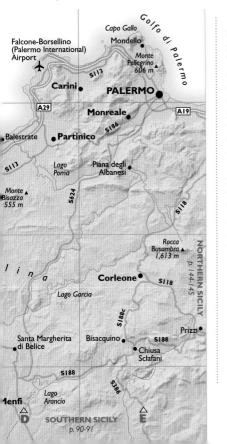

The area reflects its African links with Carthaginian settlements such as Mozia and the Arab towns of Marsala and Mazara del Vallo. But it also embraces ancient peoples of more mysterious origin, notably the shadowy Elymians (Elimi), responsible for the temple at Segesta, Sicily's most romantic ruin, and the sacred citadel of Erice, now the island's finest medieval village, but once the Mediterranean's most important temple to the goddess of love.

Further variety is apparent in the region's many landscapes, from the olive groves, vineyards, and fertile plains of the interior to the salt marshes of Trapani, the beaches of San Vito lo Capo, and the peerless coastline of the Riserva Naturale dello Zingaro, Sicily's first protected nature reserve. Equally stunning landscapes can be found on the rugged and mountainous island of Marettimo, one of the Isole Egadi (Egadi Islands), and on strange, volcanic Pantelleria, a chic island stranded halfway to Africa.

Food and wine across the region are also excellent, with superb fish, seafood, and Arab-influenced dishes such as couscous, as well as celebrated wines including Marsala and the rare dessert wines of Pantelleria. ■

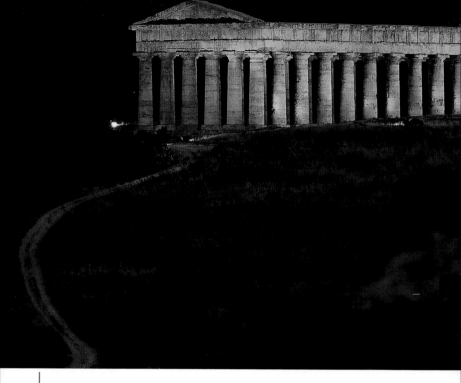

Dramatic lighting casts a glow on Segesta's glorious, unfinished temple.

Segesta

SEGESTA IS SICILY'S MOST CAPTIVATING GREEK TEMPLE, not because it is the largest or best preserved—though its appearance is one of the most perfect and harmonious imaginable—but because of its locale, rising in glorious isolation in the middle of beautiful pastoral countryside.

Tempio di Segesta

Map pp. 70–71 C3

1.25 miles (2 km) E of A 29dir (Segesta exit)

0924 952 356

9 a.m.–one hr. before sunset

$$

The ancient city of Egesta was the principal city of the Elymians, or Elimi, who also founded and settled Erice (see pp. 76-79). Some scholars believe this mysterious people originated in Spain or Liguria on Italy's west coast; others claim they came from Anatolia. The Elymians themselves, according to later Greek historians, claimed to be refugees from the Fall of Troy.

The site was probably settled in the 12th century B.C., but was rapidly hellenized after the Greeks arrived in Sicily. From about 580 B.C. it was in almost constant dispute with the Greek colony of Selinus, or Selinunte (see pp. 92-94). It looked to Athens as an ally in 426 B.C., famously deceiving the Athenian ambassadors sent to the city as to the extent of its wealth, but suffered when the Athenians were defeated by Syracuse in 420 B.C. It

Segesta's ancient Greek theater fits perfectly into the natural setting.

The temple probably dates from around 426 B.C. to 416 B.C., but evidently was left unfinished. One theory is that the temple was part of the deception designed to lure the Athenians into an alliance; built quickly and cheaply, it was left unfinished once their allegiance had been won. No ancient writings survive, however, to reveal the true story.

There is a parking lot, ticket office, and bar at the entrance. A ticket also will give you access to the **theater,** the only other major survivor of ancient Egesta, located 1.2 miles (2 km) away or a 20-minute walk. *(Road is closed to cars, but in summer a shuttle bus runs every 30 min.; tickets are sold at the bar.)*

Views from the road and theater are superb. The area is being extensively excavated, with remains of buildings from a range of eras being unearthed. The theater probably dates from the mid-third century B.C, when the city was coming under Roman domination. It is 207 feet (63 m) across and has room for 3,200 spectators. Concerts and plays are staged here in summer *(tel 0924 950 012 or box office 0924 950 144, www.calatafimise gesta.com).* ■

rose again under Carthaginian protection, only to massacre its Carthaginian garrison during the First Punic War (264–241 B.C.) between Rome and Carthage. Thereafter it became the first Sicilian city to declare its allegiance to the burgeoning Roman Empire.

The city's subsequent history is sketchy. Nor is much known about the area's majestic Doric **temple,** its air of mystery only adding to its appeal. Framed by mountains, the 36-column monolith sits on a low hill, close to the ravine into which troops from Syracuse are said to have catapulted 8,000 of the colony's inhabitants after their victory here in 307 B.C. Beautiful open countryside dotted with *bagli*, or traditional fortified farms, stretches all around. Early morning or evening visits are magical.

Riserva Naturale dello Zingaro

MUCH OF SICILY'S ONCE OUTSTANDING COASTLINE HAS been lost to industry, roads, and developers, making the glorious Zingaro Nature Reserve all the more remarkable, for it preserves a pristine pocket of beaches, coves, cliffs, and mountains filled with a rich variety of flora, fauna, and hiking trails.

Ruins of former tuna fisheries dot the coastline in and around the Zingaro reserve.

Riserva Naturale dello Zingaro
🅰 Map pp. 70–71 C3
Visitor information
www.riservazingaro.it
✉ Via Segesta 137, Castellammare del Golfo
☎ 0924 35 108
💲 $

The Zingaro reserve was Sicily's first protected area, created in 1981 after a mass demonstration by environmentalists against proposals to build a coastal road between Scopello and San Vito lo Capo. For years, it is claimed, the Mafia used the coast's many secret coves and beaches to smuggle drugs and other contraband. (The whispered implication is that the reserve was only possible with tacit Mafia sanction.) Whatever its history, the reserve was the catalyst for more than 25 other parks and protected areas in Sicily.

The Zingaro covers an area of 4,076 acres (1,650 ha), with the most popular access from the coast road that ends just beyond **Scopello** in the south. (The less busy entrance is at the end of the road from **San Vito lo Capo** in the north.) Scopello and San Vito are worth visits in their own right —San Vito in particular, a small resort with fine beaches and a large, picturesque bay.

The reserve has a parking lot and information center (*tel 0924 35 093, variable hours Sept.–May*) near the Scopello entrance.

Most local visitors come here for the beaches, making this a popular destination on summer weekends, but there are also plenty of good hiking trails that allow you to escape the sunbathers.

Because cars are banned, and most visitors don't walk beyond the first beach **(Punta della Capreria),** successive beaches at **Cala della Disa, Berretta, Marinella,** and **Torre dell'Uzzo** are also usually quieter.

Spring *(April–early June)* is the best time for hiking and enjoying the flora and fauna. Some 670 reserve (39 species have been recorded). Especially notable are rare raptors including peregrine falcons, Bonelli's eagles, and griffon vultures, together with seabirds such as Cory's and Manx shearwaters, and Europe's smallest seabird, the storm-petrel.

There are hiking trails to suit all ages and abilities, and though

species of plants, trees, and shrubs flourish here, including the dwarf fan palm, Europe's only indigenous palm. The craft of weaving baskets from the palm fronds has been practiced for centuries. In the past, local people also exploited trees such as olive, carob, and manna ash, the last for its nutritious sugary sap, and utilized the thick, plumed grass (known locally as *disa*) as string or wound pasta around its woody stems to give macaroni its shape.

The area's rugged shoreline, rocks, caves, and thick vegetation provide cover for a wide variety of birds, present in ever greater numbers since the creation of the the map available from the visitors' kiosk is poor, the trails are fairly self-evident, especially the well-worn coastal path.

An obvious loop involves following this path in one direction and returning by a more strenuous inland route via Borgo Cusenza, Contrada Sughero, and Pizzo del Corvo, a round-trip of 10 miles (16 km), with a change in altitude of 2,000 feet (604 m) *(allow 5 hrs.).*

Be sure to take plenty of food and water on this and other hikes *(none is available in the reserve),* and bear in mind that there is little by way of shade if you do the hike in hot weather. ■

The Zingaro reserve's diverse acres can be explored on foot or on horseback.

The Castello di Venere offers an overlook on the mist-shrouded village of Erice.

Erice

ERICE IS EASILY SICILY'S MOST ATMOSPHERIC VILLAGE, a magnificent mountaintop settlement that seems more Tuscan than Sicilian, more pagan than Christian. It has a mythical and sacred foundation, stupendous views as far as Tunisia and Etna, and narrow medieval streets that are a sheer pleasure to explore.

A holy place since time immemorial, Erice was home to one of the most significant cults and divinities of the classical age. Even today, its cobbled streets have a feeling of mystery, especially in winter, when mist swirls and the wind chills. The Italian writer Carlo Levi (1902-1975), author of *Christ Stopped at Eboli* (1945), compared it to Assisi in central Italy, another town of centuries-

old sanctity. Erice, he wrote, is "the Assisi of the south, full of churches, convents, silent streets, and of the extraordinary accumulation of mythological memories."

Erice, however, has far older roots than Assisi. One of the reasons is its position, a virtually impregnable eyrie 2,463 feet (751 m) above Sicily's west coast —precisely the sort of site that would have suggested itself both as a stronghold and the potential seat of a cult and temple. The cult in question was that of the god-

dess of love and fertility—Astarte to the Phoenicians, Aphrodite to the Greeks, and Venus to the Romans—and her temple at Erice, ancient Eryx, was known and revered across the classical and western Mediterranean world.

It was mentioned by the Greek writer Virgil in the *Aeneid.* Another myth has Hercules (or Heracles) taking the city on his return to Greece. Yet another has Erice as the place in which Daedalus landed.

Some of the site's earliest inhabitants were the Elymians, a

Erice

🅰 Map pp. 70–71
   B2–B3

Visitor information

✉ Viale Conte Pepoli 11

☎ 0923 869 388

Chiesa Madre, one of ten churches in Erice

The cult reached its zenith under the Romans, who built temples to the goddess in Rome itself, but even much later invaders appropriated its sacred nature.

Today, Erice is one of those happy places that clings to its charm in the face of mass tourism. The local population is in decline, but in summer its streets are as full of visitors, dubious souvenirs, and second-home owners as any Tuscan or Umbrian hill town. None of these factors reduces its appeal, however, but winter, fall, or early spring remain the ideal times to appreciate the village at its strange and otherworldly best.

If you do come off-season, however, pick a clear day, for some of Erice's most memorable sights are its views. These unfold as you approach from Trapani or Valderice, and extend over the Egadi Islands to the west and the headlands of Monte Cofano and Capo San Vito to the northeast.

Leave your car in the parking lot outside Porta Trapani, the main southwest entrance to town, and be sure to bring comfortable shoes for the cobbles and climbs, and a sweater (or more substantial warm clothing in winter) for the breezes and evening chill.

Erice has few specific sights, but any walk around the village is entrancing, wending through the ancient labyrinth and negotiating alleys *(vanelle)* so narrow they often are only wide enough for one person.

The facades of the houses may look foreboding, but they conceal secret courtyards, or boast delicate balconies and other baroque or medieval details. Much of their stone has been used and reused, and many buildings contain the fragmentary ghosts of Elymian and Carthaginian walls or Roman and Greek temples.

mysterious 15th- to 8th-century B.C. people who also settled Segesta (see pp. 72-73). They probably first introduced the fertility cult that would be adopted and adapted by subsequent Phoenician, Carthaginian, Greek, and Roman invaders. All revered the goddess, and all contributed to the famously rich treasury of her temple—a temple so sacrosanct that it remained undesecrated by invaders over several centuries.

Start a tour at **Porta Trapani,** the town's 14th-century gateway, which has Norman roots and is built over Elymian fortifications. From here Via Vittorio Emanuele II climbs toward Piazza Umberto I, the main square. En route it passes Erice's main church, the 14th-century **Chiesa Matrice,** also known as Santa Maria della Assunta. Its detached bell tower predates the main church and was built in about 1315 as an Aragonese watchtower. The church's lovely porch (1426) is Gothic, unusual in predominantly baroque Sicily, but the "Gothic" interior is actually a pastiche, completed in 1852.

Piazza Umberto I has a spread of outdoor café tables in summer and is home to the Municipio, or town hall (on the left, or west, side), which contains the small **Museo Cordici** (tel 0923 860 048, closed Sat.–Sun. & Tues.–Thurs. p.m.). This museum features minor archaeological finds, miscellaneous paintings and sculptures from different eras, and a fine relief of the "Annunciation" (1525) by the Sicilian sculptor Antonello Gagini.

Among the collection are coins bearing doves, Erice's ancient symbol—white doves having been sacred to Venus. Hundreds of the birds were released from the temple once a year toward the goddess's sister temple, Sicca Veneria, in present-day El Kef, Tunisia. Doves were supposed to accompany the goddess when she moved south for the winter, her return to Sicily signifying the advent of spring. The doves were released in mid-August, and it can be no coincidence that the feast day of Erice's Christian patroness, Our Lady of Custonaci, is August 16.

Other places worth seeing include **Piazza San Domenico** and its pretty church, and the village's pastry shops, Erice being famous for its *dolci ericini* (sweet almond and marzipan cakes and candies). Once these were the preserve of local novice nuns, but the convent in question closed in 1975. The shop of Maria Grammatico *(Via Vittorio Emanuele II 14, tel 0923 869 390),* who was brought up by the nuns of San

Carlo, is now the place to indulge.

Other craft products include *frazzate,* bright cotton rugs made by local women and available for sale in outlets around the village.

Erice's best views can be had from the **Giardino del Balio** (1870), communal gardens in the village's southeast corner. From here a ramp leads past the privately owned Castello Pepoli, a Norman keep, to the crag-top **Castello di Venere,** a 12th-century castle built over the remains of the once great temple to Venus (Venere). Whether it fell into ruin, or the Norman ruler, Roger I, hastened its demise in the 11th century, eager to erase its pagan associations, is unknown. ■

View of the sea from the hilltop town of Erice

Isole Egadi

Favignana's main harbor (below) contrasts with the island's barren western shore (right).

THE ISOLE EGADI—FAVIGNANA, LEVANZO, AND MARETTIMO —are the closest islands to Sicily, and the easiest to access. Only Favignana offers significant facilities for travelers, leaving its two beautiful but disparate neighbors largely unvisited and unspoiled.

Isole Egadi

🅜 Map pp. 70–71 A3–A4

Visitor information

www.egadi.com
www.isoladimarettimo.it
www.marettimoresidence.it

✉ Piazza Matrice, Favignana

☎ 0923 922 585 or 0923 921 647

Getting there

Several companies operate daily ferries and hydrofoils from Trapani to all three islands. For information, contact visitor center.

Favignana is the Egadi's largest and most populated island, covering an area of 8 square miles (20.7 sq km). It lies 10 miles (17 km) from Trapani, the port of embarkation for all three islands. Formerly, its economy rested on tufa, a soft, easily worked stone that was exported across the region, and on tuna.

Old tuna canneries are the first thing you see as you sail into Favignana town, the island's main settlement, followed by the faded **Palazzo Florio** (1876), built by the Marsala Florio wine dynasty, which bought the Egadi Islands from the Genoese Pallavicini family, who had acquired them from the Spanish in 1637 in lieu of a business debt.

Favignana has relatively little to see or do save for some good beaches and swimming, notably at **Cala Burrone, Cala Azzurra, Cala Rossa, Cala Rotonda,** and **Cala Grande.** Bikes are easily rented and many fishermen offer boat trips around the island.

Levanzo is much smaller than Favignana (at just 2 square miles/5.2 sq km), but its austere, rocky landscape has more in the way of isolated island charm. Although it is bisected by just one road and has only one tiny community, it offers numerous coastal and inland trails, including one leading to **Pizzo del Monaco** (912 feet/278 m), the island's highest point, and boasts plenty of little bays and pebble beaches for swimming and snorkeling.

Many visitors come here for the **Grotta Genovese,** a

La Mattanza

La Mattanza is a centuries-old collective hunt that involves the slaughter of many hundreds of tuna as they swim south to spawn in the waters around Sicily. Once intrinsic to a traditional way of life and the economic mainstay of many communities, the mattanza now only survives off Favignana, where it is in danger of becoming a cruel spectacle played out for tourists.

Tuna live for much of the year in the Atlantic, but at the beginning of spring, they start their migration through the Mediterranean toward their warm-watered spawning grounds off the coast of Sicily. Since

Phoenician times, and possibly the Bronze Age, fisherman have waited for them, though it took the arrival of the Arabs in the ninth century to educate the Sicilians in fishing for creatures that can weigh up to 1,300 pounds (600 kg). The Arabs, for example, taught the islanders that tuna rarely take bait before spawning, and they introduced them to the technique of drift-netting, the method at the heart of the mattanza.

Around May, when the local *favinio* (wind that brings flowers) begins to blow, tuna begin to run in the channels near Favignana. Teams of fishermen set out in traditional flat boats with nets up to 10 miles (16 km) long,

Migrating tuna swim into a drift net (above), which fishermen haul to the surface for the traditional killing of the fish—a ritual known as the *mattanza* (below).

preparing a series of corridors and holding pens that force the tuna into a closed *camera della morte*, or chamber of death. When a hundred or so fish are trapped, the head fisherman orders the 60-strong crew to haul the 100-foot-deep (30 m) net to the surface. This is done to the rhythmic chant of ancient songs, the *cialoma*, or *scialome*, that date to Arab times or earlier. As the frenzied mass of fish rises to the surface, the tuna are clubbed, speared, and hooked until the sea froths with a bloody foam. (The word "mattanza" suggests slaughter, a description that any spectator, and there are many, would not refute.)

Cultural significance aside, there is a considerable cruelty element in the ritual. Tuna tend to dive when panicked; many are already stunned or severely injured through collision as they are dragged to the surface in their *sarabanda della morte*, or dance of death. This dance may take 15 minutes and death is usually slow, though some fish die quickly from heart attacks or too much oxygen.

This cruelty might be more tolerable were fishing the economic mainstay it once was, but these days only one of Sicily's 50 former *tonnare*, or tuna stations, is still working. (In Favignana's heyday, 150,000 tons of tuna might have been caught and processed: today the figure is between 1,000 and 1,500 tons.) These days the ritual barely survives—there may be one or two held between May and June. Contact the local visitor center for information. ∎

cave with some of Italy's most important cave paintings, dating back between 6,000 and 10,000 years. These can only be seen with an official guide *(tel 0923 924 032)*, who organizes trips by foot, boat, Jeep, or donkey. Price and schedule vary according to demand.

While Levanzo has a couple of hotels, magical **Marettimo** (4 square miles/10.4 sq km) has just a handful of sleepy trattorias and a few rooms for rent in local houses *(reservations needed in summer; at other times you may be met by locals offering rooms)*. The 300 or so residents are mostly fishing families, some of whom offer boat trips around the island's tremendous coastline.

On Marettimo, however, the mountains and breathtakingly

Sicily's Egadi Islands offer rocky shores and moody views of the hills above Trapani.

beautiful interior are the main attraction. The island was long the haunt of pirates, which discouraged settlement; today its near-pristine state is protected by a regional nature reserve. The relatively luxuriant vegetation, with some 515 species of plants, provides cover for thousands of migrating and nesting birds.

Forest rangers care for much of the island, with the result that many paths are marked and maintained. Hiking is, therefore, possible, with recommended trails to the **Case Romane** (old Roman earthworks), **Cala Sarde** and **Cala Nera,** the summit of **Pizzo Falcone** (2,251 feet/686 m), and the ruined fortress at **Punta Troia.** Rough maps of the island can usually be obtained from local cafés and the ferry ticket office in Marettimo town. ■

Pantelleria

Pantelleria

🗺 68 A2

Visitor information

www.pantelleria.it

www.comune.pantelleria.it

✉ Piazza Cavour

☎ 0923 911 838

Getting there

By air: Twice-daily, 30-minute flights from Trapani Gandalf Air, 0923 864 000, www.gandalfair.it. In summer, flights from Rome, Venice, Bologna, and Milan by Alitalia tel 800 223 5730 (U.S.), www.alitaliausa.com

By car ferry: Daily service (5 hrs.) from Trapani. Siremar, tel 0923 540 515 or 199 123 199 (toll-free Italy), www.gruppotirrenia.it

By hydrofoil: Daily, (2.5 hrs.) service from Trapani. Ustica Lines, tel 0923 22 200, www.usticalines.it

PANTELLERIA IS THE LARGEST AND MOST WESTERLY OF Sicily's offshore islands, a fascinating outpost with a rich history, dramatic coastline, fertile volcanic interior, and the sort of isolated and bohemian charm that has begun to attract such high-profile visitors as Sting, Madonna, and Giorgio Armani.

Pantelleria owes its prosperity to its dark, volcanic soils. These attracted Neolithic visitors, who built the 18th-century B.C. rock tombs, or *sesi,* that are unique to the island. It also benefited from its position, just 52 miles (84 km) from Tunisia, tempting African traders such as the Phoenicians, who called it Hiranin, or the Place of Birds, after the many species that still use it as a migratory staging post.

To the Greeks it was Kossyra (the Small One), though its present name derives from the Arabic Bint er-rhia, or Daughter of the Winds. During their 400-year occupation, the Arabs introduced palms, cotton, vegetables, and citrus fruits, as well as the distinctive walled gardens and low-trained vines designed to protect against the wind that gave Pantelleria its name. They may also have introduced, or refined, the island's *dammusi,* dwellings whose distinctive vaulted design helps keep them cool in summer.

Later, Mussolini described the island as an "unsinkable aircraft carrier," a strategic merit that prompted the Allies to bomb it for a month before its capture on June 11, 1943. As a result, the rebuilt main town and harbor, also called Pantelleria, are a depressing prelude to what otherwise is a wonderful island.

Visitors are not here to lounge on beaches; there are none, though the water is sublime and coves, cliffs, and inlets abound. Instead, they come to hike, bird-watch,

snorkel, dive (the diving is world-class), cruise around the majestic coastline, stay in dammusi, soak in natural hot pools, and enjoy some excellent food and wine. Small farms sell wine, oil, figs, capers, and other products.

At 32 square miles (83 sq km), Pantelleria is not so large that you need a car, though cars, bikes, and scooters can be rented. Buses run to most points, and there are many hiking trails, not least the one to **Montagna Grande** (2,742 feet/ 836 m), the island's ancient crater and highest point. May, June, September, and October are the best months to visit, when the water is warm and you can enjoy the birds, wildflowers, and calm beauty without the crowds and summer heat.

The best of the megalithic sesi are off the coastal road just southwest of Pantelleria town, 1.8 miles (3 km) beyond Mursia (Villaggio Neolithico). Once, the island probably had some 500 of these elliptical burial mounds, but their stones have been pilfered over the centuries, mostly to build the island's dammusi, whose angular stone blocks match almost exactly those of the 27 surviving sesi.

The west-coast hamlets of Scauri, Nikà, and the more barren southern coast (known as the Dietro Isola) are all good for panoramic views. Here and elsewhere are numerous hot springs and caves, notably at **Bagno Asciutto, Grotta di Sataria, Favara Grande,** and **Grotta di**

Nikà. They are well known and the visitor center can direct you.

The island's loveliest settlement is **Gadir** on the northeast coast (Giorgio Armani has a villa nearby), connected by a scenic inland road to Tracino to the south. Nearby **Kamma** and the ghost village of **Mueggen** (*accessible by a walking trail*) are also captivating.

Other good inland destinations are the **Specchio di Venere,** a hot-water lake, and the **Valle di Monastero** and **Valle della Ghirlanda** below Montagna Grande, two pretty, verdant valleys for hiking. **Sibà,** on the Montagna's west slopes, is a fine, crumbling village with some of the island's oldest dammusi. ■

Fishermen harvest crayfish along the rocky coast of Pantelleria, Sicily's largest island.

From Trapani to Marsala, the coastal road is lined with salt pans.

More places to visit in western Sicily

MARSALA

The mostly modern town of Marsala is syn-onymous with the dessert wine of the same name. You can visit several producers, in-cluding **Florio** *(Via Vincenzo Florio 1, tel 0923 781 111, www.cantineflorio.com);* **Pellegrino** *(Via del Fante 39, tel 0923 719 911, www.carlopellegrino.it);* and **Rallo** *(Via Vincenzo Florio 2, tel 0923 721 633, www .donnafugata.it).* Also worth seeing are the **cathedral** (1176); the small **Museo degli Arazzi** *(Via Giuseppe Garraffa 57, tel 0923 712 903, closed Mon.);* and the **Museo Baglio Anselmi** *(Lungomare Boeo, tel 0923 952 535, closed Mon., Tues., & Thurs. p.m.),* home to the only existing Carthaginian ship (241 B.C.). ⬛ Map pp. 70-71 B2 **Visitor information** www.comune marsala.it ✉ Via XI Maggio 100 ☎ 0923 714 097

MAZARA DEL VALLO

Once one of the Arabs' most important Sicilian outposts—it was the first Sicilian settlement conquered and the last surren-dered—this town has a lovely palm-lined waterfront, booming fishing industry (see the day's catch unloaded and sold in the market on **Piazza dello Scalo),** and a delightful old center; some of the streets have a decided North African air. **Piazza della Repubblica** offers a fine ensemble of baroque and other buildings, as does the **Piazza Plebiscito,** home to the **Museo**

del Satiro *(tel 0923 808 111).* Above the dock stands **San Nicolò Regale** (1124), an outstanding Norman church.
⬛ Map pp. 70–71 B1 **Visitor information** www.comune.mazara-del-vallo-.tp.it ✉ Piazza Santa Veneranda 2 ☎ 0923 941 727

MOZIA

Mozia, or Motya, is Sicily's only surviving Carthaginian site. Founded by the Phoe-nicians in the eighth century B.C., it became a major trade center. Razed in 397 B.C., it was rediscovered after 1913 by James Whitaker, a Marsala wine magnate and amateur archaeol-ogist. A foundation in his name owns and manages the island *(tel 091 682 0522).*

Adding appeal to the site, with its fine small **museum** *(tel 0923 712 598, closed daily p.m. Nov.–March),* is its location on the **Isola San Pantaleo,** an island in the **Isole dello Stagnone**—a lagoon, salt flats, and nature reserve between Trapani and Marsala. From the minor SP 21, where you get the ferry to the island, you'll see old windmills and salt pans that testify to the centuries of salt production.

Leave time to visit the **Museo del Sale di Nubia** *(tel 0923 867 142, closed Sun. p.m.)* on the mainland, an interesting museum de-voted to the salt industry and housed in the 300-year-old home of a local salt worker.
⬛ Map pp. 70–71 B2 **Visitor information** www. apt.trapani.it or www.trapani-sicilia.it. ✉ Piazza Saturno, Trapani ☎ 0923 29 000 ■

Although southern Sicily is one of the island's quietest corners, marked by hinterland and a sprinkling of sleepy towns and villages, the region boasts two major sights: Agrigento's Greek temples and the Roman mosaics at the Villa Imperiale del Casale.

Southern Sicily

Roman mosaic from the Villa Imperiale del Casale

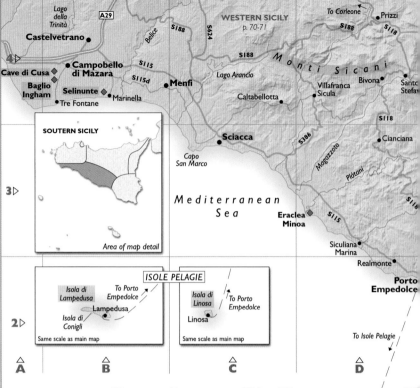

Southern Sicily

SOUTHERN SICILY IS THE MOST ENIGMATIC REGION OF AN ENIGMATIC
island, its miles of lonely coast and empty beaches, classical ruins, and insular fishing villages backed by wheat-rich plains that give rise to mostly deserted mountains. While major
attractions are few, those that are here—notably the temples of Agrigento and mosaics of
Casale—rank among Europe's finest Greek and Roman sites.

The often dry, sparsely populated coast that
looks to Africa may be less verdant than much
of Sicily, but its hills and plains are rich fertile
agricultural land—the lure that in the sixth
century B.C. first tempted ancient Greek settlers. Today, some of those once great cities are
gone, notably Eraclea Minoa, now visited as
much for its magnificent beach and position as
its partially excavated ruins. Others, such as
Selinunte have been excavated or retain monuments to their past. One—Agrigento—is still a
large town, and today boasts the greatest Greek
remains outside Greece itself.

Inland, a monument from another era, the
Villa Imperiale del Casale, contains Europe's
finest Roman mosaics, a well-preserved site
that demands a visit. The villa, easily
approached via Enna or Catania, hints at one
of the dilemmas of any visit to the south—the
planning of an itinerary in a region that has little outside its main centers with few conces-
sions to visitors.

Here are none of the autostrada of Sicily's
other coasts, just the old, slow S 115 road, a
highway on which interest is largely incidental:
salty, no-nonsense fishing towns such as Sciacca
or Licata; long, empty stretches of beach; and
the occasional patch of industrial blight.

Inland routes through the mountains are
slower, but also rewarding in their way, bringing
you face to face with slumbering (occasionally
shabby) hill villages, sweeping panoramas, and
a Sicily that hasn't changed in a hundred years.
Finally are the islands—Linosa and Lampedusa,
or Isole Pelagie (Pelagie Islands), increasingly
popular among divers and snorkelers. ∎

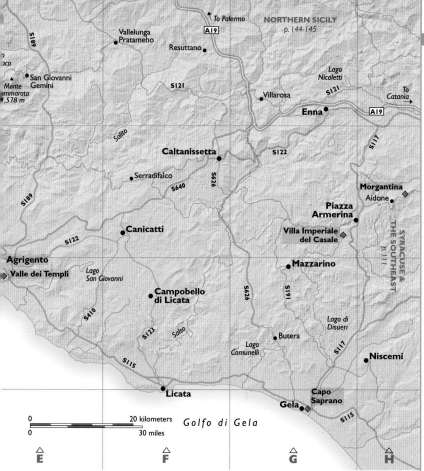

To Palermo
NORTHERN SICILY
p. 144-145

Vallelunga
Pratameho

Resuttano

San Giovanni
Gemini

Monte
ammarata
,578 m

S121

Lago
Nicoletti

Villarosa

S121

To
Catania

Enna

A19

Caltanissetta

S122

Serradifalco

S640

S626

Morgantina
Aidone

Piazza
Armerina

Canicatti

S122

Villa Imperiale
del Casale

Agrigento

Valle dei Templi

Lago
San Giovanni

Mazzarino

SYRACUSE & THE SOUTHEAST

p.111

Campobello
di Licata

S626

S191

S410

S123

Salso

Lago di
Disueri

Butera

Lago
Comunelli

S117

Niscemi

S115

Licata

Capo
Saprano

Gela

S115

0   20 kilometers
0   30 miles

Golfo di Gela

E   F   G   H

Beach near Selinunte on Sicily's south coast

Selinunte

Selinunte

⬛ Map pp. 90–91 B4

Visitor information

✉ Entrance North of Marinella off Via Caboto (S 115d)

☎ 0924 46 251
Ticket Office:
0924 46 277

§ $$

WHILE SOME ARCHAEOLOGICAL SITES IN SICILY ARE compromised by their modern surroundings, Selinunte rivals Segesta for the beauty and unsullied romance of its setting. Edged by the sea to the south, its eight ruined temples and ancient acropolis occupy a lovely pastoral setting scattered with wildflowers, aromatic herbs, and the wild celery (*selinon* in Greek) that gave the colony its name.

Ancient Selinus probably was founded in 651 B.C. by settlers from Megara Hyblaea (a colony north of Syracuse), attracted by the area's fertile floodplain. The colony prospered for 200 years, but in time attracted the covetous Segesta whose own territories were close by.

In 409 B.C., after Selinunte sided with Syracuse against Carthage, a North African power, the Segestans allied themselves with the Carthaginians, unleashing a force of over 100,000 on the unsuspecting city. Selinunte fell in nine days, with 16,000 of its inhabitants butchered and 5,000 sold into slavery.

The colony was never quite the same, and though it staggered on for another 150 years, it eventually was abandoned. In later years, only a Byzantine and tenth-century Arab settlement took temporary root among the ruins. The near-total destruction of the city, however, is not believed to have been entirely the result of Segesta's assault, but a consequence of countless earthquakes.

The site was rediscovered in the 16th century, and excavations began in the 1820s under two Englishmen, Samuel Angel and William Harris. Organized excavations began in the 1950s and continue to this day.

The ruins are divided into three: the trio of temples on the Collina Orientale, or East Hill; the five temples of the ancient Acropoli (central citadel); and the sacred area of the Santuario della Malophoros. The eight temples have been designated by letters, as archaeologists do not know to which gods they were dedicated.

The **Collina Orientale** is entered through landscaped earthworks at the site entrance and parking lot. Here, adjoining **Temples E** (480–460 B.C.) and **F** (560–540 B.C.) are the best preserved, but it is the

ruins of the third, **Temple G—** just a single column remains standing—that most capture the imagination. This was Sicily's second largest temple, after the Tempio di Zeus Olimpico (Giove) in Agrigento (see pp. 99–100), 17 columns long and 8 wide (an arrangement matched only by the Parthenon in Athens), and measuring 373 feet by 178 feet (110 m by 50 m). Each column was 53 feet (16 m) high and 12 feet (3.5 m) in diameter, and made up of several 100-ton stone drums.

From the Collina Orientale it is a ten-minute walk or short drive west on the Strada dei Templi to the **Acropoli.** En route you pass the colony's old silted-up harbor. The Acropoli would have held many of the main civic and religious buildings, along with one or two houses of its most prominent citizens. The colossal walls were built in 306 B.C., too late to withstand the Carthaginians, while the early sixth-century B.C. **Temple C** is the site's earliest and best preserved monument. The celebrated frieze panels in Palermo's Museo Archeologico Regionale (see p. 61) came from this temple.

A ten-minute walk west brings you to the **Santuario della Malophoros** (575 B.C.), a sanctuary centered on a large sacrificial altar and devoted to the goddess

Ruins of one of Selinunte's eight Greek temples greet the sun.

Above: A pastoral setting complements Selinunte's ancient temples. Below: Stone rubble reveals the scale of a single column.

Demeter Malophoros ("the bearer of pomegranates"). The environs are covered in an unexcavated ne-cropolis that stretches several miles to the west. Also unexcavated is the ancient city proper, which extended north of the Acropoli.

After seeing the site, visit the sandy **beach** that runs west from

the adjacent village-resort of **Marinella.** *(Follow the path from the site's second parking lot.)* Even if you don't wish to swim, you could have lunch in one of the trattorias on Via Marco Polo above the beach. Alternatively, consider a picnic in the shady valley between the Acropoli and Collina Orientale; tables are available.

CAVE DI CUSA

If Selinunte is lovely, then the Cave di Cusa, the quarry from which the city's stone was mined, is even more delightful. To reach it, drive 2.5 miles (4 km) north of Selinunte on the S 115d and turn left (west) at the junction on the unclassified road to Campobello di Mazara. From there, continue south towards Tre Fontane for just over a mile (2 km) and the quarry road is on the right at the ruins of Baglio Ingham. The total distance is about 12 miles (20 km).

Surrounded by olive and orange groves, the quarries are a mile (1.6 km) long and little more than 100 yards (91 m) wide. Quarrying stopped here abruptly and permanently after the Segestan and Carthaginian sack of the mother city. Everywhere are stone drums, stumps, and partly carved capitals, tossed as if at random by some giant hand. Especially impressive are the deep cavities created by quarried stone, and the partially cut column fragments that are still part of the ambient rock. Slaves and oxen pulled the finished drums, on iron-strengthened wooden rollers, the 12 miles (20 km) to Selinunte. ■

Agrigento

BELOW THE TOWN OF AGRIGENTO LIES SICILY'S MOST important archaeological site—the Valle dei Templi, or Valley of the Temples, part of the ancient city of Akragas. Once, this "loveliest of mortal cities", as the Greek writer Pindar described it, was among the wealthiest of Sicily's Greek colonies. Today, its former grandeur is still apparent in the valley's nine temples, a UNESCO World Heritage site and the finest classical remains outside Greece.

Agrigento
🅰 Map pp. 90–91 E2
Visitor information
www.agrigentosicilia.it
www.agrigentoweb.it
✉ Piazzale A. Moro 7
☎ 0922 20 454

Syracuse was the most powerful of Sicily's Greek colonies, but second ranked Akragas (or Acragus) was by far the most decadent: Its people, Pindar famously observed, "built for eternity but lived as if there were no tomorrow."

Founded in about 580 B.C., it eventually had a population of around 200,000 (the figure for the modern town is 55,450), and prospered until 406 B.C., when it was besieged and sacked by the Carthaginians. It rose again under the Romans in the third century B.C., when it was the only city to thrive among Sicily's former Greek colonies. Nemesis came with the Byzantines and early Christian settlers, who probably ravaged the site and many of its "pagan" temples. Earthquakes inflicted further damage. By the eighth century little more than a village remained.

Today, Agrigento presents the dilemma of many celebrated destinations: On one hand the main attraction—in this case, the **Valle dei Templi** (*Piazzale dei Templi, tel 0922 26191, open daily 8:30 a.m.–dusk, in summer occasionally open until 11 p.m., $$. If you also plan to visit Museo Archeologico Regionale, buy discounted combination adm. ticket*)—is unmissable, but on the other its popularity means that it can be uncomfortably crowded during peak times.

In Agrigento, there is the added fact that the contemporary surroundings, namely the present town and its ugly approaches, slightly compromise the splendor of the ancient remains.

The solution is to turn a blind eye to the depredations of the modern age and to visit the pretty, pastoral temple site off-season—January and February, when the almond trees are in blossom, is a lovely time. Failing that, come early in the morning or late in the afternoon, but bear in mind that you will need several hours to do the large site and associated museum justice.

The ancient city was enclosed by a defensive wall, part of which embraced the high ridge to the north, site of the city's ancient acropolis, an area now occupied by the medieval and modern town.

Confusingly, the Valle dei Templi is not really a valley but a second, lower ridge at the southern extent of the old city. The Greeks, wherever possible, built temples

Casa Pirandello

The birthplace of the Nobel Laureate writer Luigi Pirandello (1867–1936) (see pp. 37–38) can be visited at **Caos**, a suburb of Agrigento on the S 115 road to Porto Empedocle. The house (*tel 0922 511 826*) includes his study, editions of his work, photographs, archive film, and the grounds where his ashes were interred. ∎

where they could be seen against the skyline, particularly from the sea (most famously with the Parthenon in Athens).

Today, this ridge is divided into two sections: an open, eastern zone, and an enclosed western zone. A road, the Via dei Templi, runs from the edge of the modern town to a parking lot between the two zones (the lot also has a café and information kiosk). En route it passes through the Quartiere Ellenistico-Romano (a former residential part of the old city) and the Museo Archeologico Regionale, Agrigento's other key attraction, filled with archaeological finds from the ancient city.

It is possible to make a case for spending a little time in the present town—**Via Atenea,** the shop-lined main street is lively, for example, and churches such as **San Lorenzo, Santo Spirito,** and the **cathedral** have their moments. Without the temples, however, Agrigento is not really a place that would merit a stop on most Sicilian itineraries.

Tempio della Concordia has 34 columns each 22.5 feet high

Crepidoma, **stepped base**

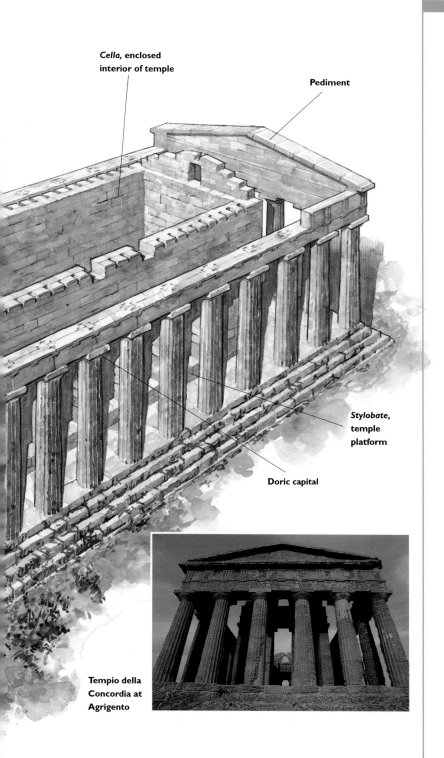

Cella, enclosed
interior of temple

Pediment

Stylobate,
temple
platform

Doric capital

Tempio della
Concordia at
Agrigento

The modern and medieval town of Agrigento overlooks the rubbled ruins of the Valle dei Templi.

THE EASTERN ZONE

This is the most intelligible part of the Valle dei Templi, with the most impressive remains and the prettiest open country. Its sights are located mainly on or just off an old lane, the Via Sacra, which heads east from the parking lot. Follow this until you come to a footbridge on the right, which crosses over rock tombs to the first of the temples, the **Tempio di Ercole** (circa 520 B.C.), or Temple of Heracles (Hercules).

This is the oldest and second largest of the temples, and would once have been about the size of the Parthenon in Athens. Nine of its original 38 columns still stand, stranded among a confusion of fallen stones, many of which show the effects of fire, possibly set by the Carthaginians following the siege of 406 B.C. Originally, the fragile golden sandstone of these and other columns would have been protected by a veneer of glazed marble stucco, then painted in bright reds and blues.

Look toward the south and just on the temple side of the S 115 road, you can see the vaguely pyramidal **Tomba di Terone,** erroneously described as the

tomb of Theron (Terone), the fifth-century B.C. tyrant ruler of Akragas, under whom the city reached its zenith. In truth it is probably a Roman monument erected to the memory of Roman soldiers who perished during the Second Punic War (218–202 B.C.) against the Carthaginians.

Returning to the Via Sacra, continue east, passing the **Villa Aurea** on the right. It now houses offices, but was once the home of Alexander Hardcastle (died 1933), the Englishman responsible for excavating much of ancient Akragas. A path alongside the villa

leads left to the site of a Greek-Roman necropolis and catacombs.

Still farther down the Via Sacra on the right is the site's highlight, the **Tempio della Concordia** (430 B.C.), or Temple of Concord, Europe's best preserved Greek temple outside the Theseion in Athens. Beautifully situated, with lovely sea views, it owes its fine state of preservation to its conversion to a Christian church in the sixth century (subsequently dismantled).

Just beyond on the left is the **Casa Pace,** a small and only occasionally open antiquarium devoted to the history of three early Christian churches found in and around the site. Should you wish to walk, a small road leads north from here for half a mile (800 m) through olives and orchards to San Nicola and the Museo Archeologico (see p. 101).

The path of the Via Sacra continues through increasingly peaceful and pretty countryside for about half a mile (800 m) to the picturesque but much ruined hilltop remains of the **Tempio di Giunone Lacinia** (circa 460 B.C.), or Temple of Juno (Hera), goddess of matrimony and childbirth. Just 25 of the original 34 columns survive. Like the Tempio di Ercole, its walls show signs (the reddish patches) of the 406 B.C. fire.

THE WESTERN ZONE
Walk west from the parking lot, and the first thing you see set back on the right is the **Altare Sacrificale,** a vast altar where anything up to a hundred sacrificial oxen could be slaughtered.

Beyond it are the jumbled ruins of the **Tempio di Zeus Olimpico,** the largest Doric temple in the Greek world, measuring 373 feet by 118 feet (113 m by 36 m). It was begun in 480 B.C., probably to celebrate Agrigento's sweeping

Artifacts and scale model displayed in the Museo Archeologico in Agrigento

victory over the Carthaginians at the Battle of Himera. Enslaved prisoners provided much of the initial labor.

The now tumbled columns were over 50 feet (15 m) high and large enough to require 20 adults standing in a circle to embrace their girth. Above them, 38 giant figures, or *telamones*, supported the architrave, taking the temple's overall height to more than 100 feet (30 m). One telamone has been reconstructed on site, and another can be seen in the Museo Archeologico.

The confusion of the site is considerable, earthquakes having felled the temple, though the ruins' scale still hints vividly at the size of the structure. The amount of debris is all the more remarkable given that colossal quantities of stone from the site were removed in the 18th century to build much of nearby Porto Empedocle.

Moving west you come to even more confusing ruins, based around four temples known collectively as the **Santuario delle Divinità Ctonie,** or the Sanctuary of the Chthonic Divinities—namely Persephone (Persefone or Kore), queen of the underworld, and her mother Demeter (Ceres), goddess of corn, fertility, and agriculture (and one of the most revered goddesses of Sicilian antiquity). All manner of shrines and altars to these and other divinities scatter the area, many from Sikel and prehistoric times, proof that the site was inhabited for centuries before the arrival of the Greeks.

The main monument in this

area, the striking **Tempio di Castore e Polluce,** or Temple of Castor and Pollux, is a pastiche, cobbled together in the 1830s from the ruins of other temples and buildings. Beyond this is the **Giardino della Kolymbetra,** formerly an artificial lake dug by Carthaginian prisoners, but now a beautifully restored garden of olive, citrus, and other trees.

Just to its north are the scant ruins of the **Tempio di Efesto** (Temple of Vulcan), the most westerly of the temples built on the imaginary east-west line across the Valle dei Templi.

MUSEO ARCHEOLOGICO REGIONALE

This major and well-presented archaeological museum *(Via dei Templi, tel 0922 401 565, $$. If you also plan to visit Valle dei Templi, buy discounted combination adm. ticket)* is partly housed in the 13th-century church and monastery of San Nicola.

Its highlights begin with finds from the early and late Bronze Age, moving quickly to the many outstanding black- and red-figure Attic vases of Room 3 and exhibits devoted to the Temple of Zeus Olimpico in Room 4. The latter includes one of the temple's telamones and three giant heads that represent the three "ethnic types" known in the period: African, Asiatic, and European.

The museum's other sculptural highlight is the "Ephebus" (circa 480 B.C.), a marble statue of a young man (perhaps a depiction of Apollo or the river god Akragas).

Allow one to two hours to see the museum and the remains of houses and other ruins in the **Quartiere Ellenistico-Romano** across the road. Once this spread of residential housing would have covered a grid of streets that extended over the whole slope between the temple ridge and the present town.

Next, head for **San Biagio,** reached by turning right off Via dei Templi north of the museum on Via Demetra. Here, it is not so much the Norman-era church (built over a Greek temple) that is interesting, as the mysterious **Tempio Rupestre di Demetra** nearby. Probably the most ancient of Agrigento's sacred sites, this cave-shrine was devoted (again) to Demeter and Persephone (and perhaps to earlier water deities), and consists of dank, atmospheric chambers reached by steps cut into the rock. ■

Doric columns mark the Tempio di Giunone Lacinia, built to honor the goddess of childbirth and fertility.

Isole Pelagie

THE ISOLE PELAGIE TAKE THEIR NAME FROM THE GREEK *pelagia*, or sea islands, and consist of three tiny scraps of land—Lampedusa, Linosa, and uninhabited Lampione. Closer in fact and feel to Africa than Europe, they have little to see, but are becoming increasing popular among visitors keen to dive, swim, and snorkel in their pristine waters.

Lampedusa is the largest of the islands, measuring 8 square miles (20.7 sq km). A fragment of Africa's continental shelf, it lies a mile closer to Monastir in Tunisia than it does to Porto Empedocle, about 127 miles (205 km) north on Sicily's mainland. Volcanic Linosa, by contrast, belongs to Europe, the last of the line of volcanoes that includes Vesuvius, Etna, and the Pontine islands between Rome and Naples.

Most people visit Lampedusa, whose population of just under 6,000 makes a living from fishing, sponges, and, increasingly, tourism. Historically, the island has been a plaything of rulers such as Charles II

Rocky shores and clear waters attract swimmers to Cala Creta and other beaches on Lampedusa.

of Spain, who in 1630 awarded Giulio di Tomasi, a Sicilian aristocrat, the title of Prince of Lampedusa. A descendant of Giulio's, Giuseppe Tomasi di Lampedusa, wrote *Il Gattopardo (The Leopard),* one of the great Sicilian novels (see p. 38).

Centuries of agricultural mismanagement and deforestation have left the interior barren, the topsoil scattered by the almost constant wind. It is the coast and its pellucid waters and largely untouched beaches that draw visitors.

Lampedusa town is the main settlement, minutes from the small airport and ferry terminal, and the place to stay—possibly in a rented *dammuso,* one of the traditional

Arab-style domed houses. It is also the place to rent bikes, scooters, cars, scuba, and other equipment.

The best beaches are all on the southern coast, the northern coast being a series of spectacular cliffs best seen on one of the highly recommended boat tours from town.

Just west of town are **Spiaggia di Guitgia,** a fine sandy crescent, and the less crowded beaches at **Cala Croce. La Tabaccara** is another glorious bay *(accessible only by boat),* though the island's best beach is the unnamed (but well-known) strand opposite the small **Isola dei Conigli.** The Isola dei Conigli is known for the loggerhead turtles that lay their eggs here. The

increasing numbers of human spectators now threaten this event. You may also see dolphins, or the March migration of the sperm whale, though note that Lampedusa is not at its best in spring or winter.

The same goes for **Linosa,** an hour away by hydrofoil, although it is to be recommended in summer, when it is quieter than Lampedusa and far from the Italian mainstream. All it boasts are pristine waters, three extinct craters, a couple of black-sand beaches, one hotel, a hundred-strong village, and lots of peace and quiet. Be warned, though, that Linosa is hot—very hot—unlike Lampedusa, where a breeze blows year-round and even summer nights have a desert chill. ∎

Isole Pelagie
 Map pp. 90–91 B2, B3

Visitor information
www.lampedusa.it
www.isoladilampedusa.it
✉ Via Anfossi 8, Lampedusa
☎ 0922 971 390

A reserve on Isola dei Conigli is home to the rare loggerhead turtle.

Getting there
By air: Daily one-hour flights on Meridiana (tel 199 111 333, www.meridiana.it) to Lampedusa from Palermo
By sea: Overnight ferry from Porto Empedocle to Linosa and Lampedusa (6 & 8 hrs. respectively). Contact Siremar (tel 0922 636 683/5 or 0922 636 777, www.siremar.it). Hydrofoil service from Porto Empedocle. Contact Ustica Lines (tel 0922 970 003, www.usticalines.it).

Villa Imperiale del Casale

THE VILLA IMPERIALE DEL CASALE IS AN ISOLATED ROMAN villa in lovely countryside a few miles from the sleepy village of Piazza Armerina. Here are preserved the world's finest Roman mosaics, a vast and almost pristine array of color and narrative drama spread over 50 rooms—an artistic wonder that was declared one of Sicily's five UNESCO World Heritage sites in 1997.

Overlooking the old town of Piazza

Visitor information

✉ Viale Muscarà Generale 1, Piazza Armerina

☎ 0935 680 201

Villa Imperiale

🅰 Map pp. 90–91 G3

✉ Casale, 3.5 miles (5.5 km) SW of Piazza Armerina

☎ 0935 680 036

💲 $$

Mosaics are not to all tastes, but even the most skeptical viewer cannot help but be impressed by the must-see Villa Imperiale. Be advised, though, that the site is extremely popular, especially in spring and summer. Note, too, that the plastic coverings raised to protect the mosaics and suggest the villa's original outlines create a sometimes stifling greenhouse effect in warm weather. The best times to visit are out of season or early or late in the day.

A visit should be combined with a trip to the nearby Greek remains at **Morgantina**, which by contrast receives only a scattering of tourists (see p. 107). If you wish to stay close to the villa, there are only a handful of local hotels, none of them outstanding, so be sure to book well ahead. Enna makes a good alternative base (see p. 155).

The villa's early history is shadowy, and scholars dispute its precise age and original ownership. The present structure dates from the late third, or early fourth century, but was built over a more humble second-century dwelling.

Most scholars believe the villa was a hunting lodge because of the mosaics' many hunting-related scenes, and also the building's position, which even today is in lovely, wooded country that once would have been rich in game.

The villa's size gives further clues as to its ownership, for only two private buildings in the Roman world of the era rival it for scale or splendor: Hadrian's second-century villa at Tivoli, near Rome, and the contemporary palace of the Emperor Diocletian in Split, in present-day Croatia. Only a man of great wealth and standing could have created such a building, which is why most scholars believe it belonged to Diocletian's co-emperor, Maximilian, who ruled between A.D. 286 and 305.

Diocletian realized that the Roman Empire was too large and unwieldy to be ruled successfully as a single entity, a realization that eventually led to its division into Western and Eastern (Byzantine) empires. Some hint of this split is perhaps contained in the Villa Imperiale, which was built far from an increasingly fractious Rome and close to northern Africa, one of Maximilian's spheres of authority in the unraveling empire.

The villa's age is also significant artistically, for within a few years the empire (under the Emperor Constantine) would recognize Christianity, and the subjects and imagery available or allowable to art would be largely religious.

Indeed, among the mosaics' many attributes are their exuberant paganism and vivid narrative variety. All the pleasures and events of everyday life are depicted, from dancing, lovemaking, and massage to hunting, sport, and children at play—none of which would have been sanctioned a few years later, at least not on such a scale. Few mosaics before or since—and little subsequent Italian art of any sort until the advent of Giotto in the 13th century—would show the same intense naturalism combined with such subtlety, intimacy, sensuality, and sheer joie de vivre.

The mosaics were probably the

work of North African artists, and many panels may have been created abroad and then shipped to Sicily. Roman mosaics tended to use simple black-and-white designs, unlike the rich polychrome panels in the villa, which were probably based on Greek paintings. At the same time, the villa's mosaics utilize monochrome backgrounds, suggesting that this was a significant and early fusing of two mosaic traditions.

Roman mosaic floor in the Villa Imperiale del Casale

Much Christian and other art vanished in the so-called Dark Ages, the five or so centuries after the sack of Rome by hostile northern invaders in 410. The villa's mosaics were luckier, first because the villa seems to have been respected by its subsequent owners, and second because they were covered in a landslide—and thus protected from the elements—in the 12th century. The site remained unknown until 1761, and almost entirely unexcavated until the late 1950s. Even today, considerable areas of the villa's slave and other quarters remain buried under the

courtyards. These are the **Thermae,** or baths (on the left of the lane as you approach the site's modern entrance); the **Peristyle,** or great central courtyard, where visitors would have been met, and in whose upper rooms they would have been housed (and around which much of the villa is arranged); the **servants quarters**

Detail from the corridor with hunting scenes

surrounding oak and hazel groves.

The site is large and confusing, the mosaics alone covering 37,600 square feet (about 3,500 sq m) in 40 distinct scenes. However, a profound knowledge of the villa's original structure is not required to appreciate its highlight—the mosaics themselves. Nor do you need to know the story, if any, behind individual mosaics, as the panels' narratives are often vivid enough for their meaning to be clear.

The villa as currently excavated has several basic components, each with many minor rooms and connecting doors, passageways, and

and **kitchens** (on the left, or north, side of the Peristyle); the main **living quarters,** including the Triclinium (a large dining room) on the south side of the Peristyle: and the **Ambulatorio,** or walkway, which runs the length of the Peristyle's eastern flank.

The Ambulatorio and its single, majestic mosaic of **"The Great Hunt"** is the villa's highlight and centerpiece, a continuous 200-foot (59 m) carpet of stone depicting the hunt and capture of wild animals of land and sea, some destined for Rome's Colosseum for use in gladiatorial games.

Staggering in its detail and animation, the rippling sea of color is crammed with human figures, tigers, elephants, ostriches, antelopes, wild boar, panthers, and creatures such as the North African lion that the Romans would eventually hunt to extinction. At the midway point, close to the steps, is a red-cloaked figure (flanked by

of Hercules," panels that vie with those of the "The Great Hunt" as the villa's masterpiece.

Also celebrated are the so-called **"Scena Erotica"**—a rather tame mosaic of a kissing couple—and the **Sala delle Dieci Ragazze** (Room of the Ten Girls) in the southeast corner of the Peristyle. The latter features

Morgantina
Seven miles (11 km) NE of Piazza Armerina in Aidone, the Museo Archeologico (Via Torre Trupia, tel 0935 87 307, closed Mon.) offers a good introduction to Morgantina (tel 0935 87 955)—a fascinating archaeological

guards) thought to be Maximilian.

Most pleasure in the villa can be had by simply wandering and admiring the mosaics, but there are one or two pieces worth tracking down: One is the **Sala della Piccola Caccia,** or Room of the Small Hunt, which depicts key episodes from a day's hunting, including an outdoor banquet. Others are the **Sala del Circo,** which portrays the events of a Roman "circus", or chariot race track (based on Rome's actual Circus Maximus), and the outstanding mosaics of the Triclinium, which illustrate the **"Labors**

a mosaic of ten women gymnasts apparently wearing bikinis some 1,700 years before they were "invented." In truth the women are probably portrayed in their underwear, which was also worn during gymnastic games.

Finally, be sure to see the "kindergarten" rooms: the **Vestibolo del Piccolo Circo,** where children are shown racing little chariots pulled by birds, and **Cubicolo dei Fanciulli Cacciatori** (Cubicle of the Child Hunters), where children are shown chasing—and being chased—by ducks and hare. ∎

site 3 miles (5 km) to the East. The site consists of the hilltop Cittadella (Citadel), once inhabited by Sikel and Bronze Age tribes, and a later Greek colony. Teams from Princeton University have been excavating the site since 1955.

Historical re-enactment in Piazza Armerian honors the Norman king, Roger I

More places to visit in southern Sicily

Much of the site of Eraclea Minoa remains unexcavated.

ERACLEA MINOA

This former Greek colony, founded in the sixth century B.C. by settlers from Selinus, occupies one of the loveliest ancient sites in Sicily. Fringed around a headland, it looks to the mouth of the Platini River on one side, and the sea and a crescent of cliff- and pine-backed white sand on the other. The **beach** is one of the best on the southern coast and worth a visit, except in July and August, when it gets crowded. You'll find more beaches just as nice, 10 miles (16 km) east at **Siculiana Marina.** Only about a third of the archaeological site *(tel 0922 846 005)* above Eraclea's beach has been excavated, revealing a theater and traces of tombs, mosaics, and city walls.
⚠ Map pp. 90–91 D3 **Visitor information**
✉ Piazzale A. Moro 7, Agrigento
☎ 0922 20 454

GELA

Gela is an appalling prospect, its environs blighted by industry, yet in the fifth century B.C. it was one of Sicily's most important Greek colonies, rivaling even mighty Syracuse. Today, a visit here is for Greek enthusiasts, who come for the ruins at **Capo Soprano** *(tel 0933 930 975)* just west of town, where the ancient Greek fortifications are the best preserved in Europe, and for the excellent

Museo Archeologico *(Corso Vittorio Emanuele II 1, tel 0933 912 626).* The museum is known mainly for its collection of red-and-black Gela ceramics, examples of which are found in many of leading museums.

Inland, the 12-mile (19 km) scenic drive to the village of **Butera** is highly worthwhile.
⚠ Map pp. 90–91 G1 **Visitor information**
✉ Via Filippo Morello 31-33 ☎ 0933 911 509

MONTI SICANI

The Sicani are wild, empty mountains, rarely visited and barely inhabited, but if you have time, they offer an interesting and scenic route toward Agrigento from the west. A good route (117 miles/189 km) follows the road from Selinunte to Sciacca by way of Menfi, then climbs to Caltabellotta (see below) and Villafranca Sicula. From south of Villafranca, minor roads lead east via Bivona to link with the S 118. A left turn at Bivona runs to Santo Stefano for the high road to San Giovanni Gemini that passes just north of Monte Cammarata (5,177 feet/1,578 m), the Sicani's highest point. Continue east to the main S 189 for the drive south to Agrigento or north to Palermo.

SCIACCA

Sciacca's **spa** *(Via Agatocle 1, tel 0925 961 111, www.termesciacca.it),* used since Greek times, is considered the world's oldest. The town's name probably derives from the Arabic *xacca,* meaning "from the waters." A thriving fishing center, the port is lively rather than pretty, with charm reserved for the old, little-visited **upper town,** worth a couple of hours of exploration. Sciacca is also known for its ceramics, available at several outlets, and for the work of Filippo Bentivegana (1888–1967), carver of thousands of heads in a strange, naive style. Many of these are now at his estate just west of town *(Castello Incantato, Via Ghezzi, tel 0925 993 044, closed Mon.).*

An essential side trip from Sciacca is the scenic 12-mile (19 km) drive northeast into the mountains to **Caltabellotta,** a majestically situated hill town (3,113 feet/949 m) with sweeping views.
⚠ Map pp. 90–91 C3 **Visitor information**
✉ Corso Vittorio Emanuele II 84
☎ 0925 21 182 ■

Southeast Sicily features the island's finest ancient city, Syracuse, full of glorious Greek, Roman, and other treasures. Architectural gems Noto and Ragusa, magnificent memorials to Sicily's baroque era, add to the region's appeal.

Syracuse & the Southeast

Column decorating the exterior of the Duomo in Syracuse

Wedding guests watch as the bride tosses her bouquet from the steps of San Giorgio in Modica. The church was rebuilt after the devastating earthquake of 1693.

Syracuse & the Southeast

SICILY'S SOUTHEAST CORNER HAS ALWAYS BEEN ONE OF THE ISLAND'S MOST fascinating enclaves, and its principal center, Syracuse (Siracusa), one of its most powerful and fascinating cities. Dotted around the region's rugged hinterland, a remote fastness dominated by the Monti Iblei, are several planned 18th-century towns—notably Ragusa, Noto, and Modica—which contain some of Europe's best baroque architecture.

The southeast has an ancient past, exemplified by the magnificent necropolis at Pantalica, a vast gorge riddled with prehistoric rock-cut tombs. Even this outstanding site, however, pales alongside Syracuse, the area's key historical player, founded as a Greek colony almost 3,000 years ago, and for centuries the most important city in the Hellenic world. Few places in Sicily are as charming to explore as the city's venerable heart, Ortygia (Ortigia), a beguiling labyrinth with sights and monuments from virtually every age.

Countless other local towns have Greek or older origins, and there are several archaeological sites—notably Megara Hyblaea near Augusta—that under other circumstances might be worth a visit. (Augusta lies close to a vast petrochemical plant that discourages a visit to the coast north of Syracuse.)

This modern desecration echoes an earlier natural disaster, the calamitous earthquake of January 11, 1693, which devastated the entire region. It was "so horrible," reported one eyewitness, "that the soil undulated like the waves of a stormy sea, and the mountains danced as if drunk."

Unlike other earthquakes in Sicily's long seismic history, the 1693 cataclysm allowed little by way of recovery or rebuilding because the destruction was almost total. But Sicily's quake resulted in some of the most compelling architecture in Europe. Why? Because the disaster occurred during a period of prosperity when baroque architecture was close to its zenith across Italy. As a result, some of the era's best architects were able to create entirely new towns, designing them according to the idealized precepts of the day, and filling them with a panoply of magnificent baroque churches, palaces, and civic buildings.

Noto is the most striking of these baroque fantasies, but Ragusa, a vaguely forlorn, gently decaying place, is ultimately more enticing. It also lies in the foothills of the Monti Iblei, limestone mountains scattered with interesting villages worth a day's exploration by car. ■

Syracuse

Syracuse
[A] Map p. III D3
Visitor information
www. apt-siracusa.it or
www. siracusa-sicilia.it
Archaeological zone
[✉] Via San Sebastiano 43
[☎] 0931 67 710

Azienda autonoma turismo
[✉] Via Maestranza 33, Ortygia
[☎] 0931 65 201

FOR SOME TWO CENTURIES SYRACUSE WAS THE MOST powerful city in the known world. This supremacy was challenged only by the Greeks, Etruscans, and Carthaginians, all of whom Syracuse defeated before succumbing to Rome. Today, its old town, Ortygia, and the extensive archaeological zone (Parco Archeologico), are essential stops on any Sicilian itinerary. Only the modern town, largely raised from the ruins of World War II bombing, is a disappointment.

The Greek historian Thucydides (circa 460–400 B.C.) claimed that emigrants from the Greek colony of Corinth founded Syracuse in 733 B.C. They were prompted, he wrote, by the urgings of Greece's Delphic oracle and attracted by the site's natural harbors, fresh springs, fertile hinterland, and the easily defended island redoubt of Ortygia. Before that it had Phoenician connections—its name may derive from Suraka, a Phoenician name for a nearby marsh—and was also inhabited by a native Sikel population.

Within 250 years it had become not only Sicily's most important colony, but also one of the most

the Greek playwright Aeschylus (525–456 B.C.) is believed to have written *Prometheus Bound* and *Prometheus Unbound* in the city.

Defeat, when it came, was at the hands of the Romans, who took the colony in 212 B.C. after a two-year siege. Even then, the city's heritage and natural advantages helped it retain some of its former importance, and it became capital of the new Roman province of Sicily. It was also prominent during the early days of Christianity, and for a brief period in the sixth century it was capital of the Byzantine Empire.

Today, Syracuse is a delightful place to visit and an excellent base for exploring southeast Sicily. Even its climate is kindly—the Roman orator Cicero (106–43 B.C.) observed that the city never knew a day without sun, even in winter. He also called it the most beautiful of all the Greek cities. This is not something you could say of the modern city, a sprawling (and generally best avoided) mainland grid between Ortygia and the Parco Archeologico, the latter a pleasing open area ranged across the site of the ancient city's recreational area, Neapolis.

ORTYGIA

The island of Ortygia, linked to the mainland and modern city by two causeways, formed the heart of Syracuse for 2,700 years. Until recently it was a moribund district, full of crumbling monuments and dilapidated streets. Recently, however, the area has undergone a renaissance, marked by extensive restoration projects and the opening of new hotels, bars, and restaurants. As a result, this is the place you should aim to stay, devoting time to the many sights, but also exploring the pretty flower-hung alleys and tree-lined waterfront promenades.

The 18th-century baroque facade of Syracuse's Duomo lights up the night.

powerful cities in the Mediterranean. In 480 B.C. under Helon, one its many despotic rulers, it defeated the Carthaginians at the Battle of Himera, while in 415 B.C. it annihilated a colossal force dispatched by a jealous Athens, the most powerful of Greece's mainland colonies, and its only rival in terms of size and beauty.

For centuries the city enjoyed military, political, and artistic supremacy, producing or attracting some of the leading cultural names of the Greek world. Plato came here in around 397 B.C. to teach philosophy; Syracuse-born Archimedes (287–212 B.C.) worked as scientist and engineer; the lyric poet Pindar (circa 518–438 B.C.) was employed as court writer; and

The Ponte Nuovo leads to Piazza Pancali and Largo XXV Luglio, home to the fragmentary **Tempio di Apollo** (circa 565 B.C.), or all that remains of the first major Doric temple built by the Greeks in Sicily. Just to the north, the covered **Antico Mercato,** the town's former 19th-century marketplace, contains a visitor center (*Via Trento 2, tel 0931 449 201,*

The 18th century facade of the city's cathedral

www.anticomercato.it). A picturesque fish market *(closed Sun.& p.m.)* is held in the surrounding streets, while Largo Graziella nearby is the focus of the old *casbah* district, a reminder of Syracuse's ninth- and tenth-century period of Arab domination.

The elegant, shop-lined Corso Matteotti leads southeast from Largo XXV Luglio to **Piazza Archimede,** Ortygia's mostly 19th-century main square. Walk south from here down Via Roma and turn

right along Via Minerva and you come to **Piazza del Duomo,** a far lovelier square (particularly at night when it is floodlit). It contains the area's most compelling monuments, chiefly the **Duomo** (*tel 0931 65 201, closed noon– 4 p.m.*), last of a succession of sacred buildings that have occupied the site for over 2,500 years.

The ancient building's magnificent decoration is long gone, pillaged or despoiled by the Romans and others, but the basic edifice was saved from ruin by its conversion into the city's cathedral in 640. Its present facade (1728–1754), one of Italy's last major baroque works, was added after the 1693 earthquake toppled the Norman frontage.

Inside, the baroque interior was largely removed in 1927, revealing the outlines of the original temple, notably its ancient columns on the left (north) side. The first chapel in the opposite (south) aisle is the baptistery, and contains a fifth-century B.C. Greek font (once a burial urn recovered from the city's catacombs), which rests on 13th-century bronze lions. The final chapel in the same aisle, the Cappella del Crocefisso, contains a 15th-century painting of St. Zosimus attributed to Antonello da Messina, Sicily's foremost Renaissance artist.

Leave Piazza del Duomo to the south on Via Picherale and you pass **Santa Lucia** on the right, a church dedicated to Syracuse's most venerated saint. Martyred in the city in A.D. 304, she was buried in the local catacombs, and is depicted in paintings across Italy, usually holding a saucer containing a pair of eyes. This alludes to the story in which she is said to have torn out her eyes after being complimented on them by an unwanted pagan suitor. Her feast day and procession on December 13 is one of Sicily's most striking.

At the end of Via Picherale is the lovely papyrus-shaded **Fonte Aretusa**, one of the most important springs in the Hellenic world. Celebrated by the poets Pindar, Virgil, and others, it was supposedly mentioned in Delphi's oracular directions that drove Corinthian exiles to found Syracuse.

It also features in the Greek myth of Arethusa, one of the nymphs of Artemis, goddess of virginity. Arethusa, so the story goes, was bathing in the Alpheus River near Olympia on the Greek mainland, when she was propositioned by Alpheus, the river's predatory god. Anxious to preserve her modesty, Arethusa appealed to Artemis for help, who saved her by turning her into a fountain. Thus transformed she was able escape under the sea to Sicily, where she emerged as the spring of the Fonte Aretusa. To

Catacombs

Syracuse's catacombs are the most extensive in Italy after those of Rome. Their main entrance is beside the ruined church of San Giovanni, west of the Museo Archeologico Regionale. In the past they have been open to the public; however, they currently are closed because of safety concerns. Inquire at a visitor center for up-to-date admission details. ∎

no avail, however, for Alpheus pursued her, mingling his river waters with those of the spring.

Myth aside, a spring of such purity so close to the sea was of great practical use, and its waters sustained Ortygia through centuries of siege and warfare. Earthquakes and new buildings

Remains of a Greek quarry used to build ancient Syracuse

Syracuse's Greek theater ranked among the largest in the ancient world.

Parco Archeologico

✉ Viale Augusto-Largo Paradiso

☎ 0931 66 206

💲 $$

Note: Two-day combination ticket available for admission to all, or any two, of the following: Museo Regionale, Parco Archeologico, and Museo Archeologico Regionale

subsequently compromised the water's purity, but the spring still flows, and continued to be used for more than two millennia—the British fleet under Adm. Horatio Nelson, for example, took on water here before its victory at the Battle of the Nile in 1798.

The fonte is the focus of the *passeggiata* (evening stroll), along with the **Foro Vittorio Emanuele II,** also known as the Marina, the lovely tree-lined waterfront promenade north of the fountain. To the south rises the **Castello Maniace,** a 13th-century fortress named after George Maniakes, the Byzantine general who recaptured the city from the Arabs in 1038. It is currently closed, but there are plans to reopen it to the public.

Walk east from the fountain on Via Capodieci and you come to the **Museo Regionale** (*Palazzo Bellomo, Via Capodieci 14, tel 0931 69 511, closed Mon. & Sun. p.m.*), Ortygia's principal museum. A mixture of artistic and archaeological exhibits, its pictorial highlights are

an "Annunciation" (1474) by Antonello da Messina and Caravaggio's superlative "Burial of St. Lucy" (1608). The museum also contains a charming collection of ceramics and other decorative arts.

After seeing the sights, be sure to spend some time just wandering the streets of Ortygia. Some of the best are **Via Roma,** the palace-lined **Via Vittorio Veneto, Via Maestranza,** and **Via della Giudecca,** heart of the old Jewish quarter. Just about any small alley, however, brings its own rewards.

PARCO ARCHEOLOGICO

The Parco Archeologico lies north of the modern city, but the walk here from Ortygia is dull, so plan to take a cab or bus No. 1 from Ortygia's Piazza della Posta. The park extends over a "new" area of the ancient city, built as a predominantly recreational zone in the third century B.C., well after the settlement of Ortygia and its hinterland.

The entrance is marked by a small visitor center and a sprawl of souvenir stands. Beyond these on the left lies the site's first major ruin, the **Ara di Ierone II** (241–217 B.C.), created as a vast sacrificial altar where up to 350 bulls could be slaughtered in a single day. Such altars to the gods were common in the Greek world. At 650 feet (200 m) in length, this was the largest such altar in Magna Graecia, and though little survives (the Spanish plundered its stone in 1526 to build the city's harbor), the structure's outlines still bear impressive witness to its enormous scale.

Far more survives of the **Teatro Greco,** an amphitheater carved from the living rock, and one of the largest and most spectacular theaters in the Greek world. It was begun in the sixth century B.C., though most of the structure dates from the third century B.C., when it was enlarged to accommodate 15,000 people in nine 59-row sections, of which 42 remain. The Romans made further alterations, partly to allow the staging of gladiatorial combats and mock sea battles (which required the flooding of the stage area).

Concerts and plays are still regularly performed here in May and June *(contact visitor centers for details).* Performances are also held in the **Anfiteatro Romano** *(S of main entrance),* the Romans' own amphitheater, built in the third century B.C. to meet an almost insatiable demand for circus and gladiatorial games.

West of the Greek theater stretches the **Latomia del Paradiso,** the largest of at least a dozen local quarries that supplied limestone both for the ancient city and for export across the Mediterranean. Today, much of its area is given over to attractive gardens, though one gargantuan cavern, the **Orecchio di Dionisio,** still offers a vivid impression of the quarries' scale. This and other quarries were long used as prisons, and it was in these *latomie* (from the Greek *lios,* stone, and *temnos,* to cut) that 8,000 Athenian prisoners captured after Syracuse's victory in 415 B.C. perished after eight years' hard labor. Only those who could recite verses from the Greek playwright Euripedes, it is said, were allowed their freedom. A neighboring cavern, the **Grotta dei Cordari,** is named after the ropemakers *(cordari)* who worked there for centuries.

MUSEO ARCHEOLOGICO REGIONALE

Italy is scattered with archaeological museums, but few are as impressive as Syracuse's Museo Archeologico Regionale, secreted in the gardens of the Villa Landolina about ten minutes' walk east of the Parco Archeologico. A museum of finds from the Parco Archeologico and elsewhere, it chronicles the history of Syracuse and eastern Sicily in general, and is one of the finest collections of Greek (and earlier) artifacts outside Athens and London. The building is modern, if a little faded, and the English labeling is limited, but there is no faulting the quality of exhibits.

Ironically, the star exhibit—the first-century "Venus Landolina"—is a Roman work, not Greek (though it was copied from a Greek original), a figure that is celebrated for the sensual pose of its protagonist. Also outstanding are the vast seventh-century burial urns; the fourth-century Sarcophagus of Adelfia; the reconstructed temple of Athena (now Syracuse's cathedral); and the striking "Mother Goddess Nursing Twins," a redoubtable statue from the sixth century B.C. ■

Museo Archeologico Regionale

✉ Viale Teocrito 66

☎ 0931 464 022 or 0931 464 023

🕐 Closed Mon. & Sun. p.m.

💲 $$

Clay bust from the fourth or fifth century B.C., one of many artifacts in the Museo Archeologico Regionale

Ornate balconies
adorn the
baroque Palazzo
Nicolaci di
Villadorata.

Noto

Noto
Map p. 111 C2
**Visitor
information**
www.comune.noto.sr.it
Piazza XVI Maggio
12
0931 573 779

NOTO IS THE FINEST BAROQUE TOWN IN SICILY, WHICH IS
to say the finest baroque town in Italy. Raised from nothing after the
earthquake of 1693, it is a gloriously theatrical architectural ensemble of grace, symmetry, tawny-stoned palaces, opulent piazzas,
sweeping vistas, and majestic churches.

Built during the golden age of the
baroque, Noto was able to adopt
the best of the 18th century's architectural ideals. Streets were laid out
on a neat grid, for example, glimpses of countryside were introduced
as unexpected features of urban
vistas, and hillsides were used to site
piazzas and staircases that played
deliberate tricks of perspective.

The town was also divided in
two, with a patrician lower section
and another more humble quarter
devoted to the accommodation of
ordinary people. Most of what you
want to see is in the former, an area
that consists of three key piazzas
and three principal streets.

The main street is **Corso
Vittorio Emanuele II,** entered
from the gardens at its eastern end
via the **Porta Reale,** a gateway
modeled on a Roman triumphal
arch and built to commemorate the
visit of Ferdinand II in 1838. Then
come **Piazza Immacolata** and
Vincenzo Sinatra's church of **San
Francesco all'Immacolata**

(1704–1748) to the right. Beyond is the more extravagant convent of **Santissimo Salvatore,** whose balconies are echoed across the street by Rosario Gagliardi's church of **Santa Chiara** (1730– 1748). Venture inside, but know that Noto's interiors tend to be rather plain.

"Plain" is not a charge that could be leveled at **Piazza Municipio,** considered Sicily's most beautiful square. To the right stands the **Duomo,** completed in 1776, and probably the work of Sinatra and Gagliardi. To the left is Sinatra's arcaded Town Hall or **Municipio** (begun 1743), also known as the Palazzo Ducezio, and the more sober 19th-century Palazzo Vescovile (Bishop's Palace) and Palazzo Landolina, former home of prominent aristocrats. At the first junction beyond the square, on the left, stands Gagliardi's church of **San Carlo** (1730), whose tower can usually be climbed for views of the town.

Follow the Via Corrado Nicolaci, right off the corso, a little way up and on the left is the **Palazzo Nicolaci di Villadorata** *(tel 0931 574 080, closed Sat.–Sun. Oct.– April),* celebrated for its magnificent exterior. The palace is open for tours, but only one room, the **Salone delle Feste,** captures the former interior splendor.

Return to the corso and the **Piazza XVI Maggio** to take in the **Teatro Comunale,** a lovely 330-seat theater, and the church of **San Domenico** (1737–1756), one of Gagliardi's finest buildings.

Also be sure to visit the simpler **upper town** (Gagliardi's **Santissimo Crocefisso** on Piazza Mazzini is the key building) and the streets parallel to the corso: Via Ducezio, with the churches of the **Carmine** and **Santa Maria dell'Arco,** and Via Cavour, known for the 1735 **Palazzo Battaglia.** ∎

Story of Noto

The story of Noto can be told twice: The first recounts the genius and good fortune that produced one of Europe's most beautiful towns. The second recounts the battle to ensure the town's survival.

Old Noto—Noto Antica—came to an end on January 11, 1693, when a catastrophic earthquake reduced the town to rubble. Three excellent architects—Rosario Gagliardi, Paolo Labisi, and Vincenzo Sinatra—were hired to create a model town from scratch, which they did, 8 miles from the old site, out of the local, soft tufa-limestone that lent itself to intricate baroque carving. The stone's dazzling white intensity weathered to a glorious honey color. Sicilians called the resulting town "a garden of stone." Little could they know that it would be susceptible to the depredations and the pollution of a later age.

Based on findings that the whole town was inherently fragile, a massive restoration project was launched in the late 1980s and UNESCO declared Noto a World Heritage site in 1996. ∎

Rosario Gagliardi's 18th-century church of San Domenico

Prickly pear cactus and other hardy plants thrive on the upland slopes of the Monti Iblei.

A drive through the Monti Iblei

The Monti Iblei are wild and rugged limestone mountains, famed for their olive oil and sweeping views, and dotted with sleepy villages and major archaeological sites.

Leave Syracuse west on the minor road toward Belvedere, pausing to visit the ruins of the fourth-century B.C. **Castel Eurialo ❶,** part of Syracuse's outer defenses. Pass under the autostrada (expressway) and turn right and then left after 3 miles (2.2 km) to the Anapo River. At the bridge, Ponte Diddino, turn right on the high, scenic road to Sortino *(Visitor information, Via Pietro Gaetani 146, tel 0931 953 359).*

From Sortino, take the minor road west toward Buccheri, which dips and climbs toward Monte Santa Venere (2,851 feet/869 m). After 10 miles (16 km), turn left to **Ferla,** where another left turn in the village center takes you 5.5 miles (9 km) above the Anapo valley to **Pantalica ❷,** Sicily's largest and most important necropolis.

The easily defended site was inhabited by the ancient Sikels between the 13th and 8th centuries B.C. It's a spectacular place, with more than 5,000 tombs honeycombed into the rock.

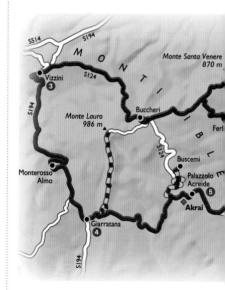

Many easy paths meander around the area or drop toward the Anapo Valley below, where the trackless line of the old Syracuse to Vizzini railroad (now a trail) can be seen.

Return to Ferla and Sortino to the Buccheri road, turning left to the mountain hamlet of **Buccheri.** From here, take the S 124 ridgetop road northwest to **Vizzini ❸,** birthplace of the 19th-century writer Giovanni Verga, who used the village as the setting for several of his novels, including *La Lupa (The She-Wolf)* and *La Cavalleria Rusticana.*

See the churches of San Sebastiano, Santa Maria del Gesù, and Chiesa Madre, and then take the road south to **Monterosso Almo,** with two fine little churches, San Giovanni and Sant'Antonio. From here continue south to **Giarratana ❹,** another hamlet with a medley of churches, and then turn left (east) toward Palazzolo Acreide.

After less than a mile (1.6 km), a minor road veers left back toward Buccheri, a lovely high route with superb views, running 7 miles (9.8 km) almost to the summit of 3,234-foot-high (986 m) **Monte Lauro,** the Iblei's highest point. You can take this route and double back for the views, or skip and go directly to **Palazzolo Acreide ❺** *(Piazza del Popolo 1, tel 0931 882 000).* The village has many good baroque buildings and an excellent museum

of Sicilian rural life, the **Museo di Antonino Uccello** *(Via Machiavelli 19, tel 0931 881 499, closed daily p.m.),* but is better known for the well-kept ruins of **Akrai** immediately to the southwest, Greek Syracuse's first inland colony. There's a charming Greek theater and extensive remains of temples, quarries, and other fragments from the seventh-century B.C. settlement.

If time allows, detour north from Palazzolo Acreide to **Buscemi** to see another fascinating ethnological "museum," the **Luoghi del Lavoro Contadino** *(tel 0931 878 528, www.museobuscemi.org).* Exhibits focus on rustic life in the Monti Iblei. Return to Syracuse on the S 124 via Solarino. ∎

▲ See area map p. 111
► Syracuse
⟷ 110 miles (175 km) plus 20-mile (20 km) detour
🕒 1 day
► Syracuse

NOT TO BE MISSED

- Pantalica
- High, scenic road to Buccheri
- Museo di Antonino Uccello
- Buscemi and museum

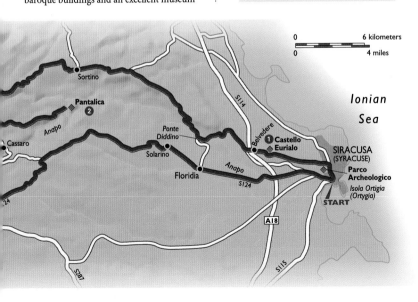

Ragusa

Ragusa

🗺 Map p. 111 B2

Visitor information

www.ragusaturismo.com or www.ragusaonline.com

✉ Via Capitano Bocchieri 33

☎ 0932 221 511

RAGUSA IS REALLY TWO TOWNS: THE UNREMARKABLE 18th-century town created in the wake of the 1693 earthquake, and Ragusa Ibla, the older hill town restored by its inhabitants after the quake to its original medieval appearance. Today, the latter has one of the most appealing and atmospheric old quarters in Sicily.

Ragusa Ibla's origins date back to Hybla Heraia, one of the ancient Sikels' principal settlements. It was then a Greek and a Roman colony, and assumed prominence under the Normans when Count Roger created a fiefdom here for his son, Roger II, in 1091. The 1693 earthquake led to a decline that has continued to this day—money, business, and people having moved to the 18th-century quarter and its ugly modern suburbs.

Decline in Ragusa Ibla, however, has been picturesque rather than catastrophic, and the town's warren of tiny streets is full of baroque and other buildings of ramshackle and wonderfully faded charm. The pace of life is slow, the views superb, and the opportunities for finding hidden nooks and crannies almost endless.

Both Ragusa Ibla and the newer town occupy a large spur between two valleys, with Ragusa Ibla set lower than its neighbor, which is known simply as Ragusa, or Ragusa Superiore. Buses and cabs run to Ragusa Ibla from Ragusa, but it is better to make for Ragusa's eastern margin and then walk into Ragusa Ibla.

Start from the church of **Santa Maria delle Scale** *(Corso Mazzini)*, and either follow the winding Corso Mazzini down to Ragusa Ibla or—a better option— take the steps (333 in all) that make the tortuous but panoramic descent to the old town. The glorious view over the rocky outcrop, the sparse limestone hills, and the sea of weathered roofs is just one of many striking vistas here.

As you descend, look first for the **Palazzo Nicastro** (1760), the town's old prison (also known as the Vecchia Cancelleria), celebrated for its lovely doorway, and (to its left) the 18th-century church of **Santa Maria dell'Itria** *(entrance on Corso Mazzini),* distinguished by the majolica tiles that decorate its little dome. A few steps below the church on the right is the 18th-century

Palazzo Cosentini, with a series of fine balconies and brackets carved with masks and caricatured figures.

From Piazza della Repubblica, a little square near the closed church of Purgatorio, either bear left to panoramic **Via del Mercato,** or become happily lost in the labyrinth of alleys, steps, and small squares behind the church (take Via Aquila Sveva as a starting point).

Either way, you will eventually stumble on **Piazza del Duomo,** the town's focal point and home to the cathedral of **San Giorgio** (1744). The visitor center is immediately behind the cathedral to the right, housed in the beautifully restored Palazzo La Rocca, known for its pretty balconies.

San Giorgio was the work of Rosario Gagliardi (1700–1770), the architect responsible for much of Noto (see pp. 118-19), and is one of the masterpieces of Sicilian baroque. Forty years in the making, its beauty is all in the pink-stoned facade—the interior is dull. The same is true of the smaller but otherwise similar church of **San Giuseppe** *(Piazza Pola)*, also attributed to Gagliardi, a few steps down Corso XXV Aprile.

Follow the corso farther downhill and you come to the **Giardino Ibleo** (1858), delightful public gardens which occupy the town's eastern tip. In and around them is a trio of little churches, though the main distractions here, as so often in the town, are the sweeping views. ■

Modern electric lights illuminate the medieval town of Ragusa Ibla.

More places to visit in southeast Sicily

A baroque staircase leads to the entrance of San Pietro in Modica's upper town.

CAVA D'ISPICA

From Modica (see below), be sure to visit the Cava d'Ispica, a deep, 7-mile (12 km) gorge entered 8 miles (13 km) east of the town on the road to Rosolino. You can walk much of the lush gorge, which is riddled with rock tombs, Greek necropoli, cave dwellings, and extensive Christian catacombs.

🅰 Map p. 111 B2 **Visitor information**
☎ 0932 622 150 🕐 Closed p.m. in winter

THE COAST

The coast north of Syracuse has been spoiled, but much to the south remains appealing, whether you want a modern resort—**Marina di Ragusa** is the locals' favorite—or a nature reserve, **Riserva Naturale di Vendicari.** You'll find low-key resorts near Pachino, and along the entire southern coast, relatively undeveloped beaches, especially at **Camerina, Punta Braccetto, Punta Secca,** and **Donnalucata.**

MODICA

Modica's valley setting and multitiered old center make it well worth a visit. The lower town, **Modica Bassa,** has several baroque churches and a small **Museo Civico** *(Via Merce, tel 0932 945 081, closed Sun.)* with an archaeological

collection and (upstairs) an interesting **folk museum** *(tel 0932 752 747, closed Mon. a.m.).* The upper town, **Modica Alta,** rises in a jumble of houses, churches, and palaces, linked in part by a superb staircase (1818) off the lively Corso Umberto I. This road leads to the church of **San Giorgio** (1702–1738), the town's architectural highlight, and possibly the work of Rosario Gagliardi.

🅰 Map p. 111 B2 **Visitor information**
✉ Corso Umberto I 149 ☎ 0932 753 324

SCICLI

A lovely road links Modica to Scicli 7 miles (9 km) to the south, a sleepy market town whose baroque center dates from the 1693 earthquake. Of note on Piazza Italia, its main square, is the 18th-century baroque **Duomo of Sant' Ignazio,** and nearby, the **Palazzo Beneventano.** Additional monuments lie on or just off the town's picturesque Via Mormino Penna, notably **San Giovanni.** Be sure to walk to **San Matteo,** heart of the medieval town, for excellent views of Scicli below and (if you walk to the ridge beyond) of the Neolithic tombs and cave dwellings that honeycomb the hills.

🅰 Map p. 111 B1 **Visitor information**
✉ Via Castellana 4 ☎ 0932 932 782 ■

Eastern Sicily is Sicily at its most ancient and strange. Ancient because of the age of its towns, among which the chic resort of Taormina stands out, and strange because of the otherworldly landscape of Mount Etna, Europe's crowning volcano.

Eastern Sicily

Hardy plants thrive on Mount Etna's fertile slopes.

Vapor issues from the smoldering summit of Mount Etna, Europe's most active volcano.

Eastern Sicily

TOWNS IN EASTERN SICILY ARE THOUSANDS OF YEARS OLD, ALREADY thriving settlements when the Greeks arrived some five centuries before the birth of Christ. Some have lost their past glory, others, such as Taormina, have preserved their charm. Ancient or modern, however, faded or beguiling, all live in the shadow of the Sicily's greatest natural feature—the brooding mass of Mount Etna (Monte Etna).

Etna is unmissable. Visible from much of Sicily and the Italian mainland, its smoking and often snow-covered summit is an almost constant presence along the Ionian coast between the towns of Messina in the north and Catania to the south. Over the centuries it has been a mixed blessing for those who live on its slopes, frequently wreaking death and destruction, but also bequeathing soils of almost untold richness. As a result, Etna's foothills, covered in vines, olives, citrus groves, pistachios, and almonds, boast some of the most fertile land in Italy.

On the upper slopes the story is different, for here the almost barren landscape is an eerie expanse of blackened lava and shifting sands of ash, pumice, and other volcanic debris. The lower slopes and their interesting villages are easily seen by car or train—roads and the Circumetnea railroad almost circle the volcano—and the upper slopes, eruptions

allowing, are accessible on foot or on organized tours (with off-road vehicles) from two base stations: Piano Provenzana and the Rifugio Sapienza, high up the mountain's northern and southern slopes respectively.

If Etna makes a virtue of its strange ugliness, the same cannot be said of the towns and coast below. North of the volcano, the Monti Peloritani, some of Sicily's wildest and most intractable mountains, with scarcely a road or village to their name, squeeze highways and railroads hard against the sea, creating an almost continuous ribbon of forgettable towns and resorts between Messina and Catania.

Some crumbling, sleepy villages in the Peloritani foothills escape the blight—places like Savoca, Casalvecchio Siculo, and Forza d'Agrò—and one, Taormina, gloriously transcends it, providing a pretty, sophisticated playground that has attracted visitors for more than a hundred years. ∎

T y r r h e n i a n
S e a

Capo di
Milazzo

Golfo di Milazzo

Punta del
Faro

S113

Milazzo

A20

Messina

Stretto di Messina

A3

Golfo di Patti

A20

← To Cefalù

Patti ● S113

Barcellona
Pozzo di Grotto

A18

Reggio di
Calabria

CALABRIA

Ucria

M o n t i   P e l o r i t a n i

NORTHERN SICILY
144–145

S116

S185

Casalvecchio
Siculo

Savoca

S114

Montagna Grande
1,374 m

Francavilla
di Sicilia

Forza d'Agro

△
D

Alcantara

Randazzo

S120

Gola
dell'Alcantara

S185

Monte Tauro
398 m

Mazzarò

Taormina

Maletto

Linguaglossa

Giardini-Naxos

Piano
Provenzana

Naxos

PARCO REGIONALE

I o n i a n   S e a

S284

Bronte

Mount Etna
(Monte Etna)
3,322 m
10,899 ft ▲

DELL' ETNA
Rifugio
Sapienza

Milo

Zafferana
Etnea

Riposto

S114

S575

Adrano

Nicolosi

S284

Acireale

EASTERN SICILY

Centuripe

S121

A18

Paternò ●

S121

Aci Castello

Area of map detail

← To Enna

Simeto

☆ Catania

0   15 kilometers

A19

Ditaino

Plain of Catania
(Piana di Catania)

✈ Catania-Fontanarossa
International Airport

0   10 miles

Golfo di
Catania

△
A

SOUTHEAST SICILY
p. 111

△
B

△
C

Etna

Etna

🗺 Maps p. 127 B3
& p. 133

**Visitor
information**

✉ Pizza Annunziata,
Linguaglossa

☎ 095 643 094

🕐 Closed Sun. p.m.

✉ Via Vittorio Emanuele
II 45, Nicolosi

☎ 095 914 488

Note: Most local tourist
offices can assist
in booking Etna
excursions.

ANCIENT NAVIGATORS THOUGHT IT THE HIGHEST POINT
on Earth. To the Arabs it was *Gibel utlamat*—the mountain of
mountains. Pindar (circa 518–438 B.C.), the ancient Greek lyric poet,
described it as the column that supports the sky. Today, no trip to
Sicily is complete without a visit to Mount Etna, Europe's highest and
most spectacular volcano.

Etna is the most monumental
landform in the Mediterranean,
covering a larger area than
London or New York. On clear
days the peak is visible from over
155 miles (250 km) away. It is
around 10,900 feet (3,323 m)
high and 20 miles (32 km) in
diameter. Eruptions occur, often
with staggering ferocity, about
once every five to ten years.

For all its sinister splendor,
however, Etna is a young mountain. Geologists believe it began
life around 500,000 years ago,
bursting from the seabed of a
vanished gulf in what is now the
Plain of Catania. Over the millennia, and the last 60,000 years in
particular, it has built layer upon
layer of ash and lava to create the
colossal peak that casts its literal

distinctive coronet of smoke a familiar sight across much of Sicily and beyond. Black smoke is apparently a good sign; white smoke is a more sinister portent.

Etna's volcanic character is marked by its tendency to split at the seams, rather than explode from a central point. Over the years these ruptures have added 350 secondary, or "adventive" craters to the four larger craters near the summit. This latter quartet, however, has accounted for most of the volcanic activity of the last 30 years, in particular the so-called Bocca Nuova, or "new mouth", which has been the most active vent since the early 1990s.

It is this volcanic activity, of course, that most visitors wish to see. Etna is so large and its environs so varied that you will need at least two days to do the region justice.

One day should be devoted to getting as close to the summit as conditions allow (see p. 130). This will take you onto the barren, lunar-like upper slopes, where pumice litters the lava fields, and shifting sands and powdered ash drift across macabre hills. If you are lucky you will enjoy not only one of Europe's strangest landscapes, but also some of its most remarkable views.

Spend a second day (see pp. 132-35) exploring the volcano's very different lower slopes, best seen as a circular tour, either on the Circumetnea railroad, or on the road that parallels its tracks for much of its course. Both routes virtually encircle the volcano, passing through a succession of tiny, often picturesque villages, and offering glimpses of the dulcet, pastoral corners and lush landscapes—forests of larch and beech, vineyards, orange groves, and orchards of pistachio and almond—that have sprung from Etna's fertile soils.

Hikers follow a packed roadbed up Mount Etna's blackened slopes.

and metaphorical shadow over much of eastern Sicily.

The first recorded eruption was in 475 B.C. Since then there have been at least 250 eruptions—90 of them major ones, the last in 2003. The most catastrophic was in 1669, when the mountain was torn apart, leaving a chasm on its southern flanks 16 miles (26 km) long. Magma flowed for 122 days, engulfing the town of Catania, while ash was thrown 60 miles. The lava took eight years to cool, and local peasants, records report, were able to boil water on it long after the eruption.

Today, Etna—whose name derives from a Greek word meaning "to burn"—is almost always smoldering, if not erupting, its

Piano Provenzana
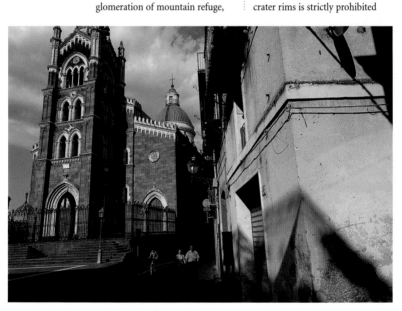 Maps p. 127 B3 &
p. 133

Rifugio Sapienza
Maps p. 127 B2 &
p. 133

SEEING THE VOLCANO

Visits to Etna's upper reaches can be made from either the north or south side of the volcano, and in particular from two base stations: **Piano Provenzana,** a ski station on the northern slope at about 5,970 feet (1,820 m), with a parking lot and winter ski lift; and the **Rifugio Sapienza,** an ugly conglomeration of mountain refuge,

the 20-person, off-road vehicles that transport visitors higher up the mountain to around 8,850 feet (2,697 m). From here, a qualified guide takes you on foot another 650 feet (198 m), with the option *(on payment of another fee, and conditions allowing)* of ascending to safe areas nearer the summit craters. Access to or around the crater rims is strictly prohibited

Etna provided the stone—black lava and yellow pumice—used to build the church of Santa Maria in Randazzo.

souvenir stands, large parking lot, and restaurants on the southern slope at 6,262 feet (1,909 m).

Both can be reached by road: the 21-mile (34 km) drive from Catania to the Rifugio via Nicolosi leads through brooding lava fields, while the similar-length route to Piano Provenzana from Taormina via Linguaglossa winds through lovely pine woods before encountering the lava wastes.

Whichever side you choose— the Rifugio Sapienza is the most popular—trips can be made in one of three ways: The first is to make your way by car or bus to the Rifugio and buy tickets on one of

after nine visitors were killed here during the eruptions of 1979.

The second option is to join a day-long organized tour, departing either from Catania or Taormina. A tour includes transport to the Rifugio Sapienza, warm clothing and sturdy footwear, and, for an additional fee, the excursion by off-road vehicle.

The third approach is to make your own way to the Rifugio and then hike to the upper slopes, a rather monotonous route that follows the vehicular tracks *(allow 4 hrs. each way).*

Note that whichever option you choose, views are better in

the early morning (a dawn hike is especially recommended), as clouds tend to form later in the day. If conditions are misty, or visibility looks questionable, do not make the trip.

Other organized tours, hikes, and off-road options are available from Piano Provenzana, though here the setup is more low key. Tours and excursions generally

upper slopes), you will need to drive or take one of the daily AST buses *(twice daily July–Aug.)* from Catania's Stazione Centrale, or main railway station. Buses usually depart around 8:15 a.m. and return from the Rifugio or Piano Provenzana at about 4:30 p.m.

However you travel, you must be well equipped. On the slopes above the Rifugio or the ski

operate from about May to September, depending on weather, volcanic activity, and summit snows.

Organized tours are the best option, if only because everything is done for you, not the least allowing you to avoid the rather chaotic scene and frequent lines for the off-road vehicle excursions at the Rifugio Sapienza. Tours can be arranged through travel agents in Taormina or Catania, or through visitor information centers in these or other towns such as Nicolosi or Linguaglossa.

If you prefer to do things under your own steam (thus allowing you more freedom and time on the

station it is always cold and blustery, with sudden changes of weather possible, even in high summer. Be sure to have good hiking shoes or boots, warm layers, and waterproof outer clothing. If you are on a tour, or are joining the vehicle excursions, padded jackets and other clothing can be rented for a few euros.

If you wish to hike beyond the well-defined vehicular tracks or explore elsewhere on the mountain, it is advisable to hire a guide. *(Contact Gruppo Guide Alpine Etna Sud, Via Etnea 49, Nicolosi, tel 095 791 4755; guides also available at Rifugio Sapienza).* ■

Rich volcanic soil has made Etna's lowest slopes perhaps the most fertile farmland in Italy.

Getting around the volcano

The best way to get an idea of Etna's enormous size and experience its remarkable scenic diversity is to drive or take the Circumetnea railroad from Catania (it leaves from its own private station), either following a clockwise circular tour around the volcano or concluding the excursion at Taormina.

The Circumetnea railroad offers fine views of Mount Etna and its lovely environs.

The train leaves from a station north of Catania's city center (*Via Caronda 352, tel 095 541 111, www.circumetnea.it*), not the main Stazione Centrale, to which it is linked by metro. It takes about 3.5 hours (with connections required at Randazzo on some runs) to reach its terminus at the coastal village of Riposto.

From here you can pick up connections on the main state (Trenitalia) network north or south to Taormina or Catania respectively. It's a delightful ride, with many superb views of the volcano, but for flexibility and the chance to explore properly, it is better to have a car.

The following drive can be picked up at several points, but is described from Catania and does not mention the many minor roads that access Etna's upper slopes. These are all highly recommended, especially those to the Rifugio Sapienza from Adrano (see below) and to **Nicolosi** (*Visitor information, Via Vittorio Emanuele II 45, tel 095 914 488*), home to the visitor center for the **Parco Regionale dell'Etna** (*Visitor information, Via Etnea 107, tel 095 821 111, www.parcoetna.it*) that protects much of

Etna. Also worthwhile are those to Piano Provenzana from Milo and Linguaglossa.

From **Catania ❶** (*Visitor information, Via Cimarosa 10-12, tel 095 730 6255, www.apt.catania.it*) take the S 121 road west to **Paternò ❷**, known for its orange groves and restored Norman castle (*tel 095 621 109, closed Mon. & Sat.–Sun. p.m.*), and then follow the S 284 to **Adrano ❸**. Founded in 400 B.C., this village is one of Etna's most ancient settlements. It boasts a castle built in 1070 by the Norman ruler Roger I. Inside is a charming archaeological **museum** (*Piazza Umberto I, tel 095 769 2660, closed Mon. & Sun. p.m.*). Stop by the adjacent **Chiesa Madre,** a Norman church with 16 basalt columns, possibly from an ancient Greek temple, then leave town northwest on the S 121 road.

After 5 miles look for signs to the **Ponte dei Saraceni ❹**, a graceful bridge of Roman origin over a peaceful stretch of the Simeto River. Two miles (3.2 km) upstream (walk or drive on minor roads from Adrano) is the beautiful **Gola di Simeto**, an 8-mile (13 km) gorge formed by lava flows and protected by the **Riserva Naturale Ingrottato Lavico del Simeto** (nature reserve).

Return to Adrano and pick up the S 284 to **Bronte ❺**, a road that offers some of the drive's best views of Etna. Bronte is the center of Italy's pistachio industry, producing 85 percent of the country's output.

The town's rather drab appearance belies its romantic history. In 1799, Ferdinand IV of Naples presented the dukedom of Bronte to Horatio Nelson in gratitude for the British admiral's help (he had whisked away the king to Palermo just as the attacking French were about to enter Naples). Nelson died before he could take advantage of his gift, although the title and estate passed through the marriage of his niece to the British Bridport family, which retained the estate until as recently as 1981.

The Nelson and the Bridport estate, the **Abbazia di Maniace** *(tel 095 690 018, open daily)*, lies just north of Bronte. Take the minor road left (west) off the gloriously high Bronte-to-Randazzo road at **Maletto**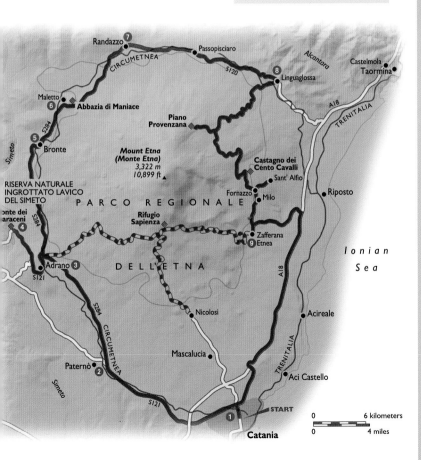
(renowned for its strawberries), where you can see the 1823 lava flow that came close to destroying the town.

The Abbazia began life as a convent in 1173, though today the building resembles an English country house, complete with appropriate (and beautiful) furnishings and a pretty English-style garden. Bronte also gave its name to the 19th-century English writers Emily, Charlotte, and Ann Brontë, their father—a passionate devotee of Nelson—having changed his surname

from Brunty in honor of his hero.

Randazzo ⑦, the closest settlement to Etna's summit (less than 10 miles/ 16 km away), has miraculously escaped

---

▲ See area map p. 127
► Catania
↔ 100 miles (160 km) round-trip
🕐 at least 1 day
► Catania or Taormina

NOT TO BE MISSED
- Adrano and environs
- Abbazia di Maniace
- Castagno dei Cento Cavalli
- minor roads to upper slopes
- Randazzo

Vegetation continues to reclaim Etna's once barren, blackened slopes (right). Advancing pastureland provides fodder for grazing goats (above).

destruction, though it was badly damaged by Allied bombing in 1943—the Nazis having made it a defensive redoubt as they sought to hold Sicily. As a result, much in the lava-black village is restored, though the streets retain a brooding medieval air. The 15th-century church of **Santa Maria** is worth a visit for its strange, dark lava columns. So, too, is the private **Museo Vagliasindi** *(tel 095 799 1611),* a mostly archaeological collection housed in the town's former castle and prison.

From Randazzo the road and railroad curve eastward, passing through some of the prettiest scenery in the Etna foothills. Just beyond **Passopisciaro** is a colossal lava flow from the 1981 eruption, but note also the olive and other trees and vegetation that flourish in the region's fertile soils.

Farther east, **Linguaglossa** ⑧ *(Visitor information, Piazza Annunziata 7, tel 095 643 094)* is the main center for exploring Etna's northern slopes, and busy ski resort. From here take the minor road south toward Piano

Provenzana, being sure to visit the **Castagno dei Cento Cavalli** or the Chestnut of a Hundred Horses *(tel 095 968 772, closed Mon.–Fri.; call to arrange guided tour during the week),* half a mile (0.8 km) before the hamlets of Fornazzo and Sant'Alfio. More than 2,000 years old, it is one of Italy's largest and most venerable trees. It takes its name from the legend that Queen Joan of Anjou once sheltered beneath its branches with a hundred horsemen. The tale may not be so far-fetched, as the combined circumference of the three linked trunks is a staggering 196 feet (60 m).

From Fornazzo the road runs south to **Zafferana Etnea** ⑨, a passable resort surrounded by vineyards and orange groves (it is renowned nationally for its orange-blossom honey). If time and weather allow, you could drive west from here to the **Rifugio Sapienza** on a steep and spectacular road returning by minor roads, or head to the A 18 autostrada to return to Catania or Taormina. ■

A café beckons at the foot of Taormina's stately church of San Giuseppe.

Taormina

TAORMINA IS SICILY'S BEST-KNOWN AND MOST URBANE resort, a beguiling and bucolic hill town that for more than a century has been a favored winter and summer retreat, offering flower-scented piazzas, charming streets, chic boutiques, subtropical gardens, and endless sea views and mountain vistas.

Taormina

Map p. 127 C3
Visitor information
www.gate2taormina.com
✉ Palazzo Corvaia, Piazza Santa Caterina
☎ 0942 23 243

Taormina's extraordinary site curves around a natural terrace 675 feet (204 m) above the sea, in the shadow of the rocky peak of Monte Tauro. History tells it has been inhabited for at least three millennia.

Its first documented settlement was the Greek colony of Tauromenion, founded in 403 B.C. by refugees from nearby Naxos, a Greek city destroyed by Syracuse.

The colony prospered quietly under the Romans and was briefly the capital of Byzantine Sicily, but it fell to the Arabs in 902 and the Normans in 1078. Thereafter it slumbered for centuries, little more than a pretty, mild-weathered village known only for its superb position and remarkable Greek theater.

Grand tourists, the English and Germans in particular, were the

somewhere to stay. Today the town boasts more than 60 hotels.

In time the village became a favored winter resort to rival similar retreats of the French Riviera. The German emperor Kaiser Wilhelm II visited in 1896, and was followed by British king Edward VII in 1906.

After World War I, writers, artists, and other exiles made it their home, including the British writer D. H. Lawrence (1885–1930), who lived here from 1920 to 1923. The town's lovely east-facing position, he declared, was "the dawn-coast of Europe." Even battle-hardened soldiers were seduced, the German field marshal Kesselring having made the town—not a place of any great strategic importance—his headquarters in 1943.

In the 1950s the village became even more chic as its growing reputation, and the advent of a film festival, drew still more celebrated visitors. Among these were Orson Welles, John Steinbeck, Greta Garbo, Rita Hayworth, Cary Grant, and Salvador Dalì. Truman Capote wrote *Breakfast at Tiffany's* and *In Cold Blood Here*, while Tennessee Williams penned *A Streetcar named Desire* and *Cat on a Hot Tin Roof.*

Today, Taormina's popularity has gotten slightly the better of it: Between about June and September, when visitors cram the beaches and tiny streets, it is best avoided altogether. April, May, and October are better, but winter and spring reveal the town at its picturesque best, with generally clear skies, carpets of wildflowers, and a chance to enjoy the genuine hill-village charm that brought visitors here in the first place.

Much of the town center is pedestrianized and parking spaces are almost impossible to come by. Most people park in outlying lots (Lumbi is the most convenient)

chief visitors during the 18th century, among them the German writer, J. W. von Goethe (1749–1832), who pronounced the town "a patch of paradise on earth." As late as 1850, however, one English visitor, W. H. Bartlett, lamenting the locals' lack of enterprise, observed that "anywhere but in Sicily a place like Taormina would be a fortune to the innkeepers, but here is not a single place where a traveller can linger to explore the spot."

All this would change after 1866, when the village was linked to Messina by rail, allowing easier access for visitors, and again after 1874, when Taormina's first hotel, the Timeo, opened (it is still in business) and provided them with and then make their way to the town center by special shuttle bus, cab, or the small cable car (*funivia*) from Mazzarò, the beach resort below the town (where there is another large parking lot). All three options leave you on the upper reaches of Via Luigi Pirandello, the

A motorcyclist roars past the Palazzo Corvaia, site of Sicily's first parliament.

long, curving road that climbs to the town from the coast.

At the end of this road, the **Porta Messina gateway** marks the beginning of Taormina's single main street, the gently climbing **Corso Umberto I,** a veritable catwalk in summer, and lined with boutiques, souvenir shops, elegant cafés, flower-filled balconies, antique stores, several churches, and lots of pretty palaces and other minor historical buildings.

Once through the gateway, the corso opens almost immediately onto **Piazza Vittorio Emanuele II,** built on the site of the old Roman forum. The **Shaker Bar** here (on the left) was a favorite of Tennessee Williams, whose habit was apparently to buy a single glass of whiskey and replenish it from a bottle bought cheaply elsewhere and kept hidden in a pocket.

The square's principal building

is the 14th-century **Palazzo Corvaia** (or Corvaja) on the right, with a central Moorish tower from the tenth century, decorated in the vividly contrasting black lava and white pumice characteristic of many local buildings.

The palace is home to the town's visitor center, and to the small **Museo Siciliano d'Arte e Tradizioni Popolari** (*tel 0942 23 243, closed Mon.*), an entertaining and occasionally eccentric collection of folk art and artifacts. The exhibits include carts, puppets, costumes, ceramics from across Sicily, handicrafts, and a variety of shepherds' accoutrements—notably some beautifully made sheep's collars in wood and horn. Also interesting are a series of ex-votos, votive paintings giving thanks for miraculous salvation from a variety of often unlikely fates (attack by cats, falling onto a stove, being blinded while playing tennis).

The palace's main salon, the Norman-era **Sala del Parlamento,** is so called because it was the seat of the Sicilian parliament in 1410, when it met to discuss a successor for the lapsed Aragon royal line.

To the left of the palace, as you face it, is the 17th-century church of **Santa Caterina,** partly built over the remains of the **Odeon,** or Teatrino Romano, a 200-seat, first-century Roman theater, the rather paltry remains of which can be seen behind the church and built into its nave.

On the opposite side of the square, Via Teatro Greco leads to the **Teatro Greco,** or Greek theater, Taormina's main sight, which deserves a more in-depth visit (see p. 141).

For now, continue along the corso, passing a tiny side street on the left (Via Naumachia) that leads quickly to the **Naumachie,** the remains of what was probably a Roman cistern or gymnasium.

Rejoining the main street, you come to **Piazza IX Aprile,** Taormina's main square, a favored place to see and be seen. Its name refers to the date in 1860 on which Taormina's citizens revolted against Bourbon rule during the battle for Italian unification. The halfway point down the corso is a good place to stop, day or night, for a drink, albeit at a far higher price than you'll probably pay elsewhere in Sicily. The money is well spent, however, both for the superb views to Etna and the sea, and for the chance to take in the square's human spectacle. The most prestigious spots are Caffè Wunderbar and the Mocambo, now rather more genteel than in the days when they were the scene of many a scandalous imbroglio and celebrity catfight.

Beyond the square and its clock tower, the corso enters the **Borgo**

Beaches

Taormina is known as a beach resort, but its main strands, in the coves around Mazzarò, are mostly pebbled. The best sandy beach is at **Giardini-Naxos,** a sprawling resort town to the south, but it is busy and popular. Most of the stretch is divided into well-kept beaches *(stabilimenti balinari),* where you pay a few euros to use the beach and shower, restaurant, and other facilities. ■

Medioevale, the oldest part of town, full of medieval palaces and the odd architectural reminder of the town's tenth-century Arab past.

Piazza del Duomo is the site of the lackluster Duomo, or cathedral, founded in the 13th century, though the piazza is more noteworthy for its **fountain** (1635), topped by a strange female

Passersby eye the goods at one of the chic boutiques along Corso Umberto I.

Taormina's Teatro Greco hosts a spectacular performance during the arts festival.

centaur, the town's symbol.

The corso ends a few steps beyond at the **Porta Catania gateway** (1440), alongside which on the left is Via del Ghetto, part of the town's Jewish quarter until the Jews were expelled from Sicily and other Spanish possessions in 1492. The little lane leads to the **Palazzo Duchi dei Santo Stefano,** a fine, 15th-century palace which hosts art and other exhibitions.

Bear left past the palace and you come to **Piazza San Domenico,** home to the San Domenico Palace hotel, opened in 1894 and still one of Taormina's top luxury hotels. Much of this part of town was badly damaged by Allied bombing in July 1943, the bombers having targeted the hotel after it was appropriated as the German headquarters of Field Marshal Kesselring.

Via Roma south of the piazza

arcs back to Piazza IX Aprile—with panoramic views en route (beware the traffic)—but it is worth returning to Porta Catania and taking one of the lanes right off the corso to the **Badia Vecchia,** home to a tiny archaeological museum *(Via Circonvallazione 30, tel 0942 620 112, closed Mon.)* with displays of finds from in and around the Teatro Greco (see below).

Continue along Via Dionisio (with the Badia on your right) and it becomes Via Circonvallazione, which runs parallel to the corso below. Some 300 yards (274 m) beyond the Badia, a signposted footpath leads left, winding steeply to the sanctuary of Madonna della Rocca and the ruined **Castello Saraceno** on Monte Tauro (1,306 feet/398 m). The views are tremendous, but the climb is not one for hot days.

The peak can also be accessed from the road (Via Leonardo da Vinci) that runs to **Castelmola,** a rock-top hamlet about 3 miles (5 km) north of Taormina—and a popular excursion (lovely off-season, horribly crowded at other times) thanks to its views and celebrated almond wine.

Winston Churchill used to come here to drink and paint (as did Kesselring), settling down at the Caffè San Giorgio *(Piazza Sant'Antonio 1, tel 0942 28 228, closed Tues. in winter),* founded in 1907 and still in business. Look at the famous autographs in the visitors' book including those of John D. Rockefeller and Mr. Rolls and Mr. Royce of luxury automobile fame.

TEATRO GRECO

Taormina's fourth-century B.C. Greek theater is a little smaller than the theater in Syracuse, but its setting is many times more magnificent, carved from the surrounding rock and with a panorama that embraces Etna, the highlands of the Sicilian interior, the azure of the Ionian Sea, and the distant, shadowy mountains of the Aspromonte on the Italian mainland. "Never did any audience, in any theater," said the German writer J. W. von Goethe in 1787, "have before it such a spectacle."

Despite its Greek origins, most of the present structure dates from the Roman period, and from alterations between the first and third centuries, when, among other things, the still well-preserved brick stage buildings *(scena)* were added and the shape of the auditorium *(cavea)* was altered to stage gladiatorial games.

Unlike its rival in Syracuse, the theater is not used to stage classical drama, but hosts musical and other performances during Taormina's arts festival, **Taormina Arte** *(Corso Umberto I 19, tel 0942 21 142, www.taormina-arte.com),* held from July to September.

Below the theater are the town's delightful public gardens at **Parco Duca di Cesarò** *(Via Bagnoli Croce),* a site that rivals the *teatro* for beauty—albeit of a quieter and more horticultural kind. An oasis of trees, shrubs, and other plants, many of them rare or exotic, the gardens were created in 1899 by Lady Florence Trevelyan, a Scotswoman "encouraged" to leave Britain hurriedly after a scandalous affair with the future King Edward VII. ■

Gola dell'Alcantara

This dramatic gorge lies 10.5 miles (17 km) west of Taormina on the S 185 road to Francavilla di Sicilia. It is commercialized, but still well worth exploring. Waders can be rented at the entrance, and an elevator is available to take you to river level. The gorge is not passable in winter or after heavy rain. ■

Walls of layered lava flows from Mount Etna distinguish Gola dell'Alcantara.

More places to visit in eastern Sicily

Isola Bella and Mazzaro beach, between Messina and Catania, draw summer crowds.

CATANIA

Sicily's second largest city, Catania lacks the sights commensurate with a place of its size. Natural disasters (earthquakes and Etna's eruptions) are partly to blame for its unappealing appearance, but so are decades of bureaucratic incompetence. Economically it is doing relatively well, but most of the city's businesses and more affluent residents have relocated to the suburbs, with the result that the inner city (despite recent efforts by more enlightened governing councils) is in a poor state.

If you do find yourself here, make sure it is not in summer, for this is one of Italy's hottest cities, with temperatures often in excess of 104° F (40° C). Devote your time to the **cathedral** (*Piazza del Duomo*), the masterpiece of Giovanni Battista Vaccarini (1702–1768), who designed much of Catania's baroque center. Also walk down **Via Crociferi,** the city's best baroque street, and **Via Etnea,** Catania's main thoroughfare. For quiet and shade, visit **Villa Bellini park** just north of the center off Via Santo Euplio and Via Pacini. Catania also offers many theaters, concerts, and festivals.

Maps p. 127 B1 & p. 133 **Visitor information** www.apt.catania.it or www.turismo. catania.it ✉ Via Cimarosa 10 ☎ 095 730 6211

MESSINA

The large coastal town of Messina, hemmed in by the Peloritani Mountains to the rear, is the first sight of Sicily for visitors approaching from the Italian mainland. As a distant prospect, it is easy to imagine the town as that in which Shakespeare set *Much Ado About Nothing.* Up close, however, Messina reveals itself as a busy and thoroughly modern place, with almost no redeeming visual features.

The fault for this is not Messina's, for the town has had a share of bad luck that is excessive even by Sicilian standards. In 1908, for example, an earthquake killed 80,000 people (out of a population of 120,000), razing the town and causing the coast to sink by 19 inches (50 cm). No sooner had rebuilding been completed than the Allies bombed it almost flat again in World War II—Messina had the unfortunate distinction of being the most heavily bombed of any town in Italy.

Apart from the rebuilt **cathedral** and its charming bell tower (*Piazza del Duomo*), the only real reason to visit is the **Museo Regionale** (*Viale della Libertà 465, tel 090 361 292, closed Wed. & Fri. p.m., & Sun.*). This rich and varied regional museum is known mainly for the five-panel polyptych of the "Madonna with St. Gregory and St. Benedict" (1473) by Antonello da Messina (1430–1479), Sicily's foremost Renaissance painter. Also outstanding are two paintings by Caravaggio (1573–1610), commissioned by the town during the year he spent here in 1609.

Map p. 127 D5 **Visitor information** www.azienturismomessina.it

✉ Piazza Cairoli 45 ☎ 090 694 780 ■

Sicily's most captivating islands, the Isole Eolie, are the highlight of northern Sicily. The region also claims the wild Madonie and Nebrodi Mountains, where rural ways of life have changed little over centuries.

Northern Sicily

Clay mask from Lipari in the Eolie Islands

Northern Sicily

The area between Palermo and Messina offers a quartet of landscapes: a highly developed coastal strip, where one town and resort, Cefalù, stands out; the glorious offshore Isole Eolie (Lipari Islands); a wall of mountains that comprises the Nebrodi and Madonie ranges; and the rolling hills and plains of Sicily's northern interior.

There are several ways to travel between east and west in northern Sicily. The most obvious is the coastal route on the A 20 expressway, but it offers only occasional glimpses of beaches, cliffs, or countryside.

Just one coastal town, Cefalù, can be unreservedly recommended, thanks to its charming streets, fine beach, and Sicily's loveliest Norman cathedral after Monreale. Other diversions include the ancient sites at Tindari and Solunto, the Norman castle at Caccamo, and the passable beach resorts of Sant'Agata di Militello, Capo d'Orlando, and Capo Zafferano.

It is still best to direct yourself through the coastal mountains—notably the Nebrodi and Madonie ranges, part of the Apennines, the mountainous spine running down the Italian peninsula. The roads are slow, but the scenic rewards are considerable, and you will discover rural ways of life vanishing elsewhere in Italy. Of the two ranges, the Madonie are the highest and have more alluring villages. They are also the more manageable, with circular driving routes possible from Cefalù.

Driving is not a realistic option on the Isole Eolie—seven tiny islets that might occupy a vacation in their own right—so plan on taking a ferry or hydrofoil.

Stromboli, with its regular volcanic eruptions, is the Eolies' main draw. All the islands, though, have their generic charms, not the least outstanding black-sand lava beaches, excellent dessert wines, and lovely scenery (boat trips around the islands are highly recommended). Regular ferries link the islands, with the least frequent services running to the most distant and most beautiful islets—the little jewels of Panarea and Alicudi. ■

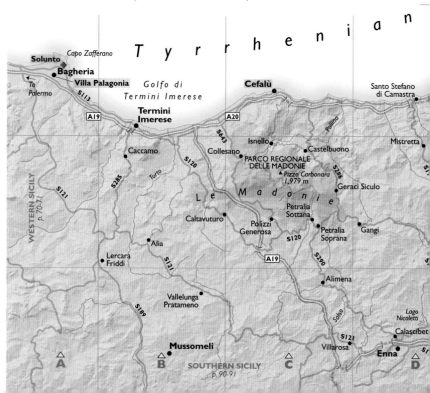

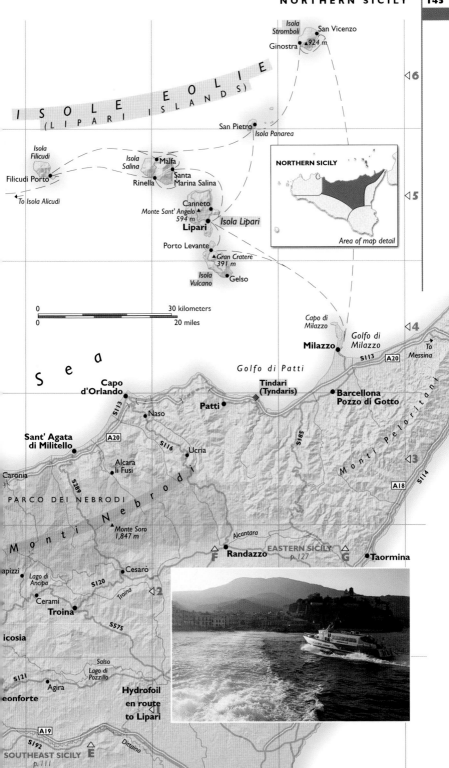

ISOLE EOLIE
(LIPARI ISLANDS)

Isola
Strömboli ● San Vicenzo
Ginostra ▲924 m

San Pietro
● Isola Panarea

Isola
Filicudi
Filicudi Porto ●
→ To Isola Alicudi

Isola
Salina ● Malfa
Rinella ● Santa
Marina Salina

Canneto ●
Monte Sant' Angelo ▲
594 m
Lipari ● *Isola Lipari*

Porto Levante ●
▲ *Gran Cratere*
391 m
Isola
Vulcano ● Gelso

NORTHERN SICILY

Area of map detail

| 0 | | | 30 kilometers |
| 0 | | | 20 miles |

*Capo di
Milazzo*

Milazzo ● *Golfo di
Milazzo*
S113 A20 → To
Messina

S   e   a

**Capo
d'Orlando** ● *Golfo di Patti*

**Tindari
(Tyndaris)**
Patti ● ● **Barcellona
Pozzo di Gotto**

**Sant' Agata
di Militello** ●
A20
S113
● Naso
S116
Ucria ●
Alcara
li Fusi ●
Caronia

PARCO DEI NEBRODI

S185

Monti Peloritani
A18
S114

▲ Monte Soro
1,847 m
Alcantara
△ **EASTERN SICILY**
F **Randazzo** *p. 127* G
● **Taormina**

apizzi
Lago di
Ancipa
Cesarò ●
Cerami ●
Troina
S120
Troina
△2
S575

icosia

Salso
Lago di
Pozzillo
● Agira
eonforte
A19
S92
Dittaino

**Hydrofoil
en route
to Lipari**
△

△ **SOUTHEAST SICILY**
E *p. 111*

Isole Eolie

Isole Eolie

🗺 Map pp. 144–45
D5–G6

**Visitor
information**

www.eolnet.it

www.amapanarea.it

www.isolasalina.com

www.isoladistromboli.com

✉ Corso Vittorio
Emanuele II 202,
Lipari

☎ 090 988 0095

Note: For ferry or hydrofoil
information from
Milazzo contact NGI,
tel 090 928 3415,
www.cormora
no.net/ngi; SIREMAR,
tel 090 928 3242,
www.siremar.it or
www.tirrenia.it;
or USTICA LINES,
tel 090 928 7821 or
info 340 902 3731,
www.usti calines.it.

SICILY HAS NUMEROUS RAVISHING OFFSHORE ISLANDS—
Pantelleria, Lampedusa, Marettimo, and others—but none are as
spectacular as the Isole Eolie (Lipari Islands), the legendary home of
Vulcan, god of fire, and Aeolus, god of the winds. The seven islets are
the remnants of volcanoes both active and extinct, and visitors come
to witness volcanic activity in the raw, and to enjoy the islands' peace
and quiet, varied landscapes, and aquamarine seas.

Ferries and hydrofoils run to the
Isole Eolie from Naples, Palermo,
Cefalù, and Messina, but the most
direct access is from Milazzo, a port
16 miles (26 km) away on the north
coast. Boats also run between the
islands, with Lipari, the largest and
most developed outpost, the hub

for most services. It is also the only island on which a car might be useful, but it is advisable to visit without one. Many of the islands have good bus service, or are small enough to explore on foot, bike, or scooter, which can be rented. You can leave your car in a garage in Milazzo such as Central *(tel 090 928 2472)* or Mylarum *(tel 090 922 4262);* or inquire at the visitor center *(Piazza Duilio Caio 10, tel 090 922 2865, www.aastmilazzo.it).*

Hiking and snorkeling are major attractions throughout the Eolie Islands, as are distinctive food and wine, hot pools and volcanic mud baths, fabulous marine and coastal landscapes, and the more intangible pleasures of small-town life and the islands' relaxed atmosphere.

You won't have the islands to yourself, however: The big three—Stromboli, Vulcano, and Lipari—are extremely popular, so you need to reserve accommodations in advance, at least during July and August. Outside these months, and other peak periods such as Easter, you should have few problems.

Hikers on Vulcano pass a steaming vent. Evidence of volcanic activity abounds in the Eolie Islands.

Night falls on lively Lipari town, the main settlement on the archipelago's largest island.

Lipari is the obvious base, with Salina a less busy alternative. Stromboli is the most popular excursion —a trip on foot to its active crater, especially at night, an unforgettable experience. Vulcano has no active crater, but its natural hot springs and volcanic mud baths make it popular with Italians. It also offers superb views and good hiking on strange volcanic landscapes. Panarea is the smallest, prettiest, and most chic of the islands; undeveloped Filicudi of greatest appeal to divers and island lovers; and Alicudi the wildest, least visited, and most far-flung of the septet. All the Eolie Islands have UNESCO World Heritage status.

Lipari is the largest and most scenically varied island, making up for what it lacks in volcanic activity with its beauty. Boats dock at busy **Lipari town,** cradled between two bays, Marina Corta and Marina Lunga, the latter with a small beach and a busy waterfront of bars, cafés, and restaurants. The town has many charming corners, and plenty of stylish accommodations, trendy nightlife, and good places to eat.

It also has the outstanding **Museo Archeologico Eoliano** *(tel 090 988 0174),* housed in four separate buildings around the 11th-century cathedral in the town's old citadel. The Eolies have been inhabited for at least 7,000 years, early settlers and traders having been attracted by obsidian, a hard volcanic rock used by Neolithic peoples to make tools and weapons. Lipari's museum has one of the world's finest collections of such items, along with other prehistoric art and artifacts.

Elsewhere, the island's highlights are **Canneto,** Lipari's second village, which has a long pebble beach, and the sandy **Spiaggia Bianca,** the island's best beach. Just north of Canneto, the coastal road passes Monte Pelato (1,416 feet/ 432 m), which is comprised partly of pumice, a light volcanic rock that is still quarried for use in the chemical, construction, and glass industries; Chicago's Sears Tower, for example, contains Lipari pumice.

It's worth taking a boat trip to see the **Cave di Pomice** (old pumice cliffs and quarries) in the lovely bay at Porticello. Also be sure to enjoy the views from the lookout at Puntazze and the still more extraordinary panorama at **Quattrocchi.** If you wish to hike, consider the climb to **Monte Sant'Angelo** (1,949 feet/594 m), an extinct crater reached from Pianoconte.

Stromboli is the island not to be missed, mainly because of the spectacular eruptions that take place from its summit cones around four times an hour. This makes it the busiest of the Eolies if you wish to stay overnight, but it is an easy day visit from Lipari, Salina, or elsewhere. Boats dock near San Vincenzo, a melancholy hamlet that with neighboring Piscità, Ficogrande, and San Bartolo forms **Stromboli Paese,** the island's main settlement.

The crater can be reached by foot with easily obtained guides *(tel 090 986 263 or 090 986 211),* but it's a long climb on a well-defined trail to the 3,031-foot (924 m) summit. Allow six to seven hours round-trip, and take plenty of water. Alternatively, hike partway or make the 30-minute walk to the **Osservatorio di Punta Labronzo** *(Via Serra, tel 090 981 1081, open by apt.)* at the north of the island to observe the volcano.

You can also admire the eruptions and smoking lava flows from a boat. The spectacle is all the more dramatic at night; many people take evening boats and camp near the summit or join guided hikes *(usually 5 p.m.–12 a.m. or 12 a.m.–dawn).* Note that volcanic activity at the crater has increased markedly since December 2002, and access may be restricted near the summit.

Vulcano, the closest island to Milazzo, takes its name from the myth that Vulcan, god of fire, kept

Bathers soak in a thermal volcanic pool near Porto Levante on the island of Vulcano.

his forge here. Its last major eruption was in 1890, but constant, low-level activity such as bubbling mud pools and fumeroles (jets of steam above and below sea level) characterizes the 8-square mile (21 sq km) island. Boats dock at Porto Levante beneath the main crater, **Gran Cratere,** or Fossa di Vulcano (1,282 feet, 391 m), easily climbed for sensational views of the crater and the rest of the island. Allow two hours roundtrip—make the hike early or late in the day for there is no shade.

Many people come for the therapeutic hot mud baths near the landing stage. *(Remove all jewelry and keep the mud out of your eyes. Then rinse off in the sea, which is superheated by underwater fumaroles; take care to avoid scalding.)* The single scenic road southwest from the port leads via the hamlet of Piano to Gelso, where there is a much less busy beach, the **Spiaggia dell'Asino.**

There is little to be said of **Panarea, Filicudi,** and **Alicudi,** other than that they are all delightful and unspoiled islets with fine coastlines, verdant interiors, and some captivating beaches. Prices are higher than elsewhere, but so—lack of volcanic activity aside—are the rewards of easy island life. ∎

Called an "island on an island" by the Arabs, the Nebrodi Mountains remain an isolated corner of Sicily.

Monti Nebrodi

THE MONTI NEBRODI, OR NEBRODI MOUNTAINS, ARE ONE of the few areas to retain the pristine appearance of a centuries-old Sicily. A belt of high, verdant wilderness, they divide the island's northeast coast from the rippling uplands of the interior, an area of thick forest, craggy summits, and upland pasture ideal for hiking or solitary, scenic drives.

The fawns that gave the Nebrodi their name—*nebros* in Greek—are long gone. So, too, are the elephant, rhinoceros, and hippopotamus whose remains have been found in fossilized form here. The last wolves vanished in the 1920s. More recent flora and fauna might also have disappeared had not this precious wilderness been embraced in 1993 by the **Parco dei Nebrodi,** a protected area that extends for about 45 miles (70 km) from near Randazzo in the east (on the slopes of Mount Etna) to Mistretta and the foothills of the neighboring Madonie Mountains to the west (see pp. 154–55).

This is not a park where you will find marked trails, visitor centers, or interpretive guides. It is still virtually untouched, with few or no historical or cultural interests, other than the insights afforded into agricultural and rural traditions fast disappearing elsewhere in Sicily. On high pastures, for example, you will still find shepherds milking by hand and making ricotta cheese in tiny outdoor camps.

It is also an area with very few roads and villages, making it ideal for those who wish to explore superb wild landscapes—and are prepared to drive long distances to do so. (Many roads twist and turn, adding miles to what might appear short distances on the map.)

One such road, the S 120, runs east-west along the mountains' southern flanks, with the medieval town of **Nicosia** the obvious inland base for the whole region. Just three roads run through the mountains from north to south: the S 116, which is at its best from Ucria to Randazzo; the magnificent S 289, which is especially attractive in its high central section; and the S 117, another high road which is a scenic delight for most of its upland run between Mistretta and Nicosia.

A fourth north-south route on a less good, but fabulously scenic road, runs from **Caronia** on the coast via Capizzi to meet the S 120 between Nicosia and **Troina.** The latter, at 3,090 feet (942 m), is one of the loftiest villages in Sicily. Any of these routes can be combined with the S 120 and the main coast road to provide rewarding circular or near-circular routes over the mountains. Side or dirt roads add spice to your exploration, such as the 2.5 mile (4 km) route off the S 289 leading close to the summit of **Monte Soro** (6,058 feet/1,847 m), the Nebrodi's highest point. Also diverting is the alternate road west from **Cesarò** almost to Cerami.

As well as ancient ways of life and fine scenery, exploring the mountains reveals ancient tracts of forest and extensive woods of beech, which flourish on limestone soils at high altitudes. These woods, together with the area's lakes and reservoirs, offer refuge for 150 species of birds, while the high crags provide nesting sites for rare raptors such as golden eagles, griffons, and Egyptian vultures. Along with hiking, the mountains offer opportunities for riding. Many small farms offer pony-trekking (*equiturismo*)—and there is even a species of horse, the *sanfratellano*, that is indigenous to the Nebrodi. ∎

Monti Nebrodi
🗺 Map pp. 144–45
    D2–F3
Visitor information
www.parks.it/parco.nebrodi
www.parcodeinebrodi.it

Caronia
✉ Via Ruggero Orlando 126
☎ 0921 333 221

Cesarò
✉ Strada Nazionale (S 120)
☎ 095 773 2061

Nicosia
✉ Municipio, Piazza Garibaldi
☎ 0935 638 139

Outdoor Activities

Sicily's mountains, coastline, and islands offer natural playgrounds for outdoor adventures. Facilities, however, are generally poorer than elsewhere in Italy and the island's environmental agencies face an uphill battle in establishing and maintaining parks, reserves, and other protected areas.

Though the first Sicilian park aimed at protecting the environment, the Zingaro reserve, was only established in 1981, Sicily's environmental groups, plus international bodies such as the Worldwide Fund for Nature (WWF), are slowly fighting back against the developers and vested interests peculiar to Sicily.

Hiking is still not as easy as elsewhere in Italy. Sicily has many centuries-old mule tracks and paths, but few marked trails, and even fewer good maps to help you find them. The exceptions are on Etna, the Zingaro reserve, Pantalica, and islands such as Marettimo. Elsewhere, such as the big Nebrodi and

Above: Dogsledding on Mount Etna. Opposite: Hiking on Stromboli in the Eolie Islands.

Madonie parks, new visitor centers can provide trail maps and advice.

Italy's excellent official park website *(www.parks.it)* is a good place to start for information on hiking and other activities, as is the site of the Club Alpino Italiano (CAI), or Italian Alpine Club *(www.cai.it)*. To learn about the excellent WWF reserves, visit www. wwfsicilia.it. The site of the environmental group Legambiente *(www.legambiente. sicilia.it)* has good general information.

Bird-watchers will find these sites helpful, along with the LIPU site *(www.lipusic ilia.it)*, run by Italy's foremost body for the protection of birds, and the Ente Fauna *(www.entefauna .siciliana.it)*, devoted to the protection of Italy's wildlife. All of these groups run field trips to their own and other reserves.

Visitor centers can provide information on **horseback riding,** which is possible from many rural centers, especially in the Nebrodi and Madonie Mountains. For information, contact the Federazione Italiano Turismo Equestre *(tel 0932 257 639, www.fiteec-ante.it)*.

Cycling is also easily possible. Bikes can be rented in many main tourist centers, and several old railroad beds have been converted into bikeways. Siciclando *(tel 091 906 086, www.siciclando.com)* organizes group and individual cycling tours of the island.

Other activities include **canyoning** in the island's many gorges *(Associazione Italiana Canyoning, tel 095 708 1995, www.canyon ing.it)*, or **caving** *(information from CAI and Legambiente; see right)*.

Offshore, **snorkeling** and **diving** are major activities, particularly on the islands of Pantelleria, Ustica, and Lampedusa. All the major islands have dive centers. **Windsurfing** is also popular, with major centers at Mondello, Cefalù, Marina di Ragusa, Scaletta, Agrigento, and elsewhere *(www.shorebreak.it and www.windsurfitalia.da.ru)*. ■

Le Madonie

Le Madonie
🔼 Map pp. 144–45
B2–C3

THE LOFTY PEAKS OF THE MADONIE MOUNTAINS ARE second only in Sicily to Mount Etna. Soaring above the northern coast, they offer tremendous hiking and touring possibilities, and command views to the Eolie Islands and across the rippling uplands of the Sicilian interior.

View of the mountain village of Petralia Sottana

Park information
www.parks.it/parco.madonie
✉ Park center, Corso Paolo Agliata 16, Petralia Sottana
☎ 0921 684 011

Castelbuono
www.comune.castelbuono .pa.it
✉ Via Umberto I
☎ 0921 671 124

Le Madonie are similar to the neighboring Nebrodi Mountains—equally wild, empty, and scenically diverse, and protected by a *parco regionale* (regional park). The main differences are that they are higher —the highest point, Pizzo Carbonara, is 6,493 feet (1,979 m)—slightly more accessible, and offer more hiking opportunities.

The Madonie also have more villages of intrinsic interest, most of them easily explored from **Cefalù** (see pp. 156–57), the best base if you only wish to devote a day's driving to the mountains. Otherwise, the area can be seen en route

between Cefalù and Enna, the latter a well-placed stopover at the heart of the island. Thereafter you can use the A19 expressway to return to Cefalù (or Palermo) or head east for Etna, Taormina, or Syracuse. Alternatively, continue to the Villa Imperiale del Casale to the south.

To begin a tour, take the A 20 or coast road east from Cefalù for 5 miles (8 km), then follow S 286 into the Madonie foothills to **Castelbuono,** 7.5 miles (12 km) south. Castelbuono is an attractive town built around a 14th-century castle *(tel 0921 671 211)* that is now used for exhibits. It also has an interesting museum, the **Museo Minà Palumbo** (*Via Roma 52, tel 0921 671 895 or 0921 671 124, closed Mon. p.m.*), with exhibits of fossils, decorative arts, archaeological finds, and natural history.

Continuing to the south, the road passes **Geraci Siculo,**

Polizzi Generosa, a delightful village that requires a 7.5-mile (12 km) detour west, and is distinguished by its many churches and small **Museo Madonita** (*tel 0921 649 478, closed p.m.*).

The minor road north from Petralia Sottana via Isnello offers a

A traditional procession marks the celebration of the Festa dei Pastori, which takes place every seven years in Geraci Siculo.

a hill village where it's worth pausing to climb to the ruins of the castle (1072) for superb views. The road then meets the S 120, where a 2.5-mile (4 km) detour southeast leads to **Gangi,** an impressively situated town.

Retrace your steps on the S 120 and head west to the appealing **Petralia Soprana**. The views of the Madonie from here are exceptional, and the medieval streets are full of incidental interest. Continuing on, turn north on a side road to see the mountain-ringed village of **Petralia Sottana.**

Much the same can be said of

far more scenic alternative to the S 643. This spectacular road leads through the heart of the Madonie, with the best views between Piano Battaglia and Piano Zucchi.

Head south from Petralia Soprana to **Enna.** This fine town sits atop a colossal crag whose sweeping views have earned it the title of the "Belvedere di Sicilia" (Balcony of Sicily). A combination of good restaurants, reasonable hotels, and interesting sights makes this a good base. Visit the **castle** (*tel 0935 40 347*), the **Duomo,** and excellent **Museo Alessi** (*off Via Roma, tel 0935 503 165*). ∎

Polizzi Generosa
✉ Via Umberto I
☎ 0921 649 018

Enna
www.apt-enna.com or www.enna-sicilia.it
✉ Piazza Colajanni 6
☎ 0935 26 119

Cefalù, with its crowning Norman cathedral, sprawls at the foot of the crag that gave the town its name.

Cefalù

 Map pp. 144–45 C3
Visitor information
✉ Corso Ruggero 77
☎ 0921 421 050

Cefalù

CEFALÙ HAS LARGELY ESCAPED THE MODERN BUILDING that has done so much to spoil Sicily's coastline. Charming and compact, this immediately likeable town, built below an immense crag, has several pleasant beaches, one of Sicily's loveliest main squares, and a Norman cathedral graced with one of the most sublime images of Christ in Western art.

Cefalù was probably founded by the Sikels in the ninth century B.C., but takes its name from the Greek *kephalos* or *kephaloidion* (head), after the shape of the crag that overshadows the town and which formed the heart of the original settlement. The Arabs built a citadel here between 858 and 1063, but the town only came into its own when Roger II, Sicily's 12th-century Norman king, extended the settlement toward the sea.

Today, the town's charm and fine beach mean that it has become increasingly popular, so you will need to reserve accommodations in summer. Nightlife, shopping, and eating are also good here, but the commercialism has not spoiled the town, whose central medieval streets remain pretty and romantic places to stroll.

Any such stroll quickly leads to **Piazza del Duomo,** as satisfying a spot for a quiet drink as you could wish for. Palms grow in each corner, overlooked by the town's wondrous **cathedral** (1131–1240). Legend has it the building was raised to fulfill a vow by Roger II, who survived a shipwreck nearby and pledged a church to the Madonna in gratitude for his escape. The shrine was intended to be Sicily's most important religious building and a pantheon for Roger's Norman descendants, but his successors lost interest in the project, and Roger's body was eventually removed to Palermo's cathedral.

Much of the church's austere interior was stripped of its later baroque decoration in the 1970s, but has otherwise remained unchanged for over 800 years. Note the impressive wooden ceiling and the old Roman columns in the nave, both of which lead the eye to the exquisite **apse mosaic.** This depicts "Christ Pantocrater"—Christ in the Act of Blessing—and dates from 1148, making this the earliest Sicilian example of an image much repeated across the island.

In Christ's left hand is a text in Greek and Latin from John 8:12— "I am the light of the world: he who follows me will not walk in darkness". Below Christ are three tiers of figures, including the Virgin flanked by archangels and the Apostles below. The mosaics on the side walls of the choir date from the late 13th century. The marble thrones were intended for Cefalù's bishop and Roger II.

A short distance from the cathedral stands the **Museo Mandralisca** *(Via Mandralisca 13, tel 0921 421 547, www.museomandralisca.it),* a fine little collection of coins and medals, pottery, Greek and Roman artifacts, and an exceptional painting, the "Portrait of an Unknown Man" (1465–1472) by Sicily's most eminent Renaissance artist, Antonello da Messina (1430–1479). Baron Enrico di Mandralisca (1809 –1864), a local politician who once lived here, bought the painting from a pharmacy on the Eolie island of Lipari, where it had been used to form part of a cupboard door.

A walk to the crag, or **Rocca,** the site of the old citadel, offers superb views. Allow about 40 minutes, and 20 minutes to reach the so-called **Temple of Diana** en route, a fifth-century B.C. building of unknown purpose. To reach the site, take Vicolo Saraceni alongside the bank building on the east side of Piazza Garibaldi, a square at the southern end of Corso Ruggero, Cefalù's main street. On this street, look out for the Osteria Magno on the west side of the street (at the corner of Via Amendola), probably once Roger II's palace, and now used for exhibits. ■

Adjacent to the historic town, Cefalù's inviting waterfront has become a popular beach resort.

More places to visit in northern Sicily

CACCAMO

The ancient little town of Caccamo, probably founded by the Phoenicians, is prettily situated among hills and olive groves. Its **cathedral** (founded in 1090), and several of its **churches** are all worth exploring, but it is the well-preserved **castle** *(Via Termitana, tel 091 810 3111)* that provides the town's main draw.

The largest castle in Sicily—and one of the largest in Italy—it probably dates from the 11th century, but acquired numerous additions and underwent many alterations over the centuries. Although the fortress is spectacular from afar, the heavily restored interior is of less interest, most of its 130 rooms being bare and undecorated.

🅰 Map pp. 144–45 B2 **Visitor information**
✉ Comune di Caccamo, Piazza del Duomo
☎ 091 810 3248

SOLUNTO

Solunto is the shell of one of only three Punic, or Carthaginian, colonies on Sicily, the other two being Motya (Mozia) and Palermo. Founded in the eighth century B.C. by the Phoenicians, North African forerunners of the Carthaginians, it eventually fell to the Romans in 254 B.C., and was abandoned in the third century. The site was rediscovered in 1825, though much still remains to be excavated. What has been uncovered is mostly Roman, including baths, gymnasium, and the remains of houses.

As at many other Sicilian archaeological sites, the setting is as memorable as the ruins, though in this instance, you have to run the gauntlet of Palermo's very grim eastern suburbs, and the scrappy town of Bagheria in particular (see Villa Palagonia below). In recompense, the headland beyond the site, **Capo Zafferano,** is appealing—the first piece of undeveloped coastline beyond Palermo.

🅰 Map pp. 144–45 A3 **Visitor information**
✉ Rovine di Solunto, near Porticello
☎ 091 904 557 🕐 Closed Sun. p.m. 💲 $

TINDARI

Ancient Tyndaris (Tindari) was founded as a garrison outpost of Syracuse in 396 B.C., making it one of Sicily's last Greek colonies. Later, it was one of the Romans' five principal Sicilian colonies, only declining when a large portion of the site tumbled into the sea in the first century.

Today, the extensive **headland site** *(tel 0941 369 023)* is one of the island's more beautiful, scattered with mostly Roman ruins and offering lovely views of the Golfo di Patti (Gulf of Patti) and the sweep of sea, beaches, and small resorts to Capo di Milazzo. There is also a superb panorama from the adjacent **Santuario della Madonna Nera,** a blunt 1960s sanctuary built to house a Byzantine icon of the Madonna attributed with miraculous powers. Many thousands of pilgrims visit the sanctuary.

🅰 Map pp. 144-45 F3 **Visitor information**
✉ Via Teatro Greco 15 ☎ 0941 369 184

VILLA PALAGONIA

A visit to Solunto (see above) can be easily combined with one to the Villa Palagonia *(Piazza Garibaldi, Bagheria, tel 091 932 088, www.villapalagonia),* one of many large villas in and around Bagheria built in the 18th century by Palermo's patrician class as a retreat from the city. Virtually all of these are now in a scandalously poor condition, and even the better preserved examples, of which the Villa Palagonia (1705) is the most notable, are compromised by their ugly modern surroundings.

In its day, however, the Palagonia's exterior decoration of fantastic stone creatures, gargoyles, and other grotesques was infamous. The decoration was the work of Prince Francesco Gravina, a local nobleman who, according to one story, created the statues as an act of revenge, portraying his wife's lovers as cruel caricatures. Even today, despite the fact that only 65 of the original 200 statues survive, there is nothing else quite like them anywhere in Sicily.

🅰 Map pp. 144–45 B2 **Visitor information**
www.comune.bagheria.pa.it ✉ Vigili Urbani, Corso Umberto I, Bagheria ☎ 091 909 020
🕐 Closed midday 💲 $$ ■

Travelwise

**Wall mural serves as a
perfect backdrop for this
artful motorscooter by
Palermitan painter
Franco Bertolino.**

TRAVELWISE INFORMATION.

PLANNING YOUR TRIP

WHEN TO GO

High summer (July–August) in Sicily is hot, busy, and expensive, with a shortage of accommodations. The sea is warm as late as November, and in May, June, and September you can enjoy fine weather without the crowds.

Spring is delightful, especially if you are hiking or wish to spend time in the countryside. Almond and other blossoms bloom as early as February, but wildflowers are at their best in April and May. Easter is busy, but also an excellent time to visit if you are interested in festivals.

Winters are mild (but sometimes wet) along the coast; however, inland and upland areas can be cold, with snow on high ground. The visitor season for island and coastal resorts often runs only from April or May to September.

See pp. 182–83 for more details if you wish to plan your trip around one of the many religious, cultural, and other festivals and events that take place across Sicily year-round.

Additional help in planning your trip is available from Italian state tourist offices (ENIT) outside Italy (see p. 166 for details).

WEBSITES

Websites for visitor centers are provided where appropriate in the text. Other more general sites include:

www.regione.sicilia.it
www.bestofsicily.com
www.siciliaonline.it
www.insicilia.it
www.festedisicilia.it
www.siciliano.it
www.viaggioinsicilia.com
www.enit.it
www.aapit.pa.it
www.beniculturali.it
www.museionline.it
www.parks.it

CLIMATE

As a general rule, Sicily has mild winters and very hot, very dry summers. Temperatures can be especially high (up to or over 104°F/40°C) on the southern coast, especially when the hot Scirocco wind blows from North Africa.

Northern and eastern coasts have less extreme climates, but are still very hot. Upland areas are cooler, and in winter can be very cold, with temperatures below freezing at high altitudes.

Average daytime temperatures in Palermo are 50.5°F (10.3°C) in January; 65.6°F (18.7°C) in May; 77.5°F (25.3°C) in July; and 68.5°F (19.9°C) in October. Note that temperatures may often exceed these figures.

Italy uses degrees Celsius (°C) as its unit of temperature. To convert degrees Celsius to degrees Fahrenheit, multiply °C by 9, divide by 5, and add 32.

WHAT TO TAKE

You should be able to buy everything you need in Sicily. Pharmacies offer a wide range of drugs, medical supplies, and toiletries, along with expert advice, but you should bring any prescription drugs you might need with you. Many brand-name drugs are different in Italy. A pharmacy (farmacia) is indicated by a green cross outside the store.

It is also useful to bring a second pair of glasses or contact lenses if you wear them. Sunscreen and mosquito repellent products are advisable in summer.

Clothing will depend on the time of year, and the activities you plan. You will only need to dress up for the grandest restaurants, but don't be too casual, as Italians generally dress more fashionably than most U.S., Canadian, and northern European visitors. Make some effort for a meal out, and

always dress appropriately for visits to churches—no bare shoulders or shorts. Note, too, that dress codes are more conservative in Sicily than in central and northern Italy, especially in rural areas.

Bring a sweater, even in summer, because evenings can be cool. Good rain and cold-weather gear are needed year-round if you intend to hike on Mount Etna or the northern mountains. Come prepared for mostly dry conditions outside the summer months.

Hiking, camping, and other sports equipment can easily be bought or rented as needed.

Electricity in Sicily is 220V, 50 Hz, and plugs have three (sometimes two) round pins. If you bring electrical equipment, you will need a plug adapter plus a transformer for U.S. appliances.

Lastly, don't forget the essentials: passport, driver's license, tickets, traveler's checks, and insurance documents.

INSURANCE

Make sure you have adequate travel and medical coverage for treatment and expenses, including repatriation and baggage and money loss. Keep all receipts for expenses. Report losses or thefts to the police and obtain a signed statement (denuncia) from police stations to help with insurance claims.

FURTHER READING

Among the books you may want to pack or read before your vacation is The Italians by Luigi Barzini (Simon & Schuster, 1996). It was first published in 1964, but no writer before or since has produced a more penetrating or better written analysis of Italy (including Sicily).

The best Sicilian or Sicily-set literature available in translation includes The Leopard by Giuseppe Tomasi di Lampedusa; Conversation in Sicily by Elio Vittorini; The Day of the Owl, The Wine-Dark Sea, and other novels by Leonardo

Sciascia; and *The Godfather* by Mario Puzo.

Evocative travelogues, or artistic, practical, or cultural analyses include *In Sicily* and *The Honoured Society* by Norman Lewis; *On Persephone's Island: A Sicilian Journal* by Mary Taylor Simeti; *Mattanza: Love and Death in the Sea of Sicily* by Theresa Maggio; *Walking in Sicily* by Gillian Price; *Midnight in Sicily* by Peter Robb; *Sicilian Odyssey* by Francine Prose; and *The Normans in Sicily* by John Julius Norwich.

HOW TO GET TO SICILY

PASSPORTS
U.S. and Canadian citizens require a passport to enter Italy for stays of up to 90 days; no visa is required. U.K. citizens require a passport, but can remain as long as they wish.

AIRLINES
Several scheduled, charter, and low-cost airlines offer direct flights to Sicily from the U.K. and other European cities. However, at the time of writing there were no direct flights from the U.S. and Canada.

All major North American airlines have flights to Rome's Leonardo da Vinci airport (also known as Fiumicino) and Milan's Malpensa, where connecting flights with Alitalia or Meridiana operate to Palermo, Catania, and some smaller Sicilian airports. Rome is the closer and more convenient hub, and has a wider and more easily accessible network of internal flights.

Flying time to Italy is about 8–9 hours from New York, 10–11 hours from Chicago, and 12–13 hours from Los Angeles. Flying time from Rome to Sicily is about 1 hour.

USEFUL NUMBERS

IN ITALY
Rome airports, tel 06 65 951; www.adr.it
Milan airports, tel 02 7485 2200 or 02 74 851; www.sea-aero ortomilano.it
Alitalia, tel 06 65 641 or 06 65 643; www.alitalia.it
Meridiana, tel 0789 52 600 or 199 111 333 in Italy, or 0039 0789 52 682 outside Italy; www.meridiana.it

IN THE U.S. & CANADA
Alitalia (U.S.), tel 800/223-5730
Alitalia (Canada), tel 905/673-2442 or 800/268-9277
American Airlines, tel 800/433-7300; www.aa.com
Continental, tel 800/525-0280; www.continental.com
Delta, tel 800/221-1212; www.delta.com
United, tel 800/241-6522; www.ual.com

When you arrive in Sicily, you will enter at either Palermo's Falcone-Borsellino airport (previously known as Punta-Raisi) or Catania's Fontanarossa airport.

Falcone-Borsellino (tel 091 702 0127 or 24-hr. 091 702 0111, www.gesap.it) is at Punta Raisi, 19 miles (31 km) west sof the city on the A 29 expressway.

Prestia e Comande shuttle buses (tel 091 586 351 or 091 580 457, www.prestia-coman de.it) depart twice hourly from outside the terminal for the 50-minute journey to the city center. There are six intermediate stops; buses terminate at the Stazione Centrale, Palermo's main railroad station for train connections to many Sicilian destinations (see p. 162).

Catania's Fontanarossa airport (tel 095 723 9111 or toll-free in Italy 800 605 656, www.aero porto-catania.it) lies 3 miles (5 km) south of the city and is more convenient for Taormina, Syracuse, and southeastern Sicily.

Alibus (tel 095 751 7111, www.amt.ct.it) shuttles run every 20 minutes from 5:00 a.m. to 10:30 p.m. to Via Etnea and the Stazione Centrale, where you can pick up train connections for Messina and Syracuse.

Direct buses also run from the airport to Agrigento, Enna, Palermo, Ragusa, Syracuse, Taormina, and Milazzo (for the ferry to the Aeolian Islands).

Only take authorized white cabs from either airport, and ignore offers from solicitors inside or outside the terminals.

There are other smaller airports around Sicily, notably at Trapani (Birgi) and on the islands of Pantelleria and Lampedusa. These are serviced by connections at Palermo; in summer, however, there are additional direct flights from other major Italian cities.

If you are beginning your trip in the U.K., you can fly nonstop to Catania from London Gatwick airport with British Airways (tel 0870 850 9850, www.ba.com) or to Palermo (no direct flights) with Meridiana (tel 020 7839 2222 in the U.K., www. meridiana.it).

You can also fly to Palermo from Stansted with Ryanair (tel 0871 246 0000, www.ryanair. com) or with Air Malta (tel 020 8788 5164, www.airmalta.com). Travel time from London to Palermo is about 2 hours and 30 minutes.

An alternative is to fly to Naples and catch a ferry to Palermo or the Aeolian Islands. Charter flights often are available to Catania (and occasionally to Palermo) in summer.

GETTING AROUND

BY AIRPLANE
It is only worth traveling by plane if you are bound for Sicily's more distant islands such as Pantelleria or Lampedusa. A variety of small carriers operate out of Palermo and Trapani, notably Air One (tel 095 722 6193 in Catania or toll-free 199 207 080 in Italy, www. flyairone.com) or ApliEagles, (tel 0923 559 579 in Trapani or

090 344 815 in Messina,
www.alpieagles.com)

BY BUS

Buses *(pullman* or *autobus)* are
an efficient means of traveling
around much of Sicily, especially
in rural areas. Express buses
also run on highways between
all major towns. Although buses
generally look alike (they're
usually blue), they are operated
by a number of different
companies.

Buses usually depart from a
town's main square, outside a
railroad station, or from a bus
depot *(autostazione)*. In general,
you must buy your ticket, usually
from the depot or the nearest
bar or station kiosk, before
boarding the bus. Inquire at local
visitor centers for details. Note
that bus service is generally limited on Sundays.

BY CAR

Sicilian town centers, and
Palermo's in particular, may
be congested, but in rural
parts of the island you will
often have the road to yourself.
Routes are generally well
marked, from the ordinary
thoroughfare, known as a
nazionale (N) or *statale/strada
statale* (S or SS), to the four-
or six-lane expressway known
as an autostrada.

The latter are toll roads;
sometimes you pay a fixed
rate, but usually you pick up
a ticket where you enter the
expressway and pay accordingly
at the booth *(stazione)* when
you exit.

If you have to travel a substantial distance, it is advisable to
take an expressway: Most other
roads in Sicily, especially in rural
areas and in the mountains, are
slow and winding. Always allow
extra time to get to your destination when traveling along
these routes.

Maps are available at bookstores and other outlets. The
best is the Touring Club of Italy
(TCI) "Sicilia" (sheet D19).

BY FERRY

Car and passenger ferries
(traghetti) and/or hydrofoils
(aliscafi) operate between
Sicily's main ports and its many
islands. Hydrofoils are generally
twice as fast and twice as
expensive as ferries.

Services include links from
Milazzo to the Isole Eolie
(Aeolian Islands), which also
have connections with Naples
and Palermo; to the Isole Egadi
and Pantelleria from Trapani;
to Ustica from Palermo; and
from Porto Empedocle near
Agrigento to the Isole Pelagie.

If you plan to take a car, it is
essential to book ahead in summer. The main operators are
Siremar (www.siremar.it), SNAV
(www.snav.it), and Tirrenia
(www.gruppotirrenia.it).

BY TRAIN

All of Sicily's main centers are
connected by rail, but train
service is slow and infrequent
unless you take the express
Inter-City (IC) train (for which
you pay a supplementary fare)
between Palermo and Messina;
otherwise, buses are the
quicker way to go.

Trains also link some small
rural centers, notably in the
east and the villages around
Mount Etna. These services
are especially slow, but if you
have time and patience, can
be enjoyable sightseeing
excursions.

Before traveling, tickets must
be validated in the yellow or
gold machines located on train
platforms and in station ticket
halls. You risk paying the penalty
of a heavy fine if you travel with
a nonvalidated ticket.

If you intend to travel extensively by train, it's worthwhile
to buy the Orario Pozzo, a
cheap biennial schedule available in bookstores and at station kiosks. Or visit the website
(www.trenitalia.it) of the state
rail network Trenitalia, still
known widely by its former
name, Ferrovie dello Stato (FS).
A Trenitalia Flexicard train pass
is available, but it's not a good

value if you only intend to
travel in Sicily.

DRIVING
INFORMATION

If you break down, put on
emergency lights and place
a warning triangle behind
the car. Call the Automobile
Club d'Italia (ACI) emergency
number (tel 116, www.aci.it)
and provide your location,
make of car, and registration.
The car will be towed to the
nearest ACI-approved garage.
Car rental firms often have
their own arrangements for
breakdowns and accidents.;
ask for details.

Peak traffic times in Sicilian
cities and larger towns are
weekdays and Saturdays from
10:00 a.m.–1:00 p.m. and 4:00–
9:00 p.m., particularly on Friday
and Sunday evenings. Also
expect heavy traffic before
and after major public holidays, and the first and last
weekends in August, when
many Italians begin and end
their vacation.

All distances are shown in
kilometers (1 km = 0.62 mile).

Gas *(benzina)*, expensive in
Italy, is priced by the liter
(0.26 U.S. gallon). Gas stations
along autostrada are open 24
hours and generally accept
credit cards. Elsewhere, gas
stations usually close between
1:00 p.m. and 4:00 p.m., after
7:00 p.m., and all day Sunday;
many stations only accept cash.

Be sure all pump meters
are set to zero before the
attendant starts filling your
tank. Some stations have
machines that accept large-
denomination euro notes and
dispense gas automatically
during closed periods.

Parking is often difficult in
Sicilian cities and towns. This
is especially true in Palermo,
where it is better to visit without a car. In most towns, street
parking and parking lots *(par-
cheggi)* are likely to be filled
with local vehicles. Many old
centers have areas that are
completely closed to traffic;

others may have restrictions at busy times during the day. If in doubt, park in an outlying lot and walk to the center. Metered parking (parcometro) is gradually being introduced in some locales.

Car theft and theft from cars can be a problem in some areas. Try to leave your car in a supervised lot and never leave valuables in the car. Illegally parked cars, especially those in a "removal zone" (zona di rimozione), may be ticketed or towed.

U.S. and Canadian drivers in Italy must hold a national driver's license (patente) or an international driver's license. They are also required, by law, to carry a translation of the license in the event that the police ask to see it; this law is rarely enforced, however. For details of current regulations and how to obtain a translation or an international driver's license, contact any branch of the American Automobile Association or Canadian Automobile Association.

Most rules of the road in Sicily and elsewhere in Italy are similar to those in the U.S.: You drive on the right and pass only on the left. Seat belts are compulsory both in the front and back seats, and you must have with you at all times your driver's license, insurance information, registration, and other relevant documents.

The penalties for drunk driving are severe, with heavy fines and the possibility of imprisonment. A red warning triangle for use in case of accidents must be carried by law (all rental cars are provided with one; check before you leave the rental premises).

The speed limit in towns and developed areas is 50 kmph (31 mph) and 110 kmph (68 kmph) outside cities, unless otherwise indicated (generally 90 kmph or 56 mph). Limits on the autostrada are 130 kmph (80 kmph), 150 kmph (93 mph) on certain designated stretches, and 110 kmph (68

mph) for vehicles with engine capacity under 1100cc.

RENTING A CAR
It is easy to rent a car in Sicily's large towns and cities, and at the two major airports, where most international companies have offices. Costs are high by U.S. standards; it may be worthwhile to make car rental arrangements (through your travel agent or on the Internet) before leaving home.

Less expensive deals in Sicily can often be obtained through small, local companies; see listings under "Autonoleggio" in the Yellow Pages (Pagine Gialle) or online at www. paginegialle.it. Drivers must be over 21 years of age and hold a full license in order to rent a car. Most large companies do not charge a drop-off fee as long as both locations are in Sicily. This allows you to pick up a car, for example, in Palermo and drop it off in Catania: inquire about policy when renting.

TRANSPORTATION IN TOWNS & CITIES

Most historic town and city centers are small enough to explore on foot. Only one or two outlying sights in Palermo, Syracuse, and Agrigento require taking a taxi or public transport. Bicycles are available for rent in several towns. You can also rent motor scooters; however, inexperienced riders should use extreme caution.

BY BUS
The procedure for using town and city buses is the same across Sicily: You buy your ticket beforehand, usually from designated bars (look for bus company logos or bar-tobacconists (tabacchi) with a white T on a blue background. You then validate your ticket by stamping it on a machine on the bus. Generally you board a bus through the rear doors and leave through

the central doors. A bus stop is una fermata. Inspectors board buses at random; passengers without valid tickets are subject to a fine.

BY CAB
Cabs are generally difficult to hail on the street. Most congregate at taxi stands on main piazzas or outside railroad stations. It is legal for drivers to charge extra for luggage placed in the trunk; and for rides early or late in the day, on Sundays and public holidays, and to airports or outside city limits. Always ask before departing and insist that the meter is switched on and reset at the start of a trip.

Only take licensed white cabs with license numbers. In case of a dispute, note the cab number. You may wish to negotiate a non-metered price for longer trips. Cabs can usually be reserved by phone. The operator will give you the number and call sign of the cab that has been dispatched. A supplement is charged for reserved cabs. Round up tips to the nearest euro, or tip about 10 percent.

PRACTICAL ADVICE

COMMUNICATION

POST OFFICES
You can buy stamps (francobolli) from a post office (ufficio postale) or from most tabacchi, the latter indicated by a blue sign with a white T. Offices are generally open Monday through Friday from between 8 and 9 a.m. to 2 p.m., and on Saturday from 8:00 or 8:30 a.m. until noon. Main post offices in larger towns and cities usually are open Monday through Saturday until 7 or 8 p.m.

The Italian postal system (www.poste.it) can be slow. Allow 15 days for letter delivery between Italy and North America, sometimes longer for postcards. Priority post (posta prioritaria) costs more, but delivery is guaranteed—within three days to the U.S. and the next day in Europe. Use email or fax for hotel and other reservations.

Small red mailboxes (blue for priority post) marked "Poste" are found outside post offices and on walls around towns and cities. Red boxes usually have two slots: one marked *Per la città* (town or local mail), the other *Per tutte le altre destinazioni* (other destinations).

You can arrange to receive mail at general delivery *(fermo posta).* Mail should show your name and be addressed to *Ufficio Posta Centrale, Fermo Posta* plus the name of the town or city. Pick up mail at the town's main post office; you will need to show a passport or photo ID. and pay a small fee.

TELEPHONES
Italy's telephone network is operated mainly by Telecom Italia (TI). Public phone booths are found on streets, in bars and restaurants, and in TI offices in larger towns. Look for red or yellow signs with a telephone symbol. Most phones take coins and cards *(schede telefoniche),* which can be purchased at tabacchi and newspaper stands in a range of euro denominations. Cards have a small perforated corner that must be removed before use.

To make a call, pick up the phone, insert the card or money, and then dial the number. (Most booths post instructions in English.) All calls can be made direct, without operator assistance or long-distance connections.

Telephone numbers may have between four and eleven digits. Call 10 for the operator, 12 for information, 176 for assistance in English, 170 for the intercontinental operator (15 for Europe), and 172 1011 for collect calls.

Calling rates are lowest on Sundays and between 10:00 p.m. and 8:00 a.m. Monday through Friday.

Note that hotels are likely to add a significant surcharge to calls made from rooms. Cellphone network coverage is good in Sicily.

To call anywhere within Sicily or to the Italian mainland, dial the number, including the town or city code (for example, 091 in Palermo or 0931 in Syracuse). The code must also be used when calling within a city or code area. Thus in Palermo, for instance, you dial the 091 code when calling another number in the city.

To call Italy from abroad, dial the international calling code (011 from the U.S. and Canada or 00 from the U.K.), then the code for Italy (39), followed by the area code (including the initial 0) and the number.

CONVERSIONS
1 kilo = 2.2 pounds
1 liter = 0.2642 U.S. gallons
1 kilometer = 0.62 miles
1 meter = 1.093 yards

Women's clothing

U.S.	8	10	12	14	16	18
Italian	40	42	44	46	48	50

Men's clothing

U.S.	36	38	40	42	44	46
Italian	46	48	50	52	54	56

Women's shoes

U.S.	6–6½	7–7½	8–8½	9–9½
Italian	38	39	40–41	42

Men's shoes

U.S.	8	8½	9½	10½	11½	12
Italian	41	42	43	44	45	46

ETIQUETTE & LOCAL CUSTOMS
On the whole Sicilians are a little more reserved and a little more conservative than northern Italians in all matters of morals and manners. While Italians on the whole may have a reputation for being passionate and excitable, they are generally polite and considerate in public and in social situations.

Upon meeting someone, or on entering or leaving stores, bars, hotels, and restaurants, use a simple *buon giorno* (good day) or *buona sera* (good afternoon/evening). Do not use the informal *ciao* (hi or goodbye) with strangers.

"Please" is *per favore,* "thank you" is *grazie,* and *prego* means "you're welcome."

Before a meal you might say *buon appetito* (enjoy your meal), to which the reply is *grazie, altrettanto* (thank you, and the same to you). The toast before a drink is *salute* or *cin cin.*

Say *permesso* when you wish to pass people, and *mi scusi* if you wish to apologize, excuse yourself, or stop someone to ask for help.

A woman is addressed as *signora,* a young woman as *signorina,* and a man as *signore.*

For additional vocabulary, see pp. 184–85.

Kissing on both cheeks is a common form of greeting among men and women who know each other well.

Italians dress conservatively for most occasions and unusual attire will be noticed, particularly in church.

If you visit churches, respect those at worship. Tourists are welcome to explore the interiors and grounds of Sicily's chapels and churches—but only if dressed appropriately and not when services are in progress.

When waiting in line—that is, when they form them at all—Italians are generally fairly assertive. In stores, banks, and other offices you should not expect "fairness" or for people to wait their turn. Feel free to be equally assertive; such behavior generally is not considered rude in Italy.

Smoking in public places is common and usually not subject to the restrictions found in the U.S.

HOLIDAYS

Stores, banks, offices, and schools close on the following national holidays:

January 1 (New Year's Day)

January 6 (Epiphany)

Easter Sunday

Easter Monday

April 25 (Liberation Day)

May 1 (Labor Day)

June 2 (Republic Day)

August 15 (Ferragosto or Assumption)

November 1 (All Saints' Day)

December 8 (Immaculate Conception)

December 25 (Christmas Day)

December 26 (Santo Stefano)

Hours of operation may also be disrupted on either side of public holidays, especially if they fall on a Thursday or Tuesday, when Italians often make what is known as a *ponte* (bridge) and take off the day between the holiday and the weekend.

Roads, as well as planes, trains, buses, and ferries, are busy around public holidays. Local accommodations tend to fill up during major festivals or cultural events.

MEDIA

Most Italian newspapers are sold from newsstands (*edicola*), many of which—in larger towns or resorts such as Palermo, Catania, Taormina, and Cefalù— also stock American, British, and other foreign-language newspapers and periodicals. In the largest centers, these may be available after about 2 p.m. on the day of issue. Elsewhere, deliveries are likely to be a day or so late.

Airports and railroad stations often have the largest selection of foreign publications.

Among national papers, *Corriere della Sera* is one of the most authorative, while

La Repubblica is also widely read. The best-selling publications are sports papers.

Sicily has a strong tradition of regional papers, notably the Palermo-based *Il Giornale di Sicilia,* Catania's *La Sicilia,* and Messina's *La Gazzetta del Sud.* These are often a good source of information on local events, museum hours, and so forth.

MONEY MATTERS

On January 1, 1999, the euro became the official currency of Italy. Euro banknotes and coins were introduced in December 2001, replacing the Italian lira (L).

Euro notes come in denominations of 5, 10, 20, 50, 100, 200, and 500 euros. There are 100 cents to the euro. Coins come in denominations of 1 and 2 euros, and 1, 2, 5, 10, 20 and 50 cents.

Most major banks, airports, railroad stations, and tourist areas have automatic teller machines (ATM's—*Bancomat* in Italian) for money cards and international credit cards (*carta di credito*), with instructions in various languages.

Before leaving home, ask your credit card company for a four-digit number (PIN) to enable you to withdraw money.

Currency and traveler's checks—best bought in euros before you leave—can be exchanged in most banks and exchange offices (*càmbio*), but lines are often long and the process slow.

In rural areas, small towns, and throughout much of the south, ATMs and cambio facilities are rarer—and sometimes nonexistent.

Credit cards are accepted in hotels and restaurants in most major towns and cities. Look for Visa, Mastercard, or American Express symbols (Diners Card is less well known), or the Italian *Carta Sì* (literally, "yes to cards") sign.

Many businesses still prefer

cash, however, and smaller stores, hotels, and similar establishments, especially in rural areas, may not take cards. Always ask before ordering a meal or reserving a room.

American Express
In Palermo, c/o Agenzia Ruggeri, Via Emerico Amari 40, tel 091 587 144, www.americanexpress.com or www.americanexpress.it
In Catania, c/o La Duca Viaggi, Piazza Europa 2, tel 095 722 2295.

OPENING TIMES

Hours of operation present a problem in Sicily. For the most part, there are no firm schedules and you can't rely on assumptions. Opening times of museums and churches in particular can change with little or no notice.

Stores, banks, and other institutions in big cities are increasingly shifting to northern European hours (with no lunch and afternoon closing, indicated by the phrase *orario continuato*).

Use the following schedule as a general guide only:

Banks are open Monday through Friday 8:30 a.m.– 1:30 p.m. Major banks may also open for an hour in the afternoon and on Saturday morning. Hours are becoming longer and more flexible.

Churches are usually open 8 or 9 a.m.–noon and 3 or 4 p.m.–6 or 8 p.m., not including services. Many churches close on Sunday afternoon.

Gas stations are open 24 hours a day on autostrada. Elsewhere they tend to follow store hours (see p. 166).

National (state-operated) museums usually close Sunday afternoon and Monday. Most close for lunch (1–3 or 4 p.m.), although it is becoming more common for major museums to remain open 9 a.m.–7 p.m. Winter hours are shorter.

Post offices are open

Monday–Saturday 8 or 9 a.m.
–2 p.m. Major locations are
open 8 or 9 a.m.–6 or 8 p.m.

Many restaurants close
on Sunday evening and on
Monday or another weekday
(la chiusura settimanale). Many
establishments close in January
and for vacation in July
or August.

Store hours are generally
8:30 or 9 a.m.–1 p.m. and
3:30 or 4–8 p.m. Monday–
Saturday. Many stores close
on Monday morning and
another half day during the
week. Department stores
and major city stores may
be open seven days a week
9 a.m.–8 p.m.; a few stay
open until 10 p.m., but late
and Sunday hours are still
unusual.

RESTROOMS

Few public buildings have
restrooms. Generally you
will have to resort to facilities
in bars, railroad stations, and
gas stations where standards
are generally low. Ask for
il bagno (pronounced
eel BAHN-yo), take a few
tissues, and don't confuse
Signori (Men) with Signore
(Women). Tip the attendant
25 to 50 cents.

TIME

Sicily runs to CET (Central
European Time), 1 hour ahead
of Greenwich Mean Time
and 6 hours ahead of Eastern
Standard Time. Noon in Italy
is 6 a.m. in New York.

Clocks change for daylight
saving in late April/early May
(1 hour forward) and late
September/early October
(1 hour back). Italy uses the
24-hour clock.

TIPPING

In restaurants where a service
charge (servizio) is not included, leave 10–15 percent;
even if the charge is included,
you may wish to leave 5–10
percent for the waiter. In bars,
tip a few cents for drinks if
you're standing at the bar and

25–50 cents for waiter service.
In hotel bars, be slightly more
generous.

Service is included in hotel
rates, but tip chambermaids
and doormen about 50 cents
(1 euro for calling a cab), the
bellhop 1–3 euros for carrying
your bags, and the concierge
or porter around 3–7 euros
if he has been helpful. Double
these figures in the most
expensive hotels.

Tip restroom and checkroom
attendants 25 to 50 cents.
Porters at airports and railroad
stations generally work for
fixed wages, but tip up to
2 euros at your discretion.
Cab drivers expect around
10 percent. Barbers get around
2 euros, a hairdresser's assistant 2–4 euros depending on
the level of establishment.
Tip church or other custodians
1–2 euros.

TRAVELERS WITH DISABILITIES

Outside a very small minority
of better hotels and major
museums with the appropriate
facilities, Sicily is a very difficult
place to visit for those with
disabilities. Busy streets with
badly parked cars in Palermo
present obvious problems,
and old and uneven streets
in rural villages everywhere
are unwelcoming to wheel-
chairs. Towns such as Taormina,
with its steep grades, are
especially demanding.

Museums, galleries, and
public offices in bigger
towns and newly built public
buildings are making progress
in providing wheelchair access,
but there remains much to
be done.

Sicilians, including hoteliers
and restauranteurs, will always
try to be accommodating,
but only the larger luxury
hotels are equipped to deal
with wheelchairs.

Contact the Italian embassy
or consulate for information
about special procedures
required to bring a guide
dog into Italy.

Useful contacts in North
America include Wheels Up!
(tel 888/389-4335, www.
wheelsup.com), which offers
discounted air fares and
other travel arrangements;
Access-Able (www.access-
able.com), which specializes
in online advice; and agencies
that provide travel advice for
visitors with disabilities such
as SATH (tel 212/447-7284
or 212/447-0027, www.sath.
org) and Mobility International
(tel 541/343-1284, www.mi
usa.org).

VISITOR INFORMATION

ITALIAN STATE TOURIST OFFICES
www.italiantourism.com or
www.enit.it

USA
630 Fifth Ave., Suite 1565
New York, NY 10111
tel 212/245-4822
fax 212/586-9249

500 N. Michigan Ave.,
Suite 2240
Chicago, IL 60611
tel 312/644-0990
or 312/644-0996
fax 312/644-3109

12400 Wilshire Blvd., Suite 550
Los Angeles, CA 90025
tel 310/820-1898
or 310/820-9807
fax 310/820-6357

CANADA
175 Bloor St. E, Suite 907
South Tower
Toronto, ON M4W 3R8
tel 416/925-4882
fax 416/925-4799

UNITED KINGDOM
1 Princes St.
London W1R 8AY
tel 020-7408 1254
fax 020-7493 6695

EMERGENCIES

EMBASSIES & CONSULATES IN ITALY

U.S. Embassy
Via Vittorio Veneto 119/a, Rome
Tel 06 46 741
www.usembassy.it

U.S. Consulate
Via Vaccarini 1, Palermo,
Tel 091 305 857
www.usembassy.it

Canadian Embassy
Via G. Bastia de Rossi 27
Rome
Tel 06 445 981
www.canada.it or
www.dfait-maeci.gc.ca

U.K. Embassy
Via XX Settembre 80/a,
Rome
Tel 06 4220 0001
www.britain.it

U.K. Consulate
Via Cavour 117
Palermo
Tel 091 326 412
www.britishembassy.gov.uk

EMERGENCY PHONE NUMBERS

Police, tel 112
Emergency, tel 113
Fire, tel 115
Car breakdown, tel 116
Ambulance, tel 118

For legal assistance in an emergency, contact your embassy or consulate (see above) for a list of English-speaking lawyers.

For general help in English, contact the Rome-based English Yellow Pages (tel 06 474 0861, www.paginegialle.it or www.englishyellowpages.it).

WHAT TO DO IN A TRAFFIC ACCIDENT

Put on hazard lights and place a warning triangle 165 feet (50 m) behind the car. Call the police (tel 112 or 113).

At the scene, do not admit liablity or make potentially incriminating statements to police or onlookers. Ask any witnesses to remain, make a police statement, and exchange insurance and other relevant details with the other driver(s). Call the car rental agency, if necessary, to inform them of the incident

HEALTH

Check that your health insurance covers you while you are visiting Italy and that any travel insurance also includes sufficient medical coverage.

For minor complaints, first visit a drugstore or pharmacy (una farmacia), indicated by a green cross outside the store. Staff is well trained and will be able to offer advice as well as help finding a doctor (un medico), if necessary.

Also consult your hotel, the Yellow Pages, or visitor centers for help in choosing a doctor or dentist (un dentista). Bring an ample supply of any prescription drugs (medicina) you need. Should you need to refill a prescription, pharmacies will direct you to a doctor.

Visit a hospital (un ospedale) for serious complaints. Emergency treatment is provided at the Pronto Soccorso. Italian hospitals often look run-down, but the treatment standards are generally good.

Before leaving home, consider contacting the International Association for Medical Assistance to Travelers (tel 716/754-4883 in the U.S. and 416/652-0137 or 519/836-0102 in Canada, www.iamat.org), a nonprofit organization that anyone can join free of charge. Members receive a directory of English-speaking IAMAT doctors on call 24 hours a day and are entitled to services at set rates.

Common minor complaints include overexposure to the sun and insect bites. Poison ivy is not a major problem, but Italy does have poisonous snakes (vipere), though bites are usually not fatal unless you have an allergic reaction.

Tap water is generally safe. Do not drink water, however, if marked acqua non potabile, and never drink from streams in the mountains or elsewhere. Milk is pasteurized and safe.

HOSPITALS
Palermo
Palermo Policlinico
Via del Vespro
tel 091 655 1111

Ospedale Civico
Via Carmelo Lazzaro
tel 091 666 1111

LOST PROPERTY
If you lose property, go first to the local visitor center and ask for assistance. Bus, tram, train, and metro systems in cities usually have special offices to deal with lost property, but they can be hard to find and are usually only open a few hours a day. Ask for directions at visitor centers, and also try bus depots and rail stations. Hotels should be able to provide assistance as well.

To report a more serious loss or theft, go to the local police station or Questura. In Palermo the main Questura is at Piazza della Vittoria (tel 091 210 111 or 091 651 4330). Many have English-speaking staff to deal with visitors' problems. You will be asked to complete and sign a form (una denuncia) reporting any crime. Keep your copy for relevant insurance claims.

HOTELS & RESTAURANTS

Sicily offers a variety of accommodations to suit all tastes and budgets. Choose from fine hotels in centuries-old buildings to intimate, family-run establishments or from charming bed-and-breakfasts to luxurious island resorts. Italy boasts one of the world's great cuisines—and the pleasures of Italian/Sicilian food and wine are as much a part of your visit as museums and galleries. Restaurants of different type and quality, from humble pizzerias to venerable classics, are found in every town and village. Below is a selection of some of the most interesting places to sleep and eat in Sicily.

HOTELS

In general, accommodations that provide the best central locations within a town or city have been recommended. Noise can be a problem in urban areas, so when possible, quiet, out-of-town alternatives are provided as well. Hotels and other accommodations were also selected for their character, charm, or historical associations.

Note that even in the finest hotels, bathrooms may only have a shower (*doccia*) and no tub (*vasca*). Rooms are often small by U.S. standards, even in the most upscale establishments. Always ask to see a selection of rooms before you register.

All-day room service and air-conditioning are also comparatively rare.

Grading system

Hotels are officially graded from one star (the simplest accommodations) to five star (luxury). Grading criteria are complex, but in a three-star establishment and above, all rooms should have private bath/shower, a telephone, and a television. Most two-star hotels also have private bathrooms.

Reservations

It is advisable to reserve accommodations in advance, especially in major tourist areas, and particularly during high season (June–Aug.). Unless the hotel has a website or email address for reserving online, make your reservations by telephone and confirm by fax. It is a good idea to reconfirm reservations a couple of days before arrival.

Hoteliers are obliged to regis-

ter every guest, so when checking in you will be asked for your passport. It will be returned within a few hours or on the day of departure.

Checkout times range from around 10 a.m. to noon, but you should be able to leave luggage at the hotel reception and pick it up later in the day.

Prices

All prices are officially set, and room rates must be displayed by law at reception and in each room. Prices for different rooms can vary within a hotel, but all taxes and services should be included in the rate.

Hotels often levy additional charges for air-conditioning and garage facilities, while laundry, drinks from minibars, and phone calls made from rooms invariably carry large surcharges.

Price categories given in the entries are for double (*una matrimoniale*) or twin (*una camera doppia*) rooms and are for guidance only. Seasonal variations often apply, especially in coastal resorts, where high-season (summer) rates are usually higher.

At busy times, there may also be a two- or three-day minimum stay policy, and you may be obliged to take full- or half-board packages. Half-board (*mezza pensione*) includes breakfast and lunch, while full-board (*pensione completa*) includes all meals. Such packages are always priced on a per person basis.

Credit cards

Many large hotels accept the major credit cards. Smaller ones may only accept some,

HOTELS

An indication of the maximum high-season cost of a double room with breakfast is given by $ signs. Rooms may often be available for less than the indicated price.

$$$$$	Over $250
$$$$	$180–$250
$$$	$140–$180
$$	$100–$140
$	Under $100

RESTAURANTS

An indication of the cost of a three-course dinner, including interesting rather than the cheapest menu options, is given by $ signs. Less expensive meals will be available. Drinks are excluded.

$$$$$	Over $60
$$$$	$40–$60
$$$	$30–$40
$$	$20–$30
$	Under $20

as shown in their entries. Abbreviations used are AE (American Express), DC (Diners Club), MC (Mastercard), and V (Visa). Look for card symbols outside establishments, or the Italian Carta Si sign. As a general rule, AE and DC are less widely accepted than V and MC.

RESTAURANTS

The following selection of restaurants reflects the best of Sicily's regional cooking. Don't be afraid to experiment, however, especially in small towns and rural areas. If in doubt, see where the locals choose to eat and follow their lead.

Dining hours

Breakfast (*colazione*) usually consists of a cappuccino and bread roll or sweet pastry (*una brioche*) taken standing in a bar anytime between 7–9 a.m.

Lunch (*pranzo*) starts around 12:30 p.m. and ends at sometime around 2 p.m.—the infamous long lunch and siesta are increasingly a thing of the past in the urban areas.

Dinner (cena) begins about 8 p.m., with last orders taken at around 10 p.m., although dinner hours may be earlier in rural areas and small towns.

Most restaurants in every category close once a week, and many take long vacation breaks (ferie) in July or August.

Paying

The check (il conto) must be presented by law as a formal receipt. A price scrawled on a piece of paper is illegal and you are within your rights to demand an itemized ricevuta.

Bills once included a cover charge (pane e coperto), a practice the authorities are trying to ban. Many restaurants get around the law by charging for bread brought to your table whether you want it or not.

Smaller, simpler restaurants and those in rural areas are less likely to accept credit cards. It can be worth checking if your card is acceptable, even in places where window signs are displayed.

Meals

Meals traditionally begin with appetizers or hors d'oeuvres (antipasto—literally "before the meal"), a first course (il primo) of soup, pasta, or rice, and a main course (il secondo) of meat or fish. Vegetables (contorni) or salads (insalata) are often served separately with or after il secondo.

Desserts (dolci) may include or be followed by fruit (frutta) and cheese (formaggio). Italians often round off a meal with an espresso and brandy, grappa (a clear, brandylike spirit), or an amaro (a bitter digestif).

You don't need to order every course—a primo and salad is acceptable in all but the grandest restaurants. Many Italians choose to go to an ice-cream parlor (gelateria) as part of an after-dinner stroll instead of dessert.

Set menus

The menu in Italian is il menù or la lista. Fixed-price menus are available in many restaurants in tourist areas. The menù turistico usually includes two courses, a simple dessert, and half a bottle of wine and water per person. Quantity and quality of food are invariably poor. Of better value in more upscale restaurants is the menù gastronomico, where you pay a fixed price to sample a selection of the special dishes.

Bars, cafés, & snacks

Bars and cafés are perfect for breakfast and often provide snacks such as filled rolls (panini) or sandwiches (tramezzini) throughout the day. A few may offer a light meal at lunch. Stands or small stores selling slices of pizza (pizza al taglio) with different toppings are common. It always costs less to stand at the bar.

Tipping & dress

Tip between 10 and 15 percent where service has been good and where a service charge (servizio) is not included.

As a rule, Italians dress well but informally to eat out, especially in better restaurants. A relaxed casual style is a good rule of thumb. Jacket and tie for men are rarely necessary, but often the better dressed you are, the better service you receive.

Smoking

Smoking is common in Italy and there are very few non-smoking areas in restaurants. Italians will be unlikely to move or desist from smoking if you protest.

LISTINGS

The hotels and restaurants listed here have been grouped first according to their region, then listed alphabetically by price category. For disabled access, it is recommended that you check with the establishment to verify the extent of their facilities.

L = lunch   D = dinner

PALERMO

CENTRALE PALACE HOTEL
$$$$$ ★★★★
CORSO VITTORIO
EMANUELE II 327
TEL 091 336 666
FAX 091 334 881
EMAIL centrale@angala
hotels.it
www.centralepalacehotel.it
Palermo's best hotel occupies a 19th-century building two blocks west of the Quattro Canti, a busy but very central location. The rooms are well furnished, the service is excellent, and there is an attractive roof garden with restaurant.
🛏 103 🅿 🔁 📶 3 🔯
🚭 All major cards

GRAND HOTEL ET DES PALMES
$$$$ ★★★★
VIA ROMA 398
TEL 091 602 8111
FAX 091 331 545
EMAIL thi@thi.it
www.thi.it
This historic hotel's fame stems partly from its reputation as an alleged favorite among Mafia dons (including Lucky Luciano) in the 1950s and '60s, but it has always been a good, traditional hotel of belle époque elegance. Extensive renovations just completed in late 2004 greatly improved its rooms and common areas. Its slightly outlying location (four blocks north of the Museo Archeologico) is not as convenient as some.
🛏 183 🅿 🔁 📶 30 🔯
🚭 All major cards

PRINCIPE DI VILLAFRANCA
$$$$ ★★★★
VIA G. TURRISI COLONNA 4
TEL 091 611 8523
FAX 091 588 705
EMAIL info@principedi
villafranca.it

HOTELS & RESTAURANTS

www.principedivillafranca.it
A good choice for business travelers or those who wish to be away from the center, this is a recently built, polished, and professionally run hotel. It is in the "new" town district, half a mile (1 km) northwest of the Teatro Massimo.
🏨 34 P 🔁 🅢 🔽
🅢 All major cards

🏨 MASSIMO PLAZA
$$$$ ★★★★
VIA MAQUEDA 437
TEL 091 325 657
FAX 091 325 711
EMAIL booking@massimo plazahotel.com
www.massimoplazahotel.com
The Massimo Plaza is an excellent and intimate mid-range choice in the north of the city center opposite the Teatro Massimo. The renovated art nouveau palazzo has spacious soundproofed rooms and restrained and tasteful reception and public areas.
🛏 15 P 🔁 🅢
🅢 All major cards

🏨 POSTA
$$ ★★
VIA ANTONELLO GAGINI 77
TEL 091 587 338
FAX 091 587 347
EMAIL info@hotelpost apalermo.it
www.hotelpostapalermo.it
A city institution close to San Domenico, the Posta has been in business for more than 80 years and was traditionally the choice of actors, artists, and bohemians. Recently renovated, it offers good-size rooms and represents excellent value given its central location.
🛏 30 P 🔁 🅢
🅢 All major cards

🏨 GARDENIA
$$ ★★
VIA STABILE MARIANO 136
TEL 091 322 761
FAX 091 333 732
EMAIL gardeniahotel@gar deniahotel.com
www.hotelgardeniapalermo.it
The Gardenia is an intimate, welcoming and recently renovated central hotel (on the street that leads from Piazza Politeama to the port). Many rooms have balconies with views, and the facilities and furnishings are better than most hotels in the two-star range.
🛏 16 P 🅢 🅢 All major cards

🏨 LETIZIA
$$ ★★★
VIA DEI BOTTAI 30
TEL 091 589 110
FAX 091 589 110
EMAIL booking@hotelletizia .com
www.hotelletizia.com
Centrally located near Piazza Maffei, the Letizia has cozy public spaces with parquet floors and Persian rugs, and well-renovated rooms, some of which have a small internal patio.
🛏 13 P 🔁 🅢
🅢 All major cards

🏨 VILLA ARCHIRAFI
$ ★★
VIALE LINCOLN 30
TEL 091 616 8827
FAX 091 616 8631
First choice in its low-cost category, this hotel occupies a small art nouveau villa west of the railroad station on the edge of the Botanic Garden. Service is first-rate and there is a small garden where breakfast is served in good weather. Ask for rooms away from the street.
🛏 40 P 🔁 🅢 🅢 AE, MC, V

🍴 OSTERIA DEI VESPRI
$$$$$
PIAZZA CROCE DEI VESPRI
TEL 091 617 1631
www.osteriadeivespri.it
This single-room restaurant just south of San Francesco was once used to house the carriages of the Palazzo Gangi above the palace in which Luchino Visconti filmed the ballroom scene in his movie, *The Leopard*. Today it offers some of Palermo's most creative and accomplished cooking, including modern reinterpretations of traditional Sicilian meat and fish dishes. Good wine list. During the summer there is outdoor seating available.
🍴 35 (inside) 40 (outside)
🕐 Closed Sun. & part of Aug. 🅢 🅢 All major cards

🍴 GRAND GOURMET
$$$$
CORSO PISANI 30
TEL 091 659 8284
The name accurately reflects the high quality of food (with creatively prepared fish and seafood at the fore) and wine at this excellent restaurant, about a 5-minute walk southwest of the Palazzo dei Normanni.
🍴 50 🕐 Closed Sun. & mid-June–mid-Sept. 🅢
🅢 All major cards

🍴 SANTANDREA
$$$$
PIAZZA SANT' ANDREA 4
TEL 091 334 999
Close to the Vucciria market and San Domenico, Santandrea is a delightful, central restaurant with a longstanding good reputation. The food features many creative twists but never strays far from its Palermitan roots. Good wine list.
🍴 80 (inside) 80 (outside)
🕐 Closed Tues.–Wed. L in winter, Sun.–Mon. L in summer, & part of Aug.
🅢 🅢 AE, MC, V

⊞ DAL MAESTRO DEL BRODO

$$$

VIA PANNIERI 7

TEL 091 329 523

Market-fresh ingredients from the Vucciria go into traditional dishes such as *pasta con le sarde* (pasta with sardines) and *pesce spada e menta* (swordfish with mint) at this welcoming, family-run trattoria conveniently situated near the corner of Via Roma and Corso Vittorio Emanuele II.

🛏 100 🕐 Closed D except Fri.–Sat. Sept.–mid-June; also 2 weeks in Aug., Sun. in summer, & Tues. in winter.

🅢 🅢 AE, MC, V

⊞ MI MANDA PICONE

$$$

VIA ALESSANDRO PATERNOSTRO 59

TEL 091 616 0660

This appealing *enoteca* (wine bar) has a fine arched interior with two salons (one of which is nonsmoking) in a 14th-century building by San Francesco. Cheese, wine, and snacks are available at the downstairs bar, and full meals in the upper dining room.

🛏 40 (inside) 60 (outside) 🕐 Closed L, Sun., & part of Aug. 🅢 AE. MC, V

⊞ KURSAAL KALHESA

$$–$$$

FORO UMBERTO I 21

TEL 091 616 2282

A pleasant, if slightly outlying place, near the corner of Via Lincoln and Foro Italico southwest of the Galleria Regionale. It is a combination of a restaurant and a spacious arched bar, jazz venue, coffeehouse, and bookstore. There is also a garden. The cooking takes its inspiration from a variety of Mediterranean sources.

🛏 50 (inside) 70 (outside) 🕐 Closed Sun. D, Mon. & part of Aug. 🅢 AE, MC, V

⊞ CASA DEL BRODO

$$

CORSO VITTORIO EMANUELE II 175

TEL 091 321 655

This Palermitan favorite, founded in 1890, offers good value for the money, especially if you go for the *brodo* (broth or soup), several different choices of which are available each day. Or choose from the antipasti buffet laid out between the two dining rooms.

🛏 60 🕐 Closed Tues. 🅢 All major cards

⊞ ANTICA FOCACCERIA

$

VIA ALESSANDRO PATERNOS-TRO 59

TEL 091 320 264

An atmospheric, family-run tavern by San Francesco, founded in 1834, with marble tables (plus outdoor tables on the square), old mirrors, wrought iron, and wood paneling. It offers a handful of hot dishes and traditional snacks such as *panelle* (chickpea fritters), *purpa* (boiled octopus), and *meusa* (grilled beef spleen). More conventional snacks and sandwiches are also available.

🛏 200 (indoor) 200 (outdoor) 🕐 Closed Mon. 🅢 All major cards

WESTERN SICILY

ERICE

⊞ BAGLIO SANTA ⊞ CROCE

$$ ★★★

CONTRADA RAGOSIA

TEL 0923 891 111

FAX 0923 891 192

www.bagliosantacroce.it

Escape the crowds in this delightful rural retreat on Mount Erice among the olives and citrus groves, 5.5 miles (9 km) east of Erice on the SS 187 road. The converted farmhouse dates from 1637, and the

simple but appealing rooms and common areas retain old wooden beams and terra-cotta floors. The gardens offer lovely views and the restaurant serves wholesome country cooking.

🛏 25 🅿 🅢 🅢 🅢 All major cards

⊞ MODERNO

$$ ★★★

VIA VITTORIO EMANUELE II 63

TEL 0923 869 300

FAX 0923 869 139

www.pippocatalano.it

A renovated 19th-century building, this central, well-run hotel over two floors (with an annex boasting larger rooms across the street) has a roof terrace and excellent restaurant that is worth visiting whether or not you are staying here. Ask for a room with terrace or balcony.

🛏 40 🛏 100 🕐 Restaurant closed Mon. in winter 🅿 🅢 🅢 🅢 🅢 All major cards

⊞ MONTE SAN GIULIANO

$$$

VICOLO SAN ROCCO 7

TEL 0923 869 595

www.montesangiuliano.it

Enjoy eating in this rustic central restaurant in one of three dining rooms or under an arbor in a pleasant courtyard, and try regional specialties such as *sarde a beccafico* (sardines), *pesce alla griglia* (grilled fish), or *involtini di melanzane* (rolled and stuffed eggplant).

🛏 80 (inside) 100 (outside) 🕐 Closed Mon. & parts of Jan. & Nov. 🅢 🅢 🅢 All major cards

ISOLE EGADI

⊞ AEGUSA

$$$ ★★★

VIA GARIBALDI 11–17, FAVIGNANA

TEL 0923 922 430

FAX 0923 922 440
www.aegusahotel.it
Rooms in this restrained 19th-century palazzo are bright, spacious, and simply furnished, and the restaurant has its own small garden courtyard.
🛈 28 🔲 🔁 🕒 Hotel & restaurant closed for parts of Jan.–Feb. 🌐 All major cards

🏨 EGADI HOTEL
🍴 $$ ***
VIA CRISTOFORO COLOMBO 17, FAVIGNANA
TEL 0923 921 232
FAX 0923 921 232
www.albergoegadi.it
Bright, well-kept, and refurbished rooms provide a simple and intimate base. The restaurant, although plain in appearance, is highly regarded.
🛈 12 🛏 80 🔲 🕒 Closed from Oct.–Easter
🌐 All major cards

🍴 EL PESCADOR
$$$$
PIAZZA EUROPA 38, FAVIGNANA
TEL 0923 921 035
Photographs and décor in this rustic fish restaurant recall Favignana's fishing traditions, a heritage reflected in fine fish and seafood dishes such as spaghetti pescador. In summer, you can dine outside on a small piazza. The simpler and less expensive **La Bettola** trattoria nearby (Via Nicotera 47, tel 0923 921 988, closed Thurs.) is also recommended.
🛏 40 (inside) 90 (outside) 🕒 Closed Jan.–Feb. & Wed. except in high season.

PANTELLERIA

🏨 MONASTERO
$$$$ ****
CONTRADA KASSÀ, SCAURI ALTA
TEL 0923 916 655
www.directa.net/sicilia/
agrigento/hotels/monastero.html
Five traditional houses (*dammusi*) have been converted into this unusual and striking hotel, a favored retreat of celebrities such as Sting and Madonna.
🛈 4 villas 🔲 🌐 All major cards

🏨 MURSIA
🍴 $$ ***
LOCALITÀ MURSIA
TEL 0923 911 217
FAX 0923 911 026
www.mursiahotel.it
Just 2.5 miles (4 km) from Pantelleria town (to which there is a free hotel boat shuttle), this striking resort offers a pool, private beach, diving center, windsurfing school, tennis courts, and other outdoor facilities. Its **Le Lampare** restaurant offers Sicilian & classic Italian, and Arab-influenced dishes. The 1970s-vintage **Cossyra** (tel 0923 911 154, www.cossyrahotel.it) nearby, and under the same management, has similar facilities and prices.
🛈 74 🅿 🔁 🔲 🏊 🌐 All major cards

🏨 PAPUSCIA
🍴 $$ **
LOCALITÀ TRACINO SOPRA PORTELLA 28
TEL 0923 915 463
FAX 0923 915 463
EMAIL papuscia@meditel.it
www.papuscia.com
The three buildings in this family-run hotel are built around a converted, 18th-century *dammuso* dwelling. They overlook a pretty garden and a terrace with views of the sea (just over half a mile/1 km away). The simple restaurant has a veranda for summer dining.
🛈 11 🕒 Closed mid-Jan.–Feb. 🅿 🔲 🌐 AE, MC, V

HOTELS
An indication of the maximum high-season cost of a double room with breakfast is given by $ signs. Rooms may often be available for less than the indicated price.

$$$$$	Over $250
$$$$	$180–$250
$$$	$140–$180
$$	$100–$140
$	Under $100

RESTAURANTS
An indication of the cost of a three-course dinner, including interesting rather than the cheapest menu options, is given by $ signs. Less expensive meals will be available. Drinks are excluded.

$$$$$	Over $60
$$$$	$40–$60
$$$	$30–$40
$$	$20–$30
$	Under $20

🍴 LA NICCHIA
$$$
CONTRADA SCAURI BASSO
TEL 0923 916 342
Dining here is in two rooms (one nonsmoking) in a converted *dammuso* or in the pretty garden. The cooking is often innovative; dishes might include *ravioli di ricotta e menta* (pasta stuffed with cheese and mint) or *gamberoni all'uva zibibbo* (king prawns with local grapes). Pizzas are also available.
🛏 40 (inside) 60 (outside) 🕒 Closed mid-Jan.–mid-Feb., L year-round, & Wed. in winter
🌐 All major cards

SAN VITO LO CAPO

🏨 CAPO SAN VITO
🍴 $$$$$ ****
VIA PRINCIPE TOMMASO 29
TEL 0923 972 122
FAX 0923 972 559
www.caposanvito.it
The most comfortable

location for the Zingaro reserve and the resort of San Vito lo Capo, this charming small (four floors) hotel offers panoramic views of the sea (most rooms have a terrace), garden, and a private beach. There's a small café (the **Caruso**) and a restaurant (the **Jacaranda**), both offering outdoor tables for summer dining.

🛏 36 🔵 ⬇ 🏊
🔲 All major cards

🍴 CORALLO
$$$
VIA G. AMICO 7
TEL 0923 972 827
A lovely garden forms the centerpiece of this family-run restaurant just off the main street. Fish and seafood are the mainstays of the menu.
🍽 35 🕐 Oct.–April
🔲 DC, MC, V

◼ SOUTHERN SICILY

AGRIGENTO

🏨 BAGLIO DELLA LUNA
🍴 $$$$$ ★★★★
CONTRADA MADDALUSA
TEL 0922 511 061
FAX 0922 598 802
www.esperia.it/pregiohotel
About 2.5 miles (4 km) from Agrigento (off the SS 640 road), this beautifully restored 13th- and 15th-century castle-country house is ringed by gardens, and has elegant rooms and stylish common areas furnished with antiques. In **Il Dèhor,** it boasts the region's best restaurant and a good wine list. A definite first choice in the area.
🛏 24 🍽 100 🅿 ⬇ 🔵
🔲 All major cards

🏨 VILLA ATHENA
🍴 $$$$$ ★★★★
VIA PASSEGGIATA ARCHEOLOGICA 33
TEL 092 259 6288

FAX 092 240 2180
Once Agrigento's finest hotel, the Villa Athena, a converted 18th-century villa, is dated and a little overpriced, but is still the only place to stay in the Valle dei Templi. It also has a garden and pool, an above-average restaurant (with outdoor dining in summer), and tremendous views of the Tempio della Concordia. Ask for a room with terrace and temple views.
🛏 40 ⬇ 🔵 🏊
🔲 All major cards

🏨 COLLEVERDE PARK
🍴 $$$$ ★★★★
STRADA PANORAMICA DEI TEMPLI
TEL 0922 29 555
FAX 0922 29 012
This hotel is in the archaeo-logical zone, within an easy walk of the temples (the garden overlooks them). Rooms (some with temple views) are modern and quietly elegant, the staff charming, and there is access to a private beach.
🛏 48 🅿 ⬇ 🔵 🏊
🔲 All major cards

🍴 DEI TEMPLI
$$$
VIA PANORAMICA DEI TEMPLI 15
TEL 0922 403 110
Vaulted ceilings, stone arches, and terra-cotta floors provide a rustic atmosphere in a busy but friendly restaurant near the temples. The menu is mainly fish- and seafood-based. One of the two dining rooms is nonsmoking.
🍽 100 (inside) 20 (outside)
🔵 🅿 🕐 Closed Sun. in high season & Fri. year-round 🔵 🔲 All major cards

🍴 LEON D'ORO
$$$
VIALE EMPORIUM 102
TEL 0922 414 400
Located 4.5 miles (7 km)

from central Agrigento, near the sea, in the hamlet of San Leone, this is a well-run restaurant whose menu changes frequently and mixes traditional Sicilian food and innovative fish and seafood dishes. There is a large flower-filled garden for outdoor dining, and one of the two spacious dining rooms is nonsmoking.
🍽 120 (inside) 140 (outside)
🅿 🔵 🔵 🕐 Closed Mon.
🔲 All major cards

ISOLE PELAGIE

🏨 GUITGIA TOMMASINO
🍴 $$$$$ ★★★
VIA LIDO AZZURRO 13, LAMPEDUSA
TEL 0922 970 879
FAX 0922 970 316
EMAIL info@guitgia.com
www.guitgia.com
Two Mediterranean-style buildings compose this hotel on the beach. When booking request a room with a balcony and sea views. In summer, dine on the terrace of the hotel's **Da Tommasino** restaurant, which offers a large variety of fish dishes.
🛏 36 🅿 ⬇ 🔵 🕐
Closed Nov.–Feb.
🔲 All major cards

🍴 GEMELLI
$$$$$
VIA CALA PISANA 2, LAMPEDUSA
TEL 0922 970 699
www.ristorantegemelli.it
The Moorish theme in this smart and highly professional, three-room restaurant is continued in the cooking, which blends Arab influ-ences with traditional Sicilian cuisine. Standout dishes include the homemade ravioli stuffed with prawns. There is a terrace for warm-weather dining.
🍽 40 (indoor) 40 (outdoor)
🔵 🕐 Closed L & Nov.–
Easter 🔵 🔲 AE, DC, V

HOTELS & RESTAURANTS

VILLA IMPERIALE DEL CASALE

🏨 PARK HOTEL PARADISO
$$$ ★★★★
CONTRADA RAMALDA,
PIAZZA ARMERINA
TEL 0935 680 841
FAX 0935 683 391
EMAIL info@parkhotelpar
adiso.it or booking@park
hotelparadiso.it
www.parkhotelparadiso.it
A comfortable, if unre-
markable, hotel with many
facilities (including sauna and
tennis courts) located just
north of Piazza Armerina,
a town convenient to the
Villa Imperiale del Casale
(which has few lodgings).
🛏 95 ⬛ 🅂 ⬛ 🔲
🚭 All major cards

🏨 OSTELLO DEL BORGO
$
LARGO SAN GIOVANNI 6
PIAZZA ARMERINA
TEL 0935 687 019
FAX 0935 686 943
www.ostellodelborgo.it
Not a hostel, but monks'
quarters in the former
St John's monastery that
have been converted into
comfortable rooms with
bathrooms.
🛏 13 🚭 MC, V

🍴 AL FOGHER
$$$$
CONTRADA BELLIA 1
PIAZZA ARMERINA
TEL 0935 684 123
www.alfogher.net
Two intimate rooms (one
nonsmoking) in a former
railway building are the
stage for a mixture of
regional cooking infused
with inventive touches.
The wine list is excellent
and there is a garden for
summer meals al fresco.
Al Fogher is located just
outside of Piazza Armerina
on the SS 117 bis road.
🍽 55 (inside) 30 (outside)
🅿 🅂 🚭 AE, V

SELINUNTE

🏨 ALCESTE
🍴 $ ★★★
VIA ALCESTE 21
TEL 092 446 184
FAX 092 446 143
www.hotelalceste.it
This is a simple, family-run
hotel built in the 1980s in
the old part of Marinella,
half a mile (1km) from
Selinunte. Its terrace has
a view of the sea, and the
restaurant serves more-
than-respectable traditional
Sicilian food.
🛏 26 🅿 🅂 🕐 Closed
mid-Nov. & mid-Jan.–mid-
Feb. 🚭 All major cards

🍴 PIERROT
$$$
VIA MARCO POLO 108
TEL 092 446 205
Marinella has several good
fish and general restaurants
with sea and/or Acropolis
views—and this is one of
the best. It serves meat and
fish dishes, as well as pizzas.
One of the two dining rooms
is nonsmoking.
🍽 170 (inside) 80 (outside)
🅿 🅂 🚭 All major cards

■ SYRACUSE & THE SOUTHEAST

SYRACUSE

🏨 DES ETRANGERS ET MIRAMARE
$$$$ ★★★★★
PASSEGGIO ADORNO 10–12
TEL 0931 62 671
FAX 0931 65 124
EMAIL info@medeahotels
.com
www.medeahotels.com
Syracuse's highest rated
hotel is a recently converted
19th-century palace at the
heart of the old town on
Ortygia. Rooms have
numerous high-tech and
other facilities, and there is
access to a private beach,
as well as a health club
and sauna.

🛏 80 ⬛ 🅂 ⬛ 🔲
🚭 All major cards

🏨 GRAND HOTEL
🍴 SIRACUSA
$$$$$ ★★★★
VIALE MAZZINI 12
TEL 0931 464 600
FAX 0931 464 611
EMAIL info@grandhotelsr.it
www.grandhotelsr.it
A comfortable and pleasing
hotel with a mixture of
modern and Old World
style on the northwest tip
of Ortygia. The hotel's
La Terrazza restaurant
has a roof terrace with
fine sea and harbor views.
Hotel shuttles transport
guests to and from a
private beach.
🛏 58 🅿 ⬛ 🅂
🚭 All major cards

🏨 GRAN BRETAGNA
$$ ★★★
VIA SAVOIA 21
TEL 0931 68 765
FAX 0931 449 078
EMAIL info@hotelgranbre
tagna.it
www.hotelgranbretagna.it
A welcoming and well-run
hotel that has been an
Ortygia fixture for many
years. Some of the spacious
rooms in this 18th-century
building feature preserved
frescoed ceilings.
🛏 17 🅿 🅂 🚭 All major
cards

🏨 GUTKOWSKI
$$ ★★★
VIA LUNGOMARE VITTORINI 26
TEL 0931 465 861
FAX 0931 480 505
EMAIL info@guthotel.it
www.guthotel.it
This is the perfect budget
choice in eastern Ortygia:
not luxurious, but simple,
modern, and comfortable,
with sea views from some
rooms.
🛏 15 🚭 All major cards

DON CAMILLO
$$$$$
VIA MAESTRANZA 92–100
TEL 0931 67 133
Relatively expensive, this restaurant is the top choice in Syracuse. This beautiful two-salon establishment occupies a converted 15th-century palazzo (complete with vaulted ceilings) on the eastern side of Ortygia, close to the church of San Francesco. Food is mostly, though not entirely, fish based, and features many elegant and creative touches.
🍴 100 🔆 🕐 Closed Sun., Nov., & 10 days in July 🔑 All major cards

ARCHIMEDE
$$$
VIA GEMMELLARO 8
TEL 0931 69 701
www.trattoriaarchimede.it
A Syracusan institution, Archimede has been in business in Ortygia, just south of Santa Maria dei Miracoli, since 1938. Its three, large dining rooms are adorned with historic photographs of the town. The fish and seafood cuisine is straightforward, but there is a particularly good anti-pasti buffet. A pizzeria (under the same management) is across the street.
🍴 150 🔆 🕐 Closed Sun., except in summer 🔑 All major cards

DA MARIANO
$$
VICOLO ZUCCOLÀ 9
TEL 0931 67 444
This informal restaurant is close to the Fonte Aretusa in the west of Ortygia. It consists of three, simply decorated rooms, one of which is nonsmoking. Service is warm and friendly, and the cooking draws almost entirely on local culinary traditions.
🍴 75 (inside) 40 (outside) 🔆 🔒 🕐 Closed Tues. & July 🔑 All major cards

NOTO

VILLA CANISELLO
$ *
VIA PAVESE 1
TEL 0931 835 793
FAX 0931 837 700
EMAIL canisello@tin.it
www.villacanisello.it
The restored, 19th-century farmhouse, with a large garden, is just a 10-minute walk from central Noto. The walls are thick and whitewashed, the décor simple but elegant, and the atmosphere pleasantly old-fashioned.
🛏 6 🅿 Some rooms; otherwise ceiling fans 🔒 No credit cards

CAMERE BELVEDERE
$
PIAZZA PERELLI CIPPO 1
TEL 0931 573 820
FAX 0931 573 820
EMAIL info@camerebel vedere.com
www.camerebelvedere.com/eng/f1.htm
This historic town has no hotel, so your options are a bed and breakfast—or the Camere Belvedere, a home consisting of four inexpensive, simply furnished rooms (each has a small private bathroom) with beamed ceilings and a terrace with lovely views.
🛏 4 🔆 No credit cards

CROCIFISSO DA BAGLIERI
$$
VIA PRINCIPE UMBERTO 46–48
TEL 0931 571 151
A taste of old Sicily, this simple, family-run trattoria is located in the upper town. Also good is the similar **Carmine**, with full meals, snacks, and pizzas (Via Ducezio 1a, tel 0931 838 705, closed Mon.). On the same street is **Mandolfiore** (Via Ducezio 2), the best place in town for cakes and pastries.
🍴 48 🕐 Closed Wed.,

after Easter, and Sept.
🔑 All major cards

RAGUSA

EREMO GIUBILIANA
$$$$$ ***
CONTRADA GIUBILIANA
TEL 0932 669 119
FAX 0932 669 129
www.eremodellagiubiliana.it
Since you have to stay outside of town anyway—old Ragusa has no hotels—this converted, 15th-century fortified monastery (4.3 miles/7 km south off the SP 25) is no hardship. Don't be put off by the barren landscape nearby; inside this exclusive complex, the grounds are verdant and the rooms wonderful. There is a fine restaurant ($$$$), a hotel beach, and a private boat and airstrip for special excursions.
🛏 14 🍴 130 (inside) 70 (outside) 🅿 🔄 🔆 🔒 🔑 All major cards

DUOMO
$$$$$
VIA CAPITANO BOCCHERI 31
TEL 0932 651 265
The Duomo is one of Sicily's best restaurants: elegant, intimate, sophisticated, and beautifully situated in front of the cathedral in old Ragusa. You must have reservations to secure a table in one of the four dining rooms (one is nonsmoking). The wine list is excellent and the cooking assured and based on the best of the old and new.
🍴 50 🔆 🔒 🕐 Closed L Sun. May–Sept., Mon., & part of Oct. 🔑 All major cards

ORFEO
$$$
VIA SANT'ANNA 117
Founded in 1935 and operated by the same family since 1970, Orfeo is a great trattoria of

HOTELS & RESTAURANTS

the old school. No frills, but excellent traditional Sicilian cooking.
🍴 50 🅂 🕒 Closed Sun.
🅰 All major cards

SCICLI

🏨 BAIA SAMUELE
🍴 $$$$ ★★★★
LOCALITÀ SAMPIERI
TEL 0932 848 111
FAX 0932 939 725
EMAIL Info@baiasamuele.it
www.baiasamuele.it
On a cypress-dotted hillside a half mile (1 km) from Scicli and close to the sea, this large village-style resort will not appeal to all tastes, but the tennis courts, private beach, and many other facilities are perfect for an activity-oriented or beach-based interlude. The town's small **Al Molo** restaurant (Via Perello 90, tel 0932 937 710, closed Mon.) offers a more intimate local dining experience.
ℹ 244 🅂 🅿 🔁 🚋
🅰 All major cards

MODICA

🍴 FATTORIA DELLE TORRI
$$$$
VICO NAPOLITANO 14
TEL 0932 751 928
After the Duomo in Ragusa, this is the region's best restaurant: an old structure in the historic center whose single dining room has been tastefully reworked in a modern idiom. Cooking is traditionally based, but can be elaborate, namely in dishes such as tortelli pasta stuffed with sword-fish. Excellent wine list.
🍴 40 (inside) 20 (outside)
🅂 🕒 Closed Mon.
🅰 All major cards

🍴 TAVERNA NICASTRO
$–$$
VIA SANT'ANTONIO 28
TEL 0932 945 884
This restaurant has been run by the Nicastro family in Modica Alta since 1948, with a tradition of simple country meat and other dishes, many unique to the Modica region. While in town, don't miss **Bonajuto** (Corso Umberto 1 159), a confectioners founded in 1880; a specialty is *i'mpanatigghi,* candy made from minced meat and chocolate.
🍴 100 (inside) 40 (outside)
🕒 Closed L, Sun.–Mon., & a week in mid-Aug.
🅰 All major cards

◼ EASTERN SICILY

TAORMINA

🏨 GRAND HOTEL TIMEO
🍴 & VILLA FLORA
$$$$$ ★★★★★
VIA TEATRO GRECO 59
TEL 0942 23 801
FAX 0942 628 501
EMAIL reservation.tim@framon-hotels.it
www.framonhotels.com
Better value—and arguably a better hotel—than the more famous San Domenico (see below), the Timeo has a superb terrace setting in its own peaceful park, close to the Greek theater. Rooms in the elegant and sophis-ticated 1873 villa are spacious and bright, and all have balconies and views of Mount Etna or the sea. The hotel's smart **Il Dito e la Luna** restaurant has a good reputation in its own right.
ℹ 87 🅿 🔁 🅂 🚋 📺
🅰 All major cards

🏨 SAN DOMENICO
🍴 PALACE
$$$$$ ★★★★★
PIAZZA SAN DOMENICO 5
TEL 0942 613 111

FAX 0942 625 506
www.thi.it
The great and the good, the famous and infamous, have all stayed at the San Domenico, a converted 15th-century monastery and one of Italy's most celebrated hotels. Its reputation may be overstated, but the vast public spaces, gardens, wonderful rooms, Old World patina, and sense of history and decorum are above reproach.
ℹ 108 🅿 🔁 🅂 🚋 📺
🅰 All major cards

🏨 VILLA BELVEDERE
$$$$ ★★★
VIA BAGNOLI CROCE 79
TEL 0942 23 791
FAX 0942 625 830
EMAIL info@villabelvedere.it
www.villabelvedere.it
Panoramic views distinguish this comfortable and very pleasant hotel, situated amid palms and olives a little east of the town center near the public gardens.
ℹ 49 🅿 🔁 🅂 🚋
🕒 Closed mid-Nov.–mid-March except around Christmas 🅰 All major cards

🏨 VILLA DUCALE
$$$$ ★★
VIA LEONARDO DA VINCI 60
TEL 0942 28 153
FAX 0942 28 710
EMAIL info@hotelvilladucale.it
www.hotelvilladucale.it
As pleasing as the Villa Schuler (see below) but more expensive, the Villa Ducale is a romantic hotel, with period furnishings, rooms with balconies and views, and congenial service. It is a 10-minute (uphill) walk from town center.
ℹ 12 🕒 Closed Dec.–mid-Feb. 🅿 🅂
🅰 All major cards

🏨 BEL SOGGIORNO
$$ ★★★
VIA PIRANDELLO 60
TEL 0942 23 342
FAX 0942 626 298
This garden-ringed hotel is situated in a peaceful and scenic corner, just east of the center off the town's main approach road.
🛏 30 🅿 ⬆ 🚭
🔒 All major cards

🏨 VILLA SCHULER
$$ ★★
PIAZZETTA BASTIONE-VIA ROMA
TEL 0942 23 481
FAX 0942 23 522
www.villaschuler.com
First choice among the less expensive hotels, this is a small, family-run gem of a place to stay. Just a 2-minute walk from Piazza Umberto I, it offers lovely views, fine service, and comfortable rooms, many with small balconies.
🛏 26 🅿 ⬆ 🚭
🕐 Closed mid-Nov.–Feb.
🔒 All major cards

🍴 CASA GRUGNO
$$$$$
VIA SANTA MARIA DEI GRECI
TEL 0942 21 208
www.casagrugno.it
Taormina's best restaurant occupies a lovely historic building, and offers a sophisticated menu of classic Italian and international dishes. There is just one, intimate dining room, so reservations are essential.
🍴 35 (inside) 40 (outside)
🕐 Closed L, Wed., & parts of Feb. & Dec. 🚭
🔒 All major cards

🍴 LA GIARA
$$$$$
VICO FLORESTA I
TEL 0942 23 360
Expensive, large, and upscale, with elaborate food and service—the draw here is mainly the restaurant's historical associations: Ava Gardner and other stars dined and partied here in the 1950s.
🍴 200 (inside) 80 (outside)
🕐 Closed L, Mon. except in Aug., Sun.–Thurs. Jan.–March, & Nov. 🚭
🔒 All major cards

🍴 AL DUOMO
$$$$
VICO EBREI 11
TEL 0942 625 656
Al Duomo is an excellent, lively restaurant in a small alley just off the cathedral square (with good outdoor dining options in summer). Marble tables and homey atmosphere, good service, and well-prepared local food.
🍴 40 (inside) 35 (outside)
🕐 Closed Feb. & Mon. in low season 🚭
🔒 All major cards

🍴 'A ZAMMÀRA
$$$$
VIA FRATELLI BANDIERA 15
TEL 0942 24 408
The attraction here is the chance to dine (in summer) in a lovely garden of orange and mandarin trees. Regional Sicilian cuisine and a particularly good wine list.
🍴 90 (inside) 60 (outside)
🕐 Closed Wed. except Aug. 🚭 🔒 DC, MC, V

🍴 MAFFEI'S
$$$$
VIA SAN DOMENICO DI GUZMAN I
TEL 0942 24 055
Approaches Casa Grugno on the culinary front, with the benefit of a pretty garden terrace. Fish and seafood predominate. Elegant, small (two dining rooms, one nonsmoking), and popular, so reserve in advance.
🍴 35 (inside) 45 (outside)
🚭 🕐 Closed for parts of Jan.–Feb. 🔒 All major cards

🍴 IL CICLOPE
$$$
CORSO UMBERTO I 201
TEL 0942 23 263
This central, family-run restaurant has maintained fair prices and reliable regional cooking since 1970.
🍴 50 (inside) 50 (outside)
🕐 Closed Wed. & mid-Jan.–mid-Feb. 🚭 🔒 All major cards

ETNA

🏨 BIANCANEVE
🍴 $$ ★★★
VIA ETNEA 163, NICOLOSI
TEL 095 914 139
FAX 095 911 194
EMAIL info@hotelbiancaneve.com
www.hotelbiancaneve.com
A large, modern hotel 10 miles (15 km) from Etna and the sea, with a pool, sports facilities, and views of the volcano.
🛏 83 🅿 🚭 ⬆ 🏊
🔒 All major cards

🏨 SCRIVANO
🍴 $ ★★★
VIA BONAVENTURA 2, RANDAZZO
TEL 095 921 126
FAX 095 921 433
This serviceable hotel-restaurant at the edge of Randazzo on the volcano's northern slopes recently has been enlarged and upgraded.
🛏 30 🅿 ⬆ 🚭 4 🚭
🔒 All major cards

🏨 PARCO DELL'ETNA
$ ★★
CONTRADA BORGONOVO, VIA GENERALE DALLA CHIESA I, BRONTE
TEL 095 691 907
FAX 095 692 678
A modest hotel, with a pool, built in 1990 on the western slopes of Mount Etna.
🛏 20 🅿 🚭 🏊
🔒 All major cards

🍴 VENEZIANO
$$
VIA DEI ROMANO 8, RANDAZZO
TEL 095 799 1353
Veneziano is a typical family-run trattoria which offers

HOTELS & RESTAURANTS

hearty country dishes such as *agnello al forno* (roast lamb) and *zuppa di funghi* (mushroom soup). 🍴 100 ⬛ 🕐 Closed Mon. & D Sun. 🚫 All major cards

NORTHERN SICILY

ISOLE EOLIE

LIPARI

🏨 A' PINNATA
$$$$$ ★★★★
BAIA PIGNATARO
TEL 090 981 1697
FAX 090 981 4782
EMAIL pinnata@pinnata.it
www.pinnata.it
Room terraces in this smart, new, and intimate, hotel offer views along much of Lipari's eastern coast.
ⓘ 12 🅿 ➡ ⬛
🚫 All major cards

🏨 VILLA AUGUSTUS
$$$$ ★★★
VICO AUSONIA 16
TEL 090 981 1232
FAX 090 981 2233
EMAIL info@villaaugustus.it
www.villaaugustus.it
Family-run since the 1950s, this converted patrician villa is a good, central hotel, with gardens, vistaed terrace, balconies, and spacious rooms.
ⓘ 34 🅿 ➡ ⬛ 🕐
Closed Nov.–Feb.
🚫 All major cards

🏨 ORIENTE
$$ ★★★
VIA MARCONI 35
TEL 090 981 1493
FAX 090 988 0198
EMAIL info@hoteloriente lipari.com
www.hotelorientelipari.it
A modern hotel in a quiet area just 5 minutes from the port. Rooms are bright, and there is a shady garden terrace.
ⓘ 32 🅿 ➡ ⬛
🚫 All major cards

🍴 E' PULERA
$$$$
VIA DIANA
TEL 090 981 1158
FAX 090 981 2878
www.filippino.it
E' Pulera offers often exceptional Eolian cooking, with two dining rooms, and garden and pergola for summer dining. The same owners run the larger but similarly priced **Filippino** (Piazza Municipio, tel 090 981 1002, closed Mon. in low season), a well-known, informal establishment, opened in 1910, where the cooking is almost as good.
🍴 80 ⬛ 🕐 Closed L & Feb.–April 🚫 DC, MC, V

🍴 LA NASSA
$$$$
VIA G FRANZA 36
TEL 090 981 1319
FAX 090 981 2257
www.lanassa.it
Another outstanding restaurant, also known for Eolian specialties, with a fine terrace for alfresco dining. One of the three dining rooms is nonsmoking.
🍴 45 (inside) 70 (outside)
⬛ ⬛ 🕐 Closed mid-Nov.–mid-March & L except July–Aug.
🚫 All major cards

PANAREA

🏨 LA PIAZZA
$$$–$$$$$★★★
VIA SAN PIETRO
TEL 090 983 154
FAX 090 983 003
This comfortable 1970s hotel near the sea has been recently renovated. Each room has a private terrace or balcony, and the pool and garden are superb. As with many Eolian hotels, you may have to take half- or full-board in summer—hence the pricey rating. The nearby **Cincotta** (tel 090 983 014) is similar and has a good restaurant.

ⓘ 31 🅿 ➡ ⬛ 🏊
🕐 Closed Nov.–March
🚫 All major cards

SALINA

🏨🍴 SIGNUM
$$$–$$$$$ ★★★
VIA SCALO 8, SCARIO
TEL 090 984 4222
FAX 090 984 4102
www.hotelsignum.it
A lovely and quiet hotel, the Eolian-styled Signum has a divine pool and garden, lots of antiques, and rooms with balconies or terraces.
ⓘ 30 ➡ ⬛ 🏊
🚫 All major cards

🍴 DA FRANCO
$$$$
VIA BELVEDERE 8, SANTA MARINA
TEL 090 984 3287
FAX 090 984 3684
www.ristorantedafranco .com
First-rate Aeolian fish and seafood cuisine in a delightful and scenic setting.

⊞ 120 🕐 Mon. & part of Dec. 🅰 🅑 All major cards

VULCANO

🏨 LES SABLES NOIRS
🍴 $$$$$ ★★★★
PORTO PONENTE
TEL 090 9850
FAX 090 985 2454
www.framon-hotels.com
Vulcano's oldest and best hotel is a typical, two-story Mediterranean building by a black-sand beach, from which it takes its name.
🛈 48 🅿 🅑 🅐 🌊
🅰 All major cards

🍴 MARIA TINDARA
$$$
VIA PROVINCIALE 38
TEL 090 985 3004
Go for the homemade pastas in this appealing restaurant in the hills near Pianoconte.
⊞ 80 🅿 🕐 Closed Nov.–Feb. 🅑 🅰 All major cards

LE MADONIE

🏨 PIANO TORRE PARK
🍴 $ ★★★
PIANO TORRE, NEAR ISNELLO
TEL 0921 662 671
FAX 0921 662 672
This is an excellent country retreat 5 miles (8 km) from Isnello, a small Madonie village that is also convenient to Cefalù (see below). The garden and large restaurant (worth a visit in its own right) are good, and there are tennis and other sports and outdoor facilities.
🛈 27 ⊞ 350 (inside) 50 (outside) 🅿 🅑 🅐 ⊞ 🌊 🅰 All major cards

🏨 POMIERI
$$ ★★
CONTRADA POMIERI, POLIZZI GENEROSA
TEL 0921 649 998
The Pomieri offers simple lodgings high in the mountains. Its dining room makes

a good stop for lunch if you are touring the area.
⊞ 130 (inside) 40 (outside) 🕐 Closed 3 weeks in Sept. 🅰 No credit cards

🍴 ITRIA
$$
VIA BEATO GNOFFI 8, POLIZZI GENEROSA
TEL 0921 688 790
This traditional trattoria serves robust mountain food (the village sits above 3,300 feet/1,000 m) such as *cinghiale* (wild boar) and *funghi* (mushrooms).
🛈 50 (inside) 30 (outside) 🕐 Closed Wed. & for a break in the fall 🅰 No credit cards

🏨 BERGI
🍴 $
CONTRADA BERGI, CASTELBUONO, OFF SS 286
TEL 0921 672 045
FAX 0921 676 877
www.agriturismobergi.com
This peaceful, rural retreat (*agriturismo*) lies amid orchards and olive groves 11 miles (18 km) south of Castelbuono, toward Geraci Siculo. Rooms are simple but pleasing, and much of the food served here is organic and homegrown.
🛈 14 🅿 🅑 🅰 No credit cards

🍴 NANGALARRUNI
$$$$
VIA DELLE CONFRATERNITE 5/7, CASTELBUONO
TEL 0921 671 428
The Sicilian food served at this attractive beamed and exposed-brick restaurant is some of the best in the Madonie— and beyond. There's also a good wine list. A cheaper and simpler option in the village is **Vecchio Palmento** (Via Failla 4, tel 0921 672 099, closed Mon. & part of Sept.), which also serves pizza.

⊞ 100 (inside) 20 (outside) 🅑 🕐 Closed Wed. except in Aug. 🅰 All major cards

CEFALÙ

🏨 KALURA
E $$ ★★★
VIA V CAVALLARO 13
TEL 0921 421 354
FAX 0921 423 122
www.kalura.it
About a mile (1.5 km) east of central Cefalù, this hotel occupies a superb position above the sea (with its own beach), and offers gracious rooms, tennis, and other sports facilities.
🛈 75 🅿 🅑 🅐 🌊 🅰 All major cards

🍴 LA BRACE
$$$
VIA XXV NOVEMBRE 10
TEL 0921 423 570
www.ristorantelabrace.com
Classic Sicilian cooking has been honed here for more than 20 years. Try the *bruschette di pesce* (toasts with fish), *spaghetti all'aglio* (pasta with garlic and chili), and cannoli for dessert.
⊞ 50 🅑 🕐 Closed Mon., L Tues., & mid-Dec.–mid-Jan. 🅰 All major cards

---

🅰 Nonsmoking 🅑 Elevator 🅐 Air-conditioning 🖼 Indoor/🌊 Outdoor swimming pool 🎽 Gym 🅰 Credit cards **KEY**

SHOPPING IN SICILY

Shopping is one of the great pleasures of visiting Sicily. From the smallest village in the mountains to the grandest streets of Palermo, the island's stores offer superb foods and wines, wonderful clothes, precious art and antiques, fine shoes and other leather goods, and a distinctive and colorful array of quality craft products.

STORES

Many Sicilian stores are small, family-run affairs, even in Palermo. Most neighborhoods have their own baker (panificio), fruit seller (fruttivendolo), butcher (macellaio), and food shop (alimentari). Pastry and home-made candy stores (pasticceria) are particular features of Sicilian towns. Department stores and supermarkets are found only in the largest centers.

MARKETS

Most towns and cities have at least one street market (mercato), usually open every day but Sunday from early morning to early afternoon. Smaller towns may have a 1-day market that operates on a similar schedule.

WHAT TO BUY

Wine is one of Sicily's emerging specialties (see pp. 20–21). Many of the island's regions and towns also have outstanding local foods, notably cheeses, oils, dried or candied fruits, cakes, sun-dried tomatoes, capers, and artichokes.

Inquire about import restrictions to North America if you plan to take meat and other produce home.

Sicily's antique shops are full of treasures large and small, while ceramics top the list of crafts produced here.

Coral and turquoise jewelry are good buys on the west coast, and lace and embroidery can be found in Palermo and smaller inland towns.

Rugs are a specialty of Erice, and straw and cane goods are made in Monreale.

Most larger city stores will handle packing and shipping.

In general, the more fashion-able shopping districts of Palermo, Taormina, and other resorts offer the high-quality clothes, lingerie, linens, fabrics, jewelry, kitchenware, design objects, and other items for which Italy is known.

OPENING HOURS

Most small stores are open 8 or 9 a.m. –1 p.m. and 3:30–8 p.m. Shops in city centers and tourist areas may stay open all day (orario continuato). Virtually all stores are closed on Sunday and most have a weekly closing day (giorno di riposo or chiusura settimanale). Some may also close for a half day, usually Monday morning, or, in the case of many food stores, Wednesday afternoon.

PAYMENT

Supermarkets and department stores usually accept credit cards and traveler's checks, as do larger clothing and shoe stores. Cash is required, how-ever, for virtually all transactions in small food and other shops.

EXPORTS

Many Italian products include a value-added goods and services tax known as IVA. Non-European Union residents can claim an IVA refund for purchases over 150 Euros made in any one establishment.

Shop with your passport and ask for invoices to be made out clearly, showing individual articles and tax amounts.

Keep all receipts and invoices and have them stamped at the customs office at your airport of departure, or at the point of exit from EU territory if you are traveling beyond Italy.

You then have 90 days to mail the invoice to the store, though it is easier to make the claim at the Tax Free Office in the last EU airport of your trip.

Forms, receipts—and some-times the goods themselves—must all be produced. Refunds are provided on the spot as cash or as credits to your credit card account.

Some stores are members of the Tax-Free Shopping System and issue a time-saving "tax-free check" for the amount of the rebate, which can be cashed directly at the Tax Free Office.

PALERMO

Palermo has Sicily's largest selection of stores. Tiny Via Bara all'Olivella is the street for arts and crafts, along with Via Calderai. Designer and other fashionable Italian names line Via della Libertà and nearby streets such as Via Enrico Parisi.

Via Roma, Via Maqueda, Via Ruggero Settimo, and the pedestrian-only Via Principe di Belmonte are also major shopping streets.

ARTS & CRAFTS

Angela Tripi
Corso Vittorio Emanuele II 450–52, tel 091 651 2787
Excellent source for traditional terra-cotta figurines.

De Simone
Via Lanza Di Scalea Giuseppe 698, tel 091 671 1005
Distinctive contemporary ceramics that are recognized around the world. Also available in specialty stores around the city and across Sicily.

Gramuglia
Via Roma 412, tel 091 583 262
Palermo's most sumptuous fabrics, fringes, tassels, and other home-furnishing accessories are available here.

Il Laboratorio Italiano
Via Principe di Villafranca 42, tel 091 320 282
Seller of original, high-quality ceramics.

Vincenzo Argento
Corso Vittorio Emanuele II 445,
tel 091 611 3680
The Argento family has been
making Palermo's traditional
puppets for more than 160
years.

DEPARTMENT STORE
Barone
Via Abramo Lincoln 146,
tel 091 616 5626
They've been in business for
more than 60 years, selling
mainly well-priced clothes for
men and women.

FOOD & WINE
Bar Costa
Via Gabriele d'Annunzio 15
Worth a visit for the fabulous
cakes and pastries.

Enoteca Picone
Via G Marconi 36,
tel 091 331 300
A family business since 1946,
with more than 4,000 Sicilian
and international wines from
which to choose.

**I Peccatucci di Mamma
Andrea**
Via Principe di Scordia 67,
tel 091 334 835
High-quality, homemade jams,
cakes, honeys, and other
gourmet foods, all beautifully
displayed and packaged.

JEWELERS
Di Bella
Via Carini 22, tel 091 328 031
Along with the top names in
watches, they offer fine rings,
necklaces, and other jewelry.

Fiorentino
Via Roma 315, tel 091 604 7111
Jewelers since 1890, they also
carry silverware, watches, and
other gift items. Fiorentino has
several other outlets around
the city.

Piazza Meli
This square near the Cala
has several silversmiths and
other jewelers.

MARKETS
Ballarò
Fruit, vegetables, fabrics, and
household goods are sold in
the streets around Piazza
del Carmine.

Del Capo
Famous market near Sant'
Agostino and Via Porta Carini
features clothes, shoes,
and fabrics.

I Latterini
The name comes from the
Arabic *suk-el-attarin* (grocery
market), but this is now a mixed
market for clothing and
household goods, located near
Via Calderai.

Mercato delle Pulci
Flea market is located behind
the cathedral and between
Piazza Peranni and Corso
Amedeo.

Vucciria
Palermo's oldest and most
colorful food and general
market fills the streets around
Piazza Caracciolo.

ERICE

Craft products are the best buy
in Erice, particularly the gold,
coral, and ceramic ware of
Altieri (Via Cordici 14, tel 0923
869 431), in business since 1881;
and the ceramics at **Ceramica
Ericina** (Via Guarnotta 42, tel
0923 869 440).
   For traditional cakes and candies, visit **Pasticceria Grammatico Maria** and her sister
shops (Via Vittorio Emanuele II
4 and 14, Via Guarnotta 1, tel
0923 869 390).

FAVIGNANA

On an island renowned for
tuna, a good shop for tuna
products is **La Casa del
Tonno** (Via Roma 12,
tel 0923 922 227).

AGRIGENTO

Visit **Caffè Concordia** (Via

Atenea 349, tel 0922 25 894) for
cakes and pastries, and **Zam-
buto** (Via Saponara 8, tel 0922
23 924) for assorted craft goods.

SYRACUSE

Visit **Bellomo** (Via Capodieci
15, tel 0931 61 340), one of
many shops selling the papyrus
products for which the town
has long been noted.
   A **market** is held in Ortygia
near the Tempio di Apollo
(closed Sun.).
   The **Enoteca Capriccio**
(Via Amalfitania 11, tel 0931
464 918) offers an excellent
selection of Sicilian wines.

TAORMINA

First stop for a variety of craft
items is **Panarello** (Corso Umberto I 122, tel 0942 23 910);
and for ceramics in particular,
Giuseppa Di Blasi (Corso
Umberto I 103, tel 0942 24 671).
   La Torinese (Corso
Umberto I 59, tel 0942 23321),
in business since 1936, is a first-
rate delicatessen.
   For beautiful but expensive
antique and other jewelry and
objets d'art, visit **Il Quad-
rifoglio** (CorsoUmberto I 153,
tel 0942 23 545) and **Stroscio**
(Corso Umberto I 169, tel 0942
24 865). Many clothing boutiques line Corso Umberto I.

LIPARI

A wide selection of wine,
honey, herbs, and other
foodstuffs from the Aeolian
Islands can be found at **Laise
Delizie** (Corso Vittorio
Emanuele 118, no phone).
   For cakes and pastries, visit
Subba (Corso Vittorio
Emanuele II 92, tel 090 981
1352), established in 1930.

CEFALÙ

A Lumera (Corso Ruggero
180, tel 0921 921 801) carries
an excellent selection of
ceramics from across Sicily.

ENTERTAINMENT & ACTIVITIES

ENTERTAINMENT & ACTIVITIES

Sicily has numerous fascinating and colorful festivals, religious ceremonies, historic pageants, fairs, markets, and local events. Holy Week celebrations in particular are some of the most striking in Europe, and there are several arts and cultural festivals of international renown. Most celebrations, though, are small, local affairs, restricted to a town or village, and often held in honor of a saint, an historic event, or a local product.

If you wish to plan your trip around a major event, be sure to reserve accommodations and make travel arrangements well in advance or you may find that everything is booked. Should that happen, don't worry; you will likely stumble on a *festa*, or small festival, some-where on the island, especially around Easter time or during the summer.

Most smaller religious and other festivals follow a pattern similar to the large events, beginning with processions, in which participants often dress in traditional costume, followed by church services, traditional songs and dances, fireworks, and lots of eating and drinking.

Watch for flyers advertising a festa or *sagra* (a food or wine fair). You can also consult local visitor information centers or their websites for details of upcoming events. Also visit www.festedisicilia.it.

EASTER & CARNIVAL

Holy Week celebrations in Sicily are extraordinary. Most towns and villages hold dramatic processions and *misteri* (scenes from Christ's Passion), often with robed and hooded penitents and confraternities in torchlit parade.

The most famous and striking of these celebrations are at Agrigento, Alcamo, Caltanissetta, Enna (the Good Friday procession here is remarkable), Erice, Marsala, Messina, Noto, Piana degli Albanesi, Ragusa, Scicli, and Trapani. Most events take place on Good Friday.

Carnival celebrations (usually held in Feb.) are especially colorful at Acireale, Sciacca, and Palazzolo Acreide.

ARTS & MUSIC

Concerts and performances of classical drama and ballet are held at the Greek theater in Syracuse (May–June, tel 0931 67 415 or 0931 465 831, www.indafondazione.org) and at the ancient theaters in Segesta (July–Sept., tel 0924 950 012, www.calatafimisegesta.com); at Tindari (Estate Tindari, last week of July–3rd week of Aug., tel 0941 241 136, www.patti etindari.it); and at Taormina (June–Aug).

Taormina's events are part of an important, summer-long arts festival, Taormina Arte (tel 0942 21 142; www.ta ormina-arte.com). The town also hosts a prestigious interna-tional film festival in June or July.

Other summer arts, theater, and music festivals take place annually in Catania, Enna (Estate Ennese), Erice (medieval and Renaissance music festival during 2nd week of July), Gibellina (Orestiadi festival), Noto, and Trapani (Estate Musicale Trapanese).

Marsala hosts the Marsala Doc Jazz Festival at the end of July, and Monreale has a music festival in the cathedral during November.

December sees a festival of music played on traditional instruments at Erice.

There is also usually an annual festival of plays (in Italian) by Luigi Pirandello at his birthplace at Caos, near Agrigento (see p. 95).

CALENDAR OF EVENTS

JANUARY
Epiphany
Byzantine-Orthodox Festa della Teofana celebrations in Piana degli Albanesi
(Jan.6)

San Sebastiano
Saint's day celebrations in Syracuse, Acireale, and Mistretta
(Jan. 20)

FEBRUARY
Sagra della Mandorla
Festival of the Almond Blossom with folklore and cultural events in Agrigento
(late Jan.–early Feb.)

Sant'Agata
Major procession and saint's day celebrations in Catania
(Feb. 3–5)

Carnevale
Carnival events and celebrations across Sicily
(week before Ash Wed.)

San Corrado
Saint's day celebrations in Noto
(Feb. 19)

MARCH
Cavalcata di San Giuseppe
Saint's day celebrations and procession in Scicli. Also celebrations in Salemi and Santa Croce Camertina
(March 18–19)

APRIL
Easter
Events, processions, and services in towns and villages across Sicily
(see above)

Maundy Thursday
Processions in Marsala and Caltanissetta
(Thurs. before Easter)

San Giorgio
Parades in Ragusa and Piana degli Albanesi
(April 23)

ENTERTAINMENT & ACTIVITIES/LANGUAGE GUIDE

MAY

Santissimo Crocifisso
Celebrations in Isnello in
the Madonie Mountains
(April 31–May 1)

Santa Lucia
Feast of St. Lucy celebrations in
Syracuse
(1st and 2nd Sun.)

Infiorita
Flower festival in Noto
(3rd Sun.)

Battaglia delle Milizie
Procession in period costume in
Scicli
(end of the month)

Corpus Domini
Festa della Frottola in Cefalù
(May or early June)

San Giorgio
St. George celebrations
in Ragusa Ibla
(last Sun.)

Sfilata del Carretto
Traditional painted carts and
puppet shows in Taormina
(last 3 days of the month)

JUNE

La Mattanza
Month-long ritual killing of tuna
in Favignana
(see pp. 82–83)

Madonna della Lettera
Religious celebrations in Messina
(June 3)

Festa del Mare
Festival of the Sea in Sciacca
(June 27–29)

SS. Pietro e Paolo
Celebrations honoring St. Peter
and St. Paul in Modica, Palazzolo
Acreide, and Pantelleria
(June 29)

JULY

Santa Venera
Week-long saint's festival
in Acireale
(from 1st Sun.)

San Calogero
Folklore and religious festival in
Agrigento
(1st Sun.)

Madonna della Visitazione
Religious festival in Enna
(July 2)

U Fistinu
Spectacular festival to honor
St. Rosalia in Palermo
(July 14–15)

Festa di Giacomo
Celebrations and illuminations
in Caltagirone
(July 24–25)

AUGUST

Palio del Mare
Boat procession and races
in Syracuse
(1st Sun)

Festa di San Salvatore
Religious celebration in Cefalù
(Aug. 2–6)

Festa della Spiga
Corn festival with music, theater,
and dance in Gangi
(2nd week)

Madonna della Luce
Procession of boats in Cefalù
(Aug.14)

Palio dei Normanni
Major festival with jousting
in medieval costume on
Piazza Armerina
(Aug. 13–14)

Festa di San Bartolomeo
Saint's festival with offshore
fireworks in Lipari
(Aug. 21–24)

San Giovanni Battista
Celebration honoring St. John
the Baptist in Ragusa, the
culmination of a month-long
festival of folklore in the
Iblea region
(Aug. 29)

San Corrado
Religious festival in Noto
(last Sun. of Aug. and 1st Sun.
of Sept.)

SEPTEMBER

Madonna delle Lacrime
Religious festival and pilgrimage
in Syracuse
(Aug. 29–Sept. 3)

La Madonna di Porto Salvo
Religious festival and procession
in Lampedusa
(Sept. 22)

OCTOBER

Festa di Sant'Angelo
Religious festival in Vulcano
(Oct. 2)

Festa del Pistacchio
Festival celebrating pistachio
harvest in Bronte
(early Oct.)

Ottobrata Zafferanese
Autumn food festival
in Zafferana Etnea
(each Sun. of the month)

NOVEMBER

Festa dei Morti
All Souls toy fair and children's
festival in Palermo
(Nov. 1–2)

DECEMBER

Festival di Morgana
International puppet festival
in Palermo
(end of Nov.–mid-Dec.)

Immacolata
Religious festival in Syracuse
(Dec. 8)

Santa Lucia
St. Lucy saint's day festival and
procession in Syracuse
(Dec. 13)

LANGUAGE GUIDE

Italians respond well to foreigners who make an effort to speak
their language. Many Italians
speak at least some English, and
more upscale hotels and restaurants have multilingual staff.

All Italian words are pronounced as written with each
vowel and consonant sounded.
The letter c is hard, as in the

English "car," except when
followed by *i* or *e*, when it
becomes the soft *ch* of "children," as in the toast *cin cin*.
The same applies to *g* when
followed by *i* or *e*—soft in *buon
giorno* (as in the English "giant");
hard in *grazie* as in "gate."

USEFUL WORDS & PHRASES

Yes **Sì**
No **No**
Okay/that's fine/sure **Va bene**
I don't understand **Non capisco**
Do you speak English? **Parla inglese?**
I don't know **Non lo so**
I would like...**Vorrei**...
Do you have...? **Avete...?**
How much is it? **Quant'è?**
What is it? **Che cos'è?**
Who? **Chi?**
What? **Quale?**
Why? **Perchè?**
When? **Quando?**
Where? **Dove?**
What's the time? **Che ore sono?**
Good morning **Buon giorno**
Good afternoon/good evening **Buona sera**
Good night **Buona notte**
Hello/good-bye (informal) **Ciao**
Good-bye **Arrivederci**
Please **Per favore**
Thank you **Grazie**
You're welcome **Prego**
What's your name? **Come si chiama?**
My name is... **Mi chiamo...**
I'm American (man/woman) **Sono Americano/ Americana**
How are you? (polite/informal) **Come sta/stai?**
Fine, thanks **Bene, grazie**
And you? **E lei?**
I'm sorry **Mi dispiace**
Excuse me/I beg your pardon **Mi scusi**
Excuse me (in a crowd) **Permesso**
good **buono**
bad **cattivo**
big **grande**
small **piccolo**
with **con**
without **senza**
more **più**
less **meno**

enough **basta**
near **vicino**
far **lontano**
left **sinistra**
right **destra**
straight ahead **sempre dritto**
hot **caldo**
cold **freddo**
early **presto**
late **ritardo**
here **qui**
there **là**
today **oggi**
tomorrow **domani**
yesterday **ieri**
morning **la mattina**
afternoon **il pomeriggio**
evening **la sera**
entrance **entrata**
exit **uscita**
open **aperto**
closed **chiuso**
bathroom **il bagno**
toilet **il gabinetto**
Let's go **Andiamo**

EMERGENCIES

Help! **Aiuto!**
Can you help me? **Mi puo aiutare?**
I'm not well **Sto male**
Call a doctor **Chiamate un medico**
Where is the police station? **Dov'è la polizia/ laquestura?**
first aid **pronto soccorso**
hospital **l'ospedale**

SIGHTSEEING

art gallery **la pinacoteca**
castle **il castello/la fortezza**
church **la chiesa**
garden **il giardino**
museum **il museo**
postcard **la cartolina**
stamp **il francobollo**
visitor center **l'ufficio di turismo**

IN THE HOTEL

hotel **un albergo**
room **una camera**
single room **una camera singola**
double room **una camera doppia**
room with private bathroom **una camera con bagno**
I have a reservation **Ho una prenotazione**

SHOPPING

shop/store **il negozio**
market **il mercato**
Do you have some...? **Avete un po' di...?**
this one **questo**
that one **quello**
a little **poco**
a lot **tanto**
enough **abbastanza**
too much **troppo**
Do you accept credit cards? **Accetate carte di credito?**
expensive **caro**
cheap **a buon prezzo**

STORES & SHOPS

bakery **il forno/il panificio**
bookstore **la libreria**
butcher **la macelleria/il macellaio**
cake store **la pasticceria**
delicatessen **la salumeria/ la norcineria**
drugstore/pharmacy **la farmacia**
food store **l'alimentari**
ice cream parlor **la gelateria**
post office **l'ufficio postale**
supermarket **il supermercato**
tobacconist **il tabaccaio**

MENU READER
General

breakfast **la colazione**
lunch **il pranzo**
dinner **la cena**
waiter **il cameriere**
I'd like to reserve a table **Vorrei riservare una tavola**
Have you a table for two? **Avete una tavola per due?**
I'd like to order **Vorrei ordinare**
I'm a vegetarian **Sono vegetariano/a**
The check, please **Il conto, per favore**
cover charge **il coperto**
Is service included? **Il servizio è incluso?**

The menu

l'antipasto appetizer
il primo first course
la zuppa soup
il secondo main course
il contorno vegetable, side dish
insalata salad
la frutta fruit
il formaggio cheese

i dolci sweets/desserts
la lista dei vini wine list

Menu terms
affumicato smoked
ai ferri grilled
alla griglia grilled
alla Milanese in breadcrumbs
allo spiedo on the spit
arrosto roasted
bollito boiled
costoletta chop
fritto fried
in umido stewed
ripieno stuffed/filled
stracotto braised, stewed
sugo sauce

Pasta & sauces
agnolotti large, filled pasta
   parcels
al pomodoro tomato sauce
amatriciana tomato and bacon
   sauce
arrabbiata spicy tomato sauce
bolognese veal or beef sauce
cannelloni filled pasta tubes
carbonara cream, ham, and egg
   sauce
farfalle butterfly-shaped pasta
fettucine flat, thick pasta ribbons
gnocchi potato and dough cubes
lasagne layers of meat, cheese,
   and pasta
parmigiano Parmesan cheese
   sauce
pasta e fagioli pasta and beans
penne tubular pasta
peperoncino oil, garlic, and chili
   peppers
pesto pine nuts, basil, and
   cheese
puttanesca tomato, anchovy,
   oil, and oregano sauce
ragù any meat sauce
ravioli filled pasta parcels
rigatoni large pasta tubes
spaghetti long, thin pasta
   strands
tagliatelle long, flat pasta ribbons
tagliolini thin pasta ribbons
tortellini filled pasta twists
vongole wine, clams, and parsley

Meats
agnello lamb
anatra duck
bistecca beef steak
cinghiale wild boar
coniglio rabbit
fritto misto mixed grill

maiale pork
manzo beef
ossobuco cut of veal
pancetta pork belly/bacon
pollo chicken
prosciutto cotto cooked ham
prosciutto crudo cooked
   (Parma) ham
salsiccia sausage
saltimbocca veal with ham
   and sage
trippa tripe
vitello veal

Fish & seafood
acciughe anchovies
aragosta lobster
baccalà dried salt cod
calamari squid
cappesante scallops
cozze mussels
dentice sea bream
gamberi prawns
granchio crab
merluzzo cod
ostriche oysters
pesce spada swordfish
polpo octopus
rospo monkfish
salmone salmon
sarde sardines
seppie cuttlefish
sgombro mackerel
sogliola sole
tonno tuna
triglie red mullet
trota trout
vongole clams

Vegetables
aglio garlic
asparagi asparagus
basilico basil
capperi capers
carciofi artichokes
carotte carrots
cavolo cabbage
cipolle onions
fagioli beans
funghi mushrooms
funghi porcini ceps, boletus
   mushrooms
insalata mista mixed salad
insalata verde green salad
melanzane eggplant
patate potatoes
patate fritte French fries
peperoni peppers
piselli peas
pomodoro tomato
radicchio red salad leaf

rucolo/rughetta rocket
   arucola
spinaci spinach
tartufo truffle
zucchini zucchini

Fruit
albicocca apricot
ananas pineapple
arance oranges
banane bananas
ciliegie cherries
ficchi figs
fragole strawberries
limone lemon
mele apples
melone melon
pere pears
pesca peach
pompelmo grapefruit
prugna plum

Drinking
acqua water
una birra beer
una bottiglia bottle
una mezza bottiglia
   half bottle
caffè coffee
caffè Hag/caffè decaffeinato
   decaffeinated coffee
latte milk
tè tea
vino wine
vino della casa house wine
zucchero sugar

INDEX

Bold page numbers indicate illustrations

ILLUSTRATIONS CREDITS

All photographs by Tino Soriano unless otherwise noted below:

Cover (L to R), Roger Wood/CORBIS; David Trood Pictures/Getty Images; Nik Wheeler/CORBIS.

12-13, M.L. Sinibaldi/CORBIS. 22, Time Life Pictures/Getty Images. 23, Gianni Dagli Orti/CORBIS. 24, Archivo Iconografico, S.A./CORBIS. 25 (le), Getty Images. 25 (rt), 26, & 27 (up) Hulton Archive/Getty Images. 27 (low), Time Life Pictures/Getty Images. 28-29, Gabriel Bouys/AFP/Getty Images. 33 (up), O. Louis Mazzatenta/NGS Image Collection. 37, Araldo de Luca/CORBIS. 38, Bettmann/CORBIS. 39, Sunset Boulevard/CORBIS SYGMA. 40, Bettmann/CORBIS. 52-53, Antoine Gyori/CORBIS SYGMA. 62, William Albert Allard, NGS. 78, Alfio Garozzo/CuboImages. 82-83, William Albert Allard, NGS. 83, Jeffrey L. Rotman/CORBIS. 87, Johanna Huber/SIME. 114, Alfio Garozzo/CuboImages. 152-153, Alfio Garozzo/CuboImages.

One of the world's largest nonprofit scientific and educational organizations, the National Geographic Society was founded in 1888 "for the increase and diffusion of geographic knowledge." Fulfilling this mission, the Society educates and inspires millions every day through its magazines, books, television programs, videos, maps and atlases, research grants, the National Geographic Bee, teacher workshops, and innovative classroom materials. The Society is supported through membership dues, charitable gifts, and income from the sale of its educational products. This support is vital to National Geographic's mission to increase global understanding and promote conservation of our planet through exploration, research, and education.

For more information, please call 1-800-NGS LINE (647-5463) or write to the following address:

National Geographic Society
1145 17th Street N.W.
Washington, D.C. 20036-4688
U.S.A.

Visit the Society's Web site at www.nationalgeographic.com.

Special Offer! Order today and get one year of National Geographic Traveler, the magazine travelers trust, for only $14.95. Call 1-800-NGS-LINE and mention code TRAC3A6.

Travel the world with National Geographic Experts:
www.nationalgeographic.com
/ngexpeditions

Published by the National Geographic Society
John M. Fahey, Jr., *President and Chief Executive Officer*
Gilbert M. Grosvenor, *Chairman of the Board*
Nina D. Hoffman, *Executive Vice President,*
President, Books and School Publishing
Kevin Mulroy, *Vice President and Editor-in-Chief*
Marianne Koszorus, *Design Director*
Elizabeth L. Newhouse, *Director of Travel Publishing*
Cinda Rose, *Art Director*
Carl Mehler, *Director of Maps*
Barbara A. Noe, *Series Editor*

Staff for this book:
Caroline Hickey, *Project Manager*
Kay Kobor Hankins, *Designer*
Jane Menyawi, *Illustrations Editor*
Alison Kahn, *Editor*
Alfredo Pelella, *Researcher*
Lise Sajewski, *Editorial Consultant*
Matt Chwastyk, Thomas L. Gray, Nicholas P. Rosenbach, Tibor G. Tóth, Gregory Ugiansky, and Mapping Specialists, *Map Edit, Research, and Production*
R. Gary Colbert, *Production Director*
Mike Horenstein, *Production Manager*
Meredith Wilcox, *Illustrations Assistant*
Connie D. Binder, *Indexer*
Dana Chivvis and Larry Porges, *Contributors*

Artwork by Maltings Partnership, Derby, England (pp. 96-97).

ISBN: 0-7922-9541-2

Printed and bound by Cayfosa Quebecor, Barcelona, Spain
Color separations by Quad Graphics, Alexandria, VA.

Visit the society's Web site at http://www.nationalgeographic.com.

The information in this book has been carefully checked and to the best of our knowledge is accurate. However, details are subject to change, and the National Geographic Society cannot be responsible for such changes, or for errors or omissions. Assessments of sites, hotels, and restaurants are based on the author's subjective opinions, which do not necessarily reflect the publisher's opinion. The publisher cannot be responsible for any consequences arising from the use of this book.

NATIONAL GEOGRAPHIC

TRAVELER

A Century of Travel Expertise in Every Guide

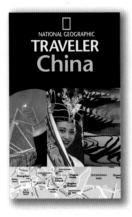

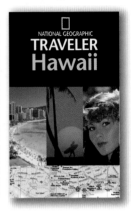

- **Amsterdam** ISBN: 0-7922-7900-X
- **Arizona** ISBN: 0-7922-3888-5
- **Australia** ISBN: 0-7922-3893-1
- **Barcelona** ISBN: 0-7922-7902-6
- **Boston & Environs** ISBN: 0-7922-7926-3
- **California** ISBN: 0-7922-3885-0
- **Canada** ISBN: 0-7922-7427-X
- **The Caribbean** ISBN: 0-7922-7434-2
- **China** ISBN: 0-7922-7921-2
- **Costa Rica** ISBN: 0-7922-7946-8
- **Cuba** ISBN: 0-7922-6931-4
- **Egypt** ISBN: 0-7922-7896-8
- **Florence & Tuscany** ISBN: 0-7922-7924-7
- **Florida** ISBN: 0-7922-7432-6
- **France** ISBN: 0-7922-7426-1
- **Germany** ISBN: 0-7922-4146-0
- **Great Britain** ISBN: 0-7922-7425-3
- **Greece** ISBN: 0-7922-7923-9
- **Hawaii** ISBN: 0-7922-7944-1
- **Hong Kong** ISBN: 0-7922-7901-8
- **India** ISBN: 0-7922-7898-4
- **Ireland** ISBN: 0-7922-4145-2

- **Italy** ISBN: 0-7922-3889-3
- **Japan** ISBN: 0-7922-3894-X
- **London** ISBN: 0-7922-7428-8
- **Los Angeles** ISBN: 0-7922-7947-6
- **Mexico** ISBN: 0-7922-7897-6
- **Miami and the Keys** ISBN: 0-7922-3886-9
- **New Orleans** ISBN: 0-7922-3892-3
- **New York** ISBN: 0-7922-7430-X
- **Paris** ISBN: 0-7922-7429-6
- **Prague & Czech Republic** ISBN: 0-7922-4147-9
- **Provence & the Côte d'Azur** ISBN: 0-7922-9542-
- **Rome** ISBN: 0-7922-7566-7
- **San Diego** ISBN: 0-7922-6933-0
- **San Francisco** ISBN: 0-7922-3883-4
- **Sicily** ISBN: 0-7922-9541-2
- **Spain** ISBN: 0-7922-3884-2
- **Sydney** ISBN: 0-7922-7435-0
- **Taiwan** ISBN: 0-7922-6555-6
- **Thailand** ISBN: 0-7922-7943-3
- **Venice** ISBN: 0-7922-7917-4
- **Washington, D.C.** ISBN: 0-7922-3887-7

AVAILABLE WHEREVER BOOKS ARE SOLD